# BEYOND BLAXPLOITATION

Contemporary Approaches to Film and Media Series
*A complete listing of the books in this series can be found online at
wsupress.wayne.edu.*

General Editor
Barry Keith Grant
*Brock University*

Advisory Editors
Robert J. Burgoyne
*University of St. Andrews*

Caren J. Deming
*University of Arizona*

Patricia B. Erens
*School of the Art Institute of Chicago*

Peter X. Feng
*University of Delaware*

Lucy Fischer
*University of Pittsburgh*

Frances Gateward
*California State University, Northridge*

Tom Gunning
*University of Chicago*

Thomas Leitch
*University of Delaware*

Walter Metz
*Southern Illinois University*

# BEYOND BLAXPLOITATION

*Edited by Novotny Lawrence and
Gerald R. Butters, Jr.*

Wayne State University Press
Detroit

© 2016 by Wayne State University Press, Detroit, Michigan 48201.
All rights reserved. No part of this book may be reproduced without formal permission.
Manufactured in the United States of America.
20 19 18 17 16        5 4 3 2 1

Library of Cataloging Control Number: 2016941943
ISBN 978-0-8143-4076-9 (paperback) | ISBN 978-0-8143-4077-6 (ebook)

Published with support from the Arthur L. Johnson Fund for
African American Studies.

Designed and typeset by Charles Sutherland E.T. Lowe
Composed in Adobe Caslon Pro

*For Professors Gregory D. Black and William Tuttle*
*We are forever grateful for your guidance and wisdom.*

# CONTENTS

*Acknowledgments*   ix

*Introduction*   1
    Novotny Lawrence

    I. Pioneer to Precursor to Blaxploitation

1. The "Black Enough" Visual Aesthetic in *Cotton Comes to Harlem*   21
    Vivian Halloran

2. Racial Exploitation in *Watermelon Man*: Contemporary Applications   41
    Charles E. Wilson, Jr.

3. *Sweetback* in Chicago   59
    Gerald R. Butters, Jr.

    II. The Canon and the Not So Canon

4. In the Beginning There Was *Shaft*   77
    Eric Pierson

5. The Blood of the Thing (Is the Truth of the Thing): Viral Pathogens and Uncanny Ontologies in *Ganja and Hess*   102
    Harrison M. J. Sherrod

6. A White Film for a Blaxploitation Audience? The Making and Marketing of *Detroit 9000*   114
   NOVOTNY LAWRENCE

7. As Foxy as Can Be: The Melodramatic Mode in Blaxploitation Cinema   137
   JOSEPH S. VALLE

III. Was, Is, or Isn't Blaxploitation

8. Stomping on Stepin Fetchit: Historicizing "Blackness" in African American Film Culture of the 1970s   157
   ALLYSON NADIA FIELD

9. Norman . . . It's Not about You: Decentering Black Gayness in *Norman . . . Is That You?*   180
   ALFRED L. MARTIN, JR.

10. Making Exploitation Black: How 1970s "Blaxploitation" Discourse Marginalized Industry History and Constructed Black Viewers' Tastes   201
    LAURA COOK KENNA

11. From Harlem to Hollywood: The 1970s Renaissance and Blaxploitation   225
    WALTER METZ

Contributors   247

Film and Television Index   251

Subject Index   255

# ACKNOWLEDGMENTS

This collection originated from years of conversation during which we discussed our bewilderment and frustrations regarding the lack of substantial blaxploitation scholarship. In the introduction to this volume, we discuss the scholars who are leading the charge in blaxploitation film studies. However, it was our editor, Annie Martin of Wayne State University Press, who emerged as our unexpected champion for this volume. From the moment that we proposed *Beyond Blaxploitation* to her at the Society for Cinema and Media Studies Conference, Annie has been a class act and a pleasure to work with. She is professional, worldly, wise, patient, and an advocate for scholars. Annie is exactly the type of editor that an academic wants to work with, and we thank her profusely for working to bring this project that means so much to us to fruition.

This volume is dedicated to Professors Gregory Black and William Tuttle. We (Novotny and Gerald) both had the same academic path through graduate school. Greg was our mentor in our master's programs at the University of Missouri–Kansas City, and he was among the first to show us the possibilities of what lay ahead for those who are interested in film studies—that you could actually make a living doing what you love. Bill was our mentor for our doctoral programs at the University of Kansas. He also taught us how to write with some very tough love in the editing processes. Bill was our advocate—both personally and professionally. He has continued to mentor us over the years, always giving us career advice when we need it. And those reference letters—let's just say that Bill wrote hundreds of them for us.

We also want to thank our spouses, Jarrett Neal and Sarah Lawrence, who are remarkably supportive of our careers. Whether we need them to listen and engage us in conversations regarding our work or to whisk us away from the world of academe, they are always with us every step of the way. Please know that you are our rocks and that we appreciate you more than we could ever express.

We also very much appreciate the members of our families—moms, dads, brothers, sisters, nieces, nephews, and others—who in myriad ways motivate us to continue doing the work. It means a great deal to us to know that you all support our endeavors, and it also motivates us to keep pressing forward.

Also, thanks to our colleagues, mentors, and friends at the institutions of higher education that employ us—Aurora University and Southern Illinois University—and across the world. It is a pleasure to work with you and to spend time discussing our various research projects at conferences. Thank you for helping enrich our scholarship and our lives.

Finally, we want to thank all of our students for making academe an exciting and fulfilling career.

# INTRODUCTION

## NOVOTNY LAWRENCE

THE BLACK EXPLOITATION (BLAXPLOITATION) MOVEMENT REMAINS ONE of the most fascinating yet oft-overlooked periods in motion picture history. Defined as films made between 1970 and 1975 by both black and white filmmakers to capitalize on the African American film audience, blaxploitation cinema emerged as a result of three social, economic, and political factors—the historic misrepresentation of blacks in cinema, the civil rights movement, and Hollywood's financial difficulties.[1] While the African American–themed pictures dominated the film industry for five years in the 1970s, initially, neither studios, producers, directors, nor actors set out to make blaxploitation films until two years after the movement was under way. Rather, the blaxploitation era marks a period when as a result of favorable conditions, the film industry briefly turned its attention to African American moviegoers, a long-ignored demographic that demonstrated its economic power by frequenting theaters in droves to view proud, assertive black movie characters that were every bit as capable as their white counterparts.

It is important that we clarify that not every film centered on African American experiences released during the early to mid-1970s is a blaxploitation film. The motion pictures that fall under the classification rely heavily on black-white revenge narratives, among other characteristics that we discuss later in this introduction. With that said, *Sounder* (1972), *Lady Sing the Blues* (1972), *Cornbread Earl and Me* (1975), and *Cooley High* (1975), among other films, function as notable examples of motion pictures geared primarily toward African American audiences that are not a part of the blaxploitation movement.

Though popular and academic accounts of blaxploitation cinema claim that the black film boom began with Melvin Van Peebles's *Sweet Sweetback's*

*Baadasssss Song* (1971), the movement actually ensued with United Artists' *Cotton Comes to Harlem*, which arrived in theaters nine months prior to *Sweetback*.[2] *Harlem* was based on Chester Himes's series of novels, *La reine de pommes*, which he hesitantly penned in France after his previous two novels, *Lonely Crusade* and *Cast the First Stone*, performed poorly in the United States.[3] Writing in the tradition of the hardboiled novelist Dashiell Hammett, Himes conceived of two black detectives, Coffin Ed Johnson and Grave Digger Jones, who work to solve crimes in the tough streets of Harlem. Readers responded so enthusiastically to Himes's African American characters that *Pommes* topped France's best-seller list and was also named best novel of the year.[4]

After learning of *Pommes'* success and reading Himes's novels, white producer Samuel Goldwyn, Jr., purchased the screen rights to the detective series with the intention of turning it into a movie franchise. His plan initially disturbed African American fans of the books who were "alarmed that the Hollywood [mogul]—fearful of raps from black integrationists—would bleach out all their hilarious 'local color,' make everybody talk General American and remove all the special flavor that gave them their special distinction."[5] With that in mind and feeling as if the white screenwriter Arnold Pearl's initial draft of *Harlem*'s script lacked authenticity, Goldwyn worked to avoid altering the characteristics that had made the Coffin Ed and Grave Digger series wildly successful by hiring the black actor and activist Ossie Davis to rewrite the screenplay.[6] Davis provided such a strong revision that Goldwyn hired him to direct the film, making it just the second time that a black man would helm a Hollywood movie.[7]

*Harlem* opens by taking viewers on a tour of the city as it follows the limousine of Reverend Deke O'Malley (Calvin Lockhart) to the site of a rally that he is holding as a part of his Back-to-Africa crusade. Convinced that his campaign is nothing more than an attempt to swindle Harlem residents out of their money, Coffin Ed Johnson (Raymond St. Jacques) and Grave Digger Jones (Godfrey Cambridge) attend to watch over the event and, more importantly, its organizer, Reverend O'Malley. All is well until armed gunmen interrupt the festivities, stealing the $87,000 that O'Malley has collected before fleeing the scene in a getaway truck. Although Coffin Ed and Grave Digger give chase, the criminals escape. The remainder of the film chronicles the detectives as they work to bring the culprits to justice and retrieve the stolen money so that they can return it to the good people of Harlem.

While its story line is fairly standard, *Harlem* presented a fresh perspective of black inner-city life while establishing the majority of the conventions that defined ensuing blaxploitation films—a black hero or heroine, a predominantly black urban setting, black supporting characters, a contemporary rhythm-and-blues soundtrack, and plot themes addressing the black experience in contemporary American society.[8] This formula proved effective at the box office as *Harlem* performed incredibly well, grossing $15,375,000 in film rentals, with black viewers accounting for 86 percent of the revenue.[9] African American viewers' strong showing at the box office captured the attention of Hollywood executives, who had traditionally geared their pictures toward white audiences. Discussing *Harlem*'s runaway success, industry analyst Ronald Gold summarized, "What this means, according to trade reasoning, is that it is now possible to make pictures aimed specifically for black filmgoers—and expect to make a substantial profit—without worrying too much about what the rest of the public will think."[10]

Gold's assessment proved accurate; however, it was not a major Hollywood release that further validated the black moviegoer's economic power. Instead, it was an independently financed film by displaced African American director Melvin Van Peebles, who broke into Hollywood's directorial ranks via France, where he shot his award-winning interracial romance *The Story of a Three-Day Pass* (1968). *Pass* garnered Van Peebles attention from the Hollywood executives who, as a result of his skin color, had previously thwarted his attempts to work in motion pictures. Considered a viable commodity after *Pass*, Van Peebles signed a three-picture deal with Columbia Pictures, where he shot *Watermelon Man* (1970), a race-themed comedy centering on a bigoted white man who awakens one morning to discover that he has turned black. Though *Man* performed moderately well at the box office, Van Peebles was unhappy with the picture, because he felt it lacked the strong and much-needed political message appropriate for an African American–themed picture created in the midst of the Black Power movement. As a result, he set out to direct a hard-hitting drama that would articulate blacks' frustrations regarding the United States' discriminatory racial practices while also transforming the African American cinematic image from one-dimensional caricature to victorious, renegade character. As Van Peebles explains, "I wanted a victorious film. A film where niggers could walk out standing tall instead of avoiding each other's eyes, looking once again like they'd had it."[11]

Significantly, the ambitious director ventured outside the studio system to bring his radical film to fruition, writing, producing, directing, scoring, editing, and starring in *Sweet Sweetback's Baadasssss Song*. "Working under the pretense of making a porno, Van Peebles used a nonunion crew (blacks, Latinos, and whites) and shot the picture in nineteen days, all on a budget of $500,000."[12] The cost represented about $100,000 of his own money in addition to funds that he borrowed and fees that he deferred. Van Peebles also received a $50,000 loan from his friend Bill Cosby, who came up with the money when it was vitally needed to continue production.[13] Van Peebles's struggles continued after he completed *Sweetback*. After he refused to submit his film to the Motion Picture Producers of America (MPAA) for review, the evaluation board automatically assigned the sexually charged *Sweetback* an X rating. The classification, which theoretically banned moviegoers under the age of seventeen from attending the film, made it difficult for Van Peebles to find a distributor. He eventually reached a deal with Cinemation, a low-budget porn company, to distribute *Sweetback*. After securing a distribution deal, Van Peebles played on the MPAA's evaluation and the tenuous racial politics of the day in the film's marketing campaign, which announced that *Sweetback* was "Rated X by an All-White Jury."

*Song* opens with a title card that reads, "This film is dedicated to all the Brothers and Sisters who have had enough of the Man," before introducing audiences to an adolescent Sweetback who has just been taken in by prostitutes working in a brothel. Shortly thereafter, he is seduced and engages in sexual intercourse with one of the women, who exclaims, "Oh God, you got a Sweetback!" The film then moves ahead several years, reintroducing the adult Sweetback (Van Peebles) who works as the star attraction in a sex show. One evening, as a favor to his manager, he allows two white policemen to take him into custody because they need a suspect in a murder case they are having trouble solving. They promise to question Sweetback as a way to appease their boss, who is frustrated because they are not making sufficient progress on their case. On the way to the police station, the cops arrest a young black militant and decide to "teach him a lesson" before taking him to jail. They take the two prisoners to a deserted oil field, where they partially uncuff Sweetback and begin beating the young militant. Sweetback becomes so enraged as he watches that he bludgeons the officers to death with his partially removed handcuffs. He then goes on the run in an attempt to cross over into Mexico. The remainder of the film is shot using an experimental aesthetic that crosscuts between Sweetback as he makes his way to the border and the police as they scour the predominantly black urban community in which he once resided in search of him. With the help of the black community and using his sexual prowess to his advantage, Sweetback manages to escape, and as the film ends, a title card flashes a warning: "Look out! Cause a bad-ass nigger is coming back to pay some dues!"

Despite the film initially opening in just two theaters after its release, *Sweetback* took the nation by storm as a large segment of the African American population connected with the film. In recounting the story of a black renegade hero who, with the help of the black community, took on white authority and in the end emerged victorious, *Sweetback* solidified the final two blaxploitation characteristics—violence and a strong display of black sexuality. Earth, Wind, and Fire's gritty, politically charged soundtrack served as the perfect musical accompaniment to the filmic image, adding to the movie's authenticity. By putting the sights, sounds, and socioeconomic problems of the black community on grand display for all to see, Van Peebles made visible what had historically gone unseen in motion pictures. African American audiences visited theaters in droves to view *Sweetback*, which grossed $4.1 million in domestic film rentals, an amazing accomplishment given the film's minuscule budget.[14]

The box-office success of *Sweetback* and *Cotton Comes to Harlem* established African Americans as a viable demographic and ignited a black film boom that remains unmatched in motion picture history. In the ensuing five years, major and independent studios such as MGM, Warner Bros., and American International Pictures (AIP) released an array of films that include, but certainly are not limited to, *Shaft* (1972), *Melinda* (1972), *Trouble Man* (1972), *Super Fly* (1972), *Slaughter* (1972), *Blacula* (1972), *Coffy* (1973), *Cleopatra Jones* (1973), *The Mack* (1973), *Hell Up in Harlem* (1973), *Foxy Brown* (1974), *Black Belt Jones* (1974), *Thomasine and Bushrod* (1974), *Boss Nigger* (1975), and *The Black Gestapo* (1975), among countless others. While only a partial list, these titles provide insight into blaxploitation's popularity, demonstrating that the movement became an industry-wide phenomenon.

Though blaxploitation cinema was a lucrative venture, after the films' releases many of them were marred in controversy, which partly led to their demise. With the exception of *Harlem*, many canonical blaxploitation films were the catalysts for fierce debates among actors, directors, critics, scholars, and activists, who argued about the impact that the films were having on the black cinematic image and, more broadly, African American life and culture. There are a number of reviews of specific films like *Sweetback* and *Coffy*, as well as commentary pieces such as "Shaft Can Do Everything, I Can Do Nothing" and "Black Film Boom: Culture or Con Game," that illustrate of the polarizing effect that the black-themed pictures had on the film industry and the African American community. For the sake of brevity, Gerald and I focus on two distinct examples that make clear the gamut of viewpoints that blaxploitation opponents and proponents held during the movement's peak years.

A 1972 *Variety* article titled "NAACP Blasts 'Super-Nigger' Trend," featuring commentary by Junius Griffin, who at the time was the president of the Beverly Hills branch of the NAACP, is arguably the most important critique of black-themed pictures. Discussing *Super Fly* and what Griffin viewed as the film's glorification of the drug trade, he asserted, "Black exploitation in films has reached devastating proportions. . . . We must tell both white and black movie producers that we will not tolerate the continued warping of our black children's minds with the filth, violence, and cultural lies that are all pervasive in current productions of so-called black movies."[15] While his comments make apparent a segment of the black population's dissatisfaction with *Super Fly*, what is most relevant to this study is that this marks the first time that the African American–oriented films were described as "black exploitation," a term that critics and industry execs subsequently combined to form the term "blaxploitation." Thus, in criticizing *Super Fly*, Griffin inadvertently coined the term "blaxploitation," which became the chic moniker that fans and scholars used to describe the black film boom during the 1970s and beyond. That the term endures in trade and popular vernacular as the name of the black film craze with little to no regard for its connotations is both a recognition of and a disservice to one of the most iconic movements in motion picture history.

In addition to the aforementioned piece, a 1972 *New York Times* article titled "Black Movie Boom—Good or Bad?" functions as a microcosm of the constant debates that plagued blaxploitation pictures. The piece features commentary from prominent African American actors, directors, screenwriters, and intellectuals who responded to questions such as "Does the recent wave of black movies . . . represent an important, if long-delayed, recognition of black artists and the right of the audiences to see movies about blacks? Or do such movies merely offer a new stereotype—blacks as studs, pimps, prostitutes, and pushers?"[16]

*Shaft* director Gordon Parks, Sr., who despised the term "blaxploitation," was among those who weighed in on the controversy: "The so-called black intellectuals' outcry against black films has been blown far out of proportion. It is curious that some black people, egged on by some whites, will use such destructive measures against black endeavors. . . . They should realize that we new black filmmakers are not yet running the big Hollywood studios, that it took many hard years to even get our foot in the door. If they would have us more subservient to their wishes, then they should bestow upon us the means or more bluntly, the money."[17] Former professional football player turned actor Jim Brown also participated in the conversation, explaining, "The so-called 'black' film has made some important contributions not only to black people but to the film industry as a whole. It has allowed black directors, black producers, black technicians, black writers, and black actors to participate on a higher level than ever before."[18] Additionally, famed movie actress and vocalist Lena Horne noted, "I see no difference between the current black films in question and their white counterparts dealing with similar dismal subjects. I have yet to see the definitive black movie."[19]

In contrast, Roy Innis, the national director of the Congress on Racial Equality (CORE), blasted blaxploitation films: "Some defenders of these Black films have defended them on the ground that they are no worse than, say, John Wayne films, that Black youth recognize them as fantasy, as escapist entertainment. But these defenders fail to see that John Wayne . . . is usually portrayed as a man with guts and strength and positive aggressiveness. He is not portrayed as the psychopathic superdude, as are the present crop of Black super-heroes."[20] Writer Amiri Baraka was equally damning in his response, asserting, "the 'soul flicks' of our times are modern nigger toys for colored adults and children."[21] Although *Sounder* screenwriter Lonne Elder III understood that blaxploitation films represented a rare opportunity for blacks working in Hollywood, he took exception with the quality of the motion pictures: "Any assessment of the current wave of exploitative, so called black films must underline one common fact—that they are nothing more than inept 'B' products by anyone's standards of excellence."[22]

"Black Movie Boom—Good or Bad" provides a representative sample of the controversy that surrounded blaxploitation cinema. As the commentary from the article's participants illustrates, the movement and its potential impact were complex, making it difficult to assess in strictly positive or negative terms. Though the constant debates more than likely encouraged some African American moviegoers to attend the films, the controversy eventually made black-themed films less desirable products for studios, especially when the films' ticket sales began to decline.

In addition to contention over blaxploitation cinema, the emergence of the blockbuster feature also led studios to cease production of the films. In *Framing Blackness*, Ed Guerrero argues that by the end of 1973, Hollywood perceived that black audiences were tiring of the endless reworking of the crime-action-ghetto formula and observes that successful black films like *Sounder* and *Lady Sings the Blues*, which toned down the black-white confrontation, attracted black and white audiences alike.[23] In short, "the film industry realized that it did not need an exclusively black vehicle to draw the large black audiences."[24] This was further emphasized in surveys that demonstrated that as much as 35 percent of the audience for the megahits *The Godfather* (1972) and *The Exorcist* (1973) was black. Therefore, Hollywood executives reasoned that the production of crossover films appealing to both white and black audiences could potentially double box-office revenue.[25] Their theory was confirmed in the ensuing years when films like *Jaws* (1975), *Star Wars* (1977), and *Saturday Night Fever* (1978) performed well with African American and white audiences.

Finally, blaxploitation's popularity played a key role in its demise. The films enjoyed such tremendous box-office success that they became an industry-wide phenomenon, with major and minor studios churning them out in great numbers. As a result, the market became oversaturated, causing studios to discontinue their production. This is a natural industry pattern that dictates the ebb and flow of Hollywood's releases. In *Film/Genre*, Rick Altman asserts, "Once a genre is recognized and practiced throughout the industry, individual studios have no further economic interest in practicing it as such (especially in their prestige productions); instead they seek to create new cycles by associating a new type of material within an existing genre, thus initiating a new round of genrification."[26]

The horror genre, which has undergone many transformations since becoming popular in the cinema, is a prime example of the process that Altman describes. In particular, in the late 1970s and throughout the 1980s, slasher films constituted the majority of the horror films that were produced in lieu of previous movies that chronicled the exploits of classic monsters such as Count Dracula, the Wolfman, and Dr. Jekyll and Mr. Hyde. Rather, a new cadre of sadistic, blade-wielding killers, including Michael Myers, Jason Voorhees, and Freddy Krueger, emerged preying on hard-partying, sexually active teens who were seemingly punished in the narratives for their illicit deeds. For approximately a ten-year period, slasher horror films like *Halloween* (1978), *Friday the 13th* (1980), and *A Nightmare on Elm Street* (1984), as well as their many sequels, featuring these menacing characters, dominated the box office, until they began losing their appeal in the late 1980s. This is not to suggest that additional sequels or remakes of these films were not produced; however, it is to say that infused with different material, this alternative rendition of the horror genre enjoyed its greatest success early on before experiencing a significant decline in box-office revenue.

Though blaxploitation was a movement composed of films from varying genres, it experienced an evolution and decline comparable to other genres after the market became oversaturated with tired retreads and cheap imitations of films like *Shaft*, *Super Fly*, and *Coffy*. As is typical with moviegoing audiences, African Americans, whom the films were geared toward, soon tired of the various blaxploitation reformulations, a fact that was evidenced at the box office when ticket sales suffered a downturn. Hollywood executives, writers, and filmmakers never attempted to infuse blaxploitation with new material as they did with other popular genres. Instead, the studios centered films in their newly discovered blockbuster cycle on white actors, once again privileging them over their equally talented African American counterparts. As a result, the blaxploitation movement came to an abrupt end, and the overwhelming majority of the directors, writers, actors, and producers who once proved so lucrative to Hollywood were cast into relative obscurity.

While some scholars might argue that blaxploitation did not experience a renewal because it was a movement and not a distinct genre, that contention is off the mark. The blaxploitation movement is comparable to film noir, a movement, cycle, or style of films that endures in both film industry and academic discourse. Film noir, like blaxploitation cinema, emerged as a result of social, economic, and political factors. Producers and directors did not deliberately set out to make noir films, which first emerged during World War II. Because the United States did not export films to France during the conflict, it was not until a year after World War II came to an end that French film critic Nino Frank coined the term "film noir" in reaction to five American films—*The Maltese Falcon* (1941), *Murder My Sweet* (1944), *Double Indemnity* (1944), *Laura* (1944), and *The Woman in the Window* (1944). These films exemplified alternative narrative, stylistic, and thematic tones from prewar Hollywood films, making them starkly different.[27] More specifically, the noir motion pictures feature ambiguously moral male protagonists, sultry femmes fatales, and pessimistic narratives that Frank attributed to the anxiety that the filmmakers and audiences were experiencing as a result of the war. The movies were also characterized by the use of voice-over narration (generally delivered by the male protagonist), while stylistically noir pictures employ low-key lighting, dramatic camera angles, and an almost Freudian obsession with water.[28] Until the late 1950s, these characteristics were on full display in an array of classic motion pictures extending across multiple genres, including *Detour* (1945), *The Big Sleep* (1946), *The Killers* (1946), *Out of the Past* (1947), *The Third Man* (1949), *Sunset Boulevard* (1950), *Kiss Me Deadly* (1955), and *A Touch of Evil* (1958).

Although film noir eventually ran its course, it remains one of the most heralded and influential film cycles in the history of motion pictures. For instance, there have been several neo-noir films produced since the movement's decline, such as *Chinatown* (1974), *Body Heat* (1981), *Blade Runner* (1982), *Devil in a Blue Dress* (1995), *L.A. Confidential* (1997), and *Sin City* (2006), that have given new life to the cycle. One way these films have reinvigorated film noir is, because of cinematic technological advancements, they were shot in color; however, the low-key lighting is still utilized and, with the color, provides a fresh visual aesthetic.

*Blade Runner* is a techno noir that shifts the story world from the contemporary settings that characterize the majority of films noir to a dark, bleak, futuristic environment. *Devil in a Blue Dress* keeps the 1940s setting intact, replacing the white male protagonist with Easy Rawlins (Denzel Washington), an out-of-work African American World War II veteran who is hired to find a mysterious woman named Daphne Monet (Jennifer Beals). As a black man operating as an amateur detective working in the racist 1940s, Rawlins encounters discrimination as he attempts to solve his case. Thus, the film functions as a racial commentary by placing at the center of the narrative a black man who cannot navigate the establishment as easily as white film noir protagonists could.

In addition to filmmakers, scholars have also enthusiastically embraced film noir, devoting a great deal of attention to the cycle of films in the form of books, chapters, and journal articles. This is not to suggest that the consideration that the cycle of films has garnered is unwarranted. Instead, Gerald and I use film noir to demonstrate its similarity to blaxploitation as a movement and to illustrate a dichotomy that, in industry and academic circles, exists between an influential cycle of films geared toward white audiences and an African American–oriented film movement that also made important cinematic strides.

Notably, blaxploitation cinema challenged Hollywood's stereotypical portrayal of blacks, demonstrating that they were much more than the tom, coon, and mammy caricatures that historically circumscribed African American performers. It is also important to point out that *Shaft* and *Super Fly* saved MGM and Warner Bros., respectively, from bankruptcy as the studios had been struggling to reverse the decline in ticket sales that plagued Hollywood since the advent of television. Finally, the blaxploitation movement represents the moment when more African Americans were working in the film industry than at any other time in history. Still, aside from a small number of parodies and action pictures such as *I'm Gonna Git You Sucka* (1988), *Undercover Brother* (2002), *Black Dynamite* (2009), *Original Gangstas* (1996), *Jackie Brown* (1997), *Shaft* (2000), *Baadasssss!* (2004), *Four Brothers* (2005), and *Django Unchained* (2012), cinematic homages and reinterpretations of blaxploitation cinema are lacking.

Not only have narrative filmmakers rarely revisited blaxploitation cinema, but documentarians have also largely ignored the movement. Isaac Julien's documentary *Baadasssss Cinema* (2002) is the most extensive nonnarrative account of blaxploitation cinema. Though the filmmaker explores some of the contours of the movement, *Baadasssss Cinema* is far from a complete or scholarly work. Despite the insights of esteemed intellectuals and writers such as Ed Guerrero, bell hooks, Armand White, and Elvis Mitchell, the documentary

INTRODUCTION

unfortunately becomes the Quentin Tarantino show as the controversial director both opens and closes the film and is given an inordinate amount of screen time throughout. Tarantino follows the common practice of emphasizing superficial blaxploitation elements such as clothes, music, and the films' cool aesthetic, over the more significant nuances characterizing the movement. Further, in *Baadasssss Cinema*, blaxploitation's demise is explained away by the neglect of Hollywood and the anti-blaxploitation forces, giving little regard for the inferior production quality of many of the films or the oversaturation of the market. Thus, Julien's film primarily functions as an enjoyable nostalgia trip rather than a complex documentation of the blaxploitation movement and its contributions to motion picture history.

Even more disturbing than the lack of sustained cinematic attention devoted to blaxploitation is that academics have long ignored the period as well. In particular, a number of survey texts chronicling the evolution of motion pictures fail to acknowledge blaxploitation at all, ignoring the films similarly to the way in which many African Americans are often marginalized in mainstream accounts of U.S. history. In the years following blaxploitation, a limited number of studies focusing on the African American cinematic experience, such as Donald Bogle's *Toms, Coons, Mulattoes, Mammies, and Bucks: An Interpretive History of Blacks in American Films* (1973), Daniel Leab's *From Sambo to Super Spade: The Black Experience in Motion Pictures* (1975), Mark Reid's *Redefining Black Film* (1993), and Ed Guerrero's *Framing Blackness: The African American Image in Film* (1993), provided the most complete academic accounts of the blaxploitation movement. However, because each of these works focuses on the entire black cinematic experience, blaxploitation is discussed in sections or as stand-alone chapters. To be clear, this observation is not a critique of the valuable cinematic contributions of Bogle, Leab, Reid, or Guerrero. Instead, it evidences that for an extended period of time, there was a need for scholars to expand on those authors' research to produce more complete analyses of the movement and cinematic history by extension.

Fortunately, intellectuals have begun filling the void in blaxploitation research, devoting a growing amount of attention to the subject. For example, since 2006, three academic texts have been published that provide much-needed in-depth examinations of the movement. In *Women of Blaxploitation: How the Black Action Heroine Changed American Popular Culture* (2006), Yvonne Sims traces the evolution of the African American actress, demonstrating how by appearing in blaxploitation films, performers such as Pam Grier, Tamara Dobson, and Jeannie Bell cut against the stereotypical mammy and sapphire stereotypes. In doing so, they "epitomized the struggles and gains of African American women in the 1960s and early 1970s and altered the onscreen perspective of African American femininity."[29] I critique the term "blaxploitation" in *Blaxploitation Films of the 1970s: Blackness and Genre* (2008), illustrating how using it as an overarching classification of black-themed motion pictures fails to consider their impact on their respective genres. Examining *Cotton Comes to Harlem*, *Blacula*, *The Mack*, and *Cleopatra Jones*, I discuss the manner in which the films' inclusion of "blackness" in the form of the protagonists, settings, and narratives, among other characteristics, revises the detective, horror, gangster, and cop action genres. Finally, in *"Baad Bitches" and Sassy Supermamas: Black Power Action Films* (2008), Stephane Dunn returns to African American actresses, highlighting the roles that the Black Power movement and feminism played in bringing black heroines to the silver screen. She analyzes films such as *Coffy*, *Cleopatra Jones*, and *Foxy Brown*, emphasizing the ways in which the movies' African American leading women displayed power and agency in patriarchal society.

Additionally, scholars have published peer-reviewed journal articles focusing on blaxploitation, further establishing the movement as an area worthy of serious academic investigation. For example, in 2005, *Screening Noir* editor Anna Everett devoted the inaugural issue of the journal to investigating the movement, with the distinct goal of expanding blaxploitation scholarly discourse. Titled "Blaxploitation Revisited," the volume features essays from scholars such as Chris Sieving, Jerry Rafiki Jenkins, and Christine Acham, discussing Pam Grier, *Blacula*, and *The Spook Who Sat by the Door* (1973), respectively. Additionally, Harry Benshoff provides a useful critique of black-themed horror films in "Blaxploitation Horror Films: Generic Reappropriation or Reinscription?" While films like *Blacula* and *Blackenstein* are generally dismissed as campy and irrelevant, Benshoff examines the intersections of race and identity in their narratives, demonstrating that the movies produced critiques of social and generic racism. In "Beyond the Black Macho: Queer Blaxploitation," Joe Wlodarz provides insightful commentary on black masculine identity, arguing that "multiple forms of critique are staged throughout blaxploitation that undercut and challenge the presumed invulnerability and 'authenticity' of the figure of the black macho."[30] Further, Racquel Gates's "Subverting Hollywood from the Inside Out: Melvin Van Peebles's *Watermelon Man*" brings much-warranted attention to Van Peebles's first Hollywood feature. More specifically, she contends that *Watermelon Man* exemplifies Van Peebles's ability to critique "Hollywood's and society's racism from the 'inside out.'"[31]

*Beyond Blaxploitation* works to sustain the momentum that blaxploitation scholarship has gained, giving it an even more prominent place in cinema

INTRODUCTION

history. Each essay in this volume approaches blaxploitation as a movement, a significant difference between this work and many others that incorrectly label it a genre. As my earlier book illustrates, there were blaxploitation detective, action, horror, and gangster pictures; therefore, this volume makes accounts of genre more complete by including films within their appropriate classifications. Further, this anthology is a much-needed pedagogical tool, informing film scholars, critics, and fans alike about blaxploitation's richness and depth. This far-reaching volume is composed of eleven essays employing historical and/or theoretical methodologies in the examination of spectatorship, marketing, melodrama, the transition of novel to screenplay, and racial politics and identity, among other significant topics. In doing so, the book fills a substantial gap that exists in the black cinematic narrative and in motion picture history, more broadly.

*Beyond Blaxploitation* is divided into three parts that feature original essays on a variety of canonic blaxploitation films and others that either influenced the movement or in some form represent a significant extension of it. Part 1, "From Pioneer to Precursor to Blaxploitation," centers on three films—*Cotton Comes to Harlem*, *Watermelon Man*, and *Sweet Sweetback's Baadasssss Song*—that ignited the African American film cycle. In "The 'Black Enough' Visual Aesthetic in *Cotton Comes to Harlem*," Vivian Halloran examines Davis's pioneering film, making clear the impact that the Black Power and Black Arts movements had on the text and ensuing African American–themed motion pictures. Through deep analysis, she demonstrates that *Harlem* established a visual and thematic aesthetic that to this day continues to inform movies featuring predominantly black casts.

Charles E. Wilson, Jr., focuses on Melvin Van Peebles's inaugural Hollywood film in "Racial Exploitation in *Watermelon Man*: Contemporary Applications." Given that most accounts of blaxploitation omit *Watermelon Man*, Wilson positions it within the blaxploitation movement before examining it as a form of prediction in retrospect. In doing so, he contends that the film is illustrative of a current segment of the U.S. population's fear about the "browning of the nation," or the notion that in the next twenty-five to fifty years, people of color will outnumber whites. Wilson draws parallels between *Watermelon Man*'s lead character and the resentment, anger, and anxiety that racist whites expressed during and after the 2008 and 2012 presidential elections that resulted in the United States' first African American commander in chief, President Barack Obama.

In "*Sweetback* in Chicago," Gerald R. Butters, Jr., expands on the discourse focusing on Van Peebles's seminal film, which has traditionally examined the motion picture's production, its violent and erotic content, and issues of representation. He goes beyond the film's thematics, exploring *Sweetback*'s impact on localized African American audiences that flocked to downtown Chicago theaters to view the motion picture, a trend that theater managers sought to capitalize on. With that in mind, Butters explores *Sweetback*'s impact on the Windy City, arguing that black filmgoing in Chicago can be classified as "BS" and "AS"—before *Sweetback* and after *Sweetback*. Furthermore, he details how "the film's enormous box-office gross and widespread controversy, which brought thousands of black Chicagoans into the Loop (the downtown district) to see the film, forever changed the racialized nature of filmgoing in the city's center."

Part 2, "The Canon and the Not So Canon," is dedicated to forging alternative considerations of some of the most highly regarded blaxploitation titles, while also bringing attention to lesser-known films that constitute the movement. The section opens with Eric Pierson's "In the Beginning, There Was *Shaft*," which centers on Gordon Parks's classic blaxploitation picture. While it is well known that Richard Roundtree became a popular-culture icon appearing as the cool, slick private detective, many scholars and fans are unfamiliar with the transition that the character underwent as he was adapted from the novel on which the film was based to the silver screen. Using archival materials in conjunction with personal interviews with the late Gordon Parks and *Shaft* producer Joel Freeman, Pierson explores the process by which an anti-Semitic, homophobic killer was transformed into one of America's most renowned film characters, John Shaft.

Harrison M. J. Sherrod provides a valuable analysis of an oft-overlooked blaxploitation horror film in "The Blood of the Thing (Is the Truth of the Thing): Viral Pathogens and Uncanny Ontologies in *Ganja and Hess*." Positioning the movie within the prestigious avant-garde cinema, he provides a reading of the text from a primarily scientific perspective. In particular, Sherrod uses germ theory to demonstrate the manner in which *Ganja and Hess*'s vampire character becomes a fecund metaphor for the plight of the black subject defined by viral prejudices, transgressing biological, cultural, and ontological boundaries.

In "A White Film for a Blaxploitation Audience?: The Making and Marketing of *Detroit 9000*," I go beyond popular blaxploitation films, exploring the General Film Corporation's foray into low-budget African American–themed pictures. More specifically, using *Detroit 9000* as a case study, I grapple with the term "blaxploitation," which begs the question, Who or what did the films exploit? In attempting to answer that query, at least in the case of *Detroit 9000*, I work through the film's conception before analyzing its most prominent themes. Finally, I discuss the film's two protagonists and its marketing campaigns to bring more attention to what I consider one of the blaxploitation movement's most intriguing yet unexplored motion pictures.

Joseph S. Valle returns to a seminal blaxploitation film in "As Foxy as Can Be: The Melodramatic Mode in Blaxploitation Cinema." Using AIP's Pam Grier vehicle *Foxy Brown*, he addresses the unbridled emotions and excessive pathos that frequently appear in many blaxploitation films, with the distinct goal of understanding the movement through the melodramatic mode, which he contends fully reveals blaxploitation heroes' and heroines' racialized suffering and their eventual triumph over racism. As Valle examines blaxploitation through the melodramatic lens, he also discusses the manner in which the Black Power movement inspired and shaped blaxploitation films, the movement's connection to serial-queen melodramas from the silent era, and the reasons that melodrama is a valid mode for considering blaxploitation beyond *Foxy Brown*.

Part 3, "Was, Is, or Isn't Blaxploitation," is composed of four essays that offer significant insights on films that are generally associated with blaxploitation but contest traditional definitions of the movement. Moreover, this part features chapters that address industrial factors that led to the creation of blaxploitation cinema and highlight the limitations of the term itself. In "Stomping on Stepin Fetchit: Historicizing 'Blackness' in African American Film Culture of the 1970s," Allyson Nadia Field focuses on African American representation, albeit in a context that is much different from previous blaxploitation discourse. She examines three films—*Watermelon Man*, *Amazing Grace* (1974), and *Car Wash* (1976)—demonstrating how each pivots on notions of "blackness" enacted through the legacy of black film history. Fields centers her examination on the appearances of three African American actors who were previously circumscribed to stereotypical roles, Mantan Moreland, Stepin Fetchit, and Clarence Muse, to reveal the complex negotiation with a significant aspect of film history as it is presented at a time when questions surrounding the legacy of black representation occupied a more prominent space in national dialogues.

Alfred L. Martin, Jr., examines the black, gay, male experience in "Norman . . . It's Not about You: Decentering Black Gayness in *Norman . . . Is That You?*" While liberating for the film image of African Americans, blaxploitation cinema followed Hollywood's traditional homophobic practices, perpetuating the most egregious gay and lesbian stereotypes in filmic representations. Martin discusses *Norman* and its duplicitous approach to black gayness in the 1970s—on the one hand, it is the first black-cast narrative film that focuses on homosexuality, yet the film decenters gayness, ultimately making *Norman* a tale of parents coming to terms with the fact that their son is gay. Hence, Martin examines the film as a sitcom, arguing that the structure of the film employs a similar strategy as sitcoms of the 1970s that engaged with homosexuality via the "Coming-Out

Episode." He then turns to the black press to illustrate the manner in which magazine articles worked to establish that the actor playing the title character was straight, thus reinforcing heteronormativity. Finally, Martin examines the ways that the film works to position homosexuality as inherently antiblack.

Laura Cook Kenna explores the industrial conditions that led to the blaxploitation movement in "Making Exploitation Black: How '70s 'Blaxploitation' Discourse Marginalized Industry History and Constructed Black Viewers' Tastes." She reconnects the history of black film criticism, exploitation film, and 1970s black cinema. In doing so, Kenna reveals how much of the aesthetic practices and marketing strategies of the black movie boom were connected to a half-century-old mode of production that was characteristic of neither "mainstream" Hollywood nor "race films."

Finally, in "From Harlem to Hollywood: The 1970s Renaissance and Blaxploitation," Walter Metz brings the collection to a close, critiquing the term "blaxploitation," which is often associated with campy, low-budget, B movies unworthy of scholarly attention. Taking that into account, he rejects the use of the reductive term "blaxploitation," contending that scholars should instead consider the films as a part of the much more highly regarded Hollywood Renaissance, composed of seminal films such as *The Graduate* (1967) and *Easy Rider* (1969). Working from that perspective, Metz provides deep analyses of the blaxploitation films *Blacula, Scream Blacula, Scream* (1973), *Ganja and Hess*, and other titles to highlight, and thus more fully celebrate, their political and aesthetic impact on cinema.

*Beyond Blaxploitation* is primarily aimed at university instructors and students and practitioners. However, it is important to note that the essays in this book are accessible; thus, fans interested in learning more about blaxploitation cinema will greatly benefit from this volume as well. Given the enormity of research that remains to be conducted on the blaxploitation movement, my coeditor, Gerald Butters, and I hope that this book will serve as a catalyst for more sustained scholarship on a subject that we feel is an incredibly important part of the black cinematic experience and motion picture history. Thus, we intend to continue doing the work to move blaxploitation cinema to a more prominent place in film's historical narrative.

## NOTES

1. Novotny Lawrence, *Blaxploitation Films of the 1970s: Blackness and Genre*. (New York: Routledge, 2007), 17, 18.
2. Paula J. Massood, *Black City Cinema: African American Urban Experiences in Film* (Philadelphia: Temple University Press, 2003), 87.

INTRODUCTION

3. Rudolph Chelminski, "'Cotton' Cashes In: All Black Comedy Is a Box-Office Bonanza," *Life*, August 28, 1970, 61.
4. Ibid.
5. Ronald Gold, "Director Dared Use Race Humor: Soul as Lure for Cotton's B. O. Bale," *Variety*, September 30, 1970, 62.
6. Ossie Davis and Ruby Dee, *With Ossie and Ruby: In This Life Together* (New York: William Morrow, 1998), 335–36.
7. In 1969, Gordon Parks, Sr., directed the autobiographical drama *The Learning Tree*, which made him the first African American to direct a Hollywood film.
8. Lawrence, *Blaxploitation Films of the 1970s*, 18–20.
9. James Robert Parish and George H. Hill, *Black Action Films* (Jefferson, NC: McFarland, 1989), 112; Gold, "Director Dared Use Race Humor," 1.
10. Gold, "Director Dared Use Race Humor," 1.
11. Qtd. in Lerone Bennett, Jr., "The Emancipation Orgasm: Sweetback in Wonderland," *Ebony*, September 1971, 112.
12. Donald Bogle, *Toms, Coons, Mulattoes, Mammies, and Bucks: An Interpretive History of Blacks in American Films* (New York: Viking, 1973), 238.
13. Ibid.
14. Parish and Hill, *Black Action Films*, 298.
15. "NAACP Blasts 'Super-Nigger' Trend," *Variety*, August 16, 1972, 2.
16. "Black Movie Boom—Good or Bad?," *New York Times*, December 15, 1972, sec. 3, p. 19.
17. Ibid.
18. Ibid.
19. Ibid.
20. Ibid.
21. Ibid.
22. Ibid.
23. Ed Guerrero, *Framing Blackness: The African American Image in Film* (Philadelphia: Temple University Press, 1993), 105.
24. Ibid.
25. Ibid.
26. Rick Altman, *Film/Genre* (London: BFI, 1999), 62.
27. Frank Krutnik, *In a Lonely Street: Film Noir, Genre, Masculinity* (New York: Routledge, 1991), 15.
28. Bruce Crowther, *Film Noir: Reflections in a Dark Mirror* (New York: Continuum, 1989), 12.
29. Yvonne Sims, *Women of Blaxploitation: How the Black Action Heroine Changed American Popular Culture* (Jefferson, NC: McFarland, 2006), 18.
30. Joe Wlodarz, "Beyond the Black Macho: Queer Blaxploitation," *Velvet Light Trap* 53 (Spring 2004): 10.
31. Racquel Gates, "Subverting Hollywood from the Inside Out: Melvin Van Peebles's *Watermelon Man*," *Film Quarterly* 68, no. 1 (2014): 9.

# WORKS CITED

Altman, Rick. *Film/Genre*. London: BFI, 1999.
Bennett, Lerone, Jr. "The Emancipation Orgasm: Sweetback in Wonderland." *Ebony*, September 1971, 106–18.
Benshoff, Harry M. "Blaxploitation Horror Films: Generic Reappropriation or Reinscription?" *Cinema Journal* 39, no. 2 (2000): 31–50.
"Black Movie Boom—Good or Bad?" *New York Times*, December 15, 1972.
Bogle, Donald. *Toms, Coons, Mulattoes, Mammies, and Bucks: An Interpretive History of Blacks in American Films*. New York: Viking, 1973.
Chelminski, Rudolph. "'Cotton' Cashes In: All Black Comedy Is a Box-Office Bonanza." *Life*, August 28, 1970.
Crowther, Bruce. *Film Noir: Reflections in a Dark Mirror*. New York: Continuum, 1989.
Davis, Ossie, and Ruby Dee. *With Ossie and Ruby: In This Life Together*. New York: William Morrow, 1998.
Dunn, Stephane. *"Baad Bitches" and Sassy Supermamas: Black Power Action Films*. Chicago: University of Chicago Press, 2008.
Gates, Racquel. "Subverting Hollywood from the Inside Out: Melvin Van Peebles's *Watermelon Man*." *Film Quarterly* 68, no. 1 (2014): 9–21.
Gold, Ronald. "Director Dared Use Race Humor: Soul as Lure for Cotton's B. O. Bale." *Variety*, September 30, 1970.
Guerrero, Ed. *Framing Blackness: The African American Image in Film*. Philadelphia: Temple University Press, 1993.
Krutnik, Frank. *In a Lonely Street: Film Noir, Genre, Masculinity*. New York: Routledge, 1991.
Lawrence, Novotny. *Blaxploitation Films of the 1970s: Blackness and Genre*. New York: Routledge, 2007.
Leab, Daniel. *From Sambo to Super Spade: The Black Experience in Motion Pictures*. Boston: Houghton Mifflin, 1975.
Massood, Paula J. *Black City Cinema: African American Urban Experiences in Film*. Philadelphia: Temple University Press, 2003.
"NCAAP Blasts 'Super-Nigger' Trend." *Variety*, August 16, 1972.
Parish, James Robert, and George H. Hill. *Black Action Films*. Jefferson, NC: McFarland, 1989.
Reid, Mark. *Redefining Black Film*. Berkeley: University of California Press, 1993.
Sims, Yvonne, *Women of Blaxploitation: How the Black Action Heroine Changed American Popular Culture*. Jefferson, NC: McFarland, 2006.
Wlodarz, Joe. "Beyond the Black Macho: Queer Blaxploitation." *Velvet Light Trap* 53 (Spring 2004): 10–25.

PART I

# PIONEER TO PRECURSOR TO BLAXPLOITATION

# 1

# THE "BLACK ENOUGH" VISUAL AESTHETIC IN *COTTON COMES TO HARLEM*

## VIVIAN HALLORAN

Historians of black film debate whether to consider Ossie Davis's film adaptation of Chester Himes's detective novel *Cotton Comes to Harlem* (1970) as a forbear to or as the first in a series of films that came to constitute the blaxploitation cinematic canon. However, most published discussions of blaxploitation include some reference to the film's impact as what Ed Guerrero calls "the first of the new black films to articulate a sense of the emerging mainstream cinema 'black style.'"[1] While I will not definitively settle the debate here, I want to offer a reading of *Cotton Comes to Harlem* as a film poised at the intersices of the discourses deployed by the Black Power and Black Arts movements to envision what might constitute an "authentic" black visual aesthetic. Though the film includes plenty of violence, nudity, and frank depictions of sexual situations as do the other two films credited with jump-starting the blaxploitation trend in filmmaking—Melvin Van Peebles's *Sweet Sweetback's Baadasssss Song* (1971) and Gordon Parks's *Shaft* (1971)—*Cotton Comes to Harlem* nonetheless promotes a vision of embodied blackness that validates both male and female desire, as well as creativity, as legitimate means through which to craft a communal, and transactional, black visual aesthetic that is situated in, but not contained by, Harlem as the iconic urban environment.

The debate regarding the relative authenticity of various characters' performance of their own sense of blackness carries over into the film's narrative structure itself, serving as a running theme or leitmotif that joins the multiple story lines together into a larger meditation on what constitutes a distinct black visual aesthetic that normalizes the Afrocentric "ghetto" lifestyle, humor, and culture on display.[2] The movie's plot establishes the genre conventions it both follows and critiques: it concerns the two police detectives' efforts to locate the evidence that will prove that Reverend Deke O'Malley's (Calvin Lockhart) back-to-Africa movement is nothing but a money-making scheme to defraud Harlemites of their hard-earned cash. Coffin Ed Johnson (Raymond St. Jacques) and Grave Digger Jones (Godfrey Cambridge) regard themselves as the advocates of the black community's best interests not only by preventing black-on-black crime, such as their interruption of the pickpocket who targets a man buying soul food during the opening back-to-Africa rally, but also by going so far as to resort to much shooting and even some extortion to restore the funds Reverend O'Malley steals from the people on their beat. However much Grave Digger Jones and Coffin Ed strive to serve and protect, they are never accepted as cultural insiders because they are law enforcement agents and also because they live elsewhere. Harlem is their beat, but it is not their home.

As a cultural text, *Cotton Comes to Harlem* breaks new ground by depicting a secondary character, the artist, as a valued member of the community. The marquee at the Apollo Theater where she performs proclaims this sense of community support and endorsement by announcing the upcoming performance of "Harlem's own Billie." The scenes featuring Billie (Mabel Robinson) set *Cotton* apart from the rest of the blaxploitation canon and demonstrate the film's engagement with the Black Arts movement's ongoing quest to determine the artist's role within, and duties to, the urban black community in crafting a recognizable black aesthetic. Though Billie is a minor character in both the novel and the film, the dancer/choreographer functions as a metacinematic stand-in for Himes as the exiled novelist and for Davis as Goldwyn's hired talent and consultant on the film project. The burlesque performance at the Apollo that is an integral component to the climax of the narrative arc represents the film and the novel as artistic undertakings subject to their respective audience's approval. By giving Billie the screen time to articulate her conflicted feelings about bringing her artistic vision to life, Davis portrays her as an empowered, successful, and even feminist icon. She represents the artist as a successful interpreter of a transactional black visual aesthetic. Chester Himes's original character, in contrast, fails to secure any community support when she explicitly advocates on behalf of black artists as a general category of people after her sultry performance. As the creative authors of a distinctly black visual aesthetic, Billie, Himes, and Davis

The Apollo Theater marquee promoting Billie's performance. (*Cotton Comes to Harlem* DVD, MGM Home Entertainment)

successfully mine the painful legacy of plantation slavery in the American South, and the popularity of cotton as a labor-intensive crop to grow and harvest, and turn it into a spectacle that chronicles the black community's ongoing effort to craft an independent and autonomous vision of urban life in the North.

## SAM GOLDWYN, JR., AS ARBITER OF THE "BLACK ENOUGH" SCREENPLAY

"Is that black enough for you?" Though this is not a phrase that is used in the novel, this line of dialogue nonetheless encapsulates the aesthetic and fiscal considerations that Ossie Davis and Samuel Goldwyn, Jr., shared about the film's appeal to black audiences. In the memoir that Davis jointly authored with his wife, Ruby Dee, *With Ossie and Ruby: In this Life Together*, he recalls that Goldwyn invited him to join the project already in development in order to ensure the film depicted black life authentically: "The movie adaptation had been written by Arnold Perl, an old friend of ours from the days of *Sholom Aleichem*, but Sam wasn't satisfied: the script wasn't black enough. He phoned me from Hollywood to ask my opinion."[3] Davis's involvement in the project of making *Cotton* "black enough" grew from his initial role as one of the actors playing the two lead detectives and evolved to reflect his increasing responsibilities first as script consultant, then as script (re)writer, and eventually as the film's director. In this capacity, Davis answered the producer's call to make the film more authentically black by featuring multiple black audiences/spectators as a collective character that punctuates shifts in action throughout the film: crowds of Harlemites assemble whenever the Reverend O'Malley begins his oratory, angry mobs demand his release from jail, and theatergoers happily applaud the interpretive dance at the Apollo that rewrites the history of southern plantation slavery. By showcasing black audiences as consumers and critics of entertainment and public rhetoric, Davis overtly affirmed their existence as a vibrant moviegoing demographic with the potential to be very profitable.

Thus, Goldwyn's deferral to Davis was not only because of his ethnicity but also because both were industry insiders with established track records in film, and Davis's experience included television and the theater as well. They spoke the common language of cinema as performance. *Cotton*'s success at the box office was seen to herald the rise of the black moviegoer as a revenue source, as noted at the time in *Variety*: "according to trade reasoning, . . . it is now possible to make pictures aimed specifically for black filmgoers—and expect to make a substantial profit—without worrying too much about what the rest of the public will think."[4] The box-office numbers quelled the concerns that had been circling the project since Goldwyn bought the rights to Himes's beloved novels. According to Ronald Gold, "fans of the books were concerned that the Hollywood moguls . . . would bleach out all their hilarious 'local color.'"[5] Though the source material was written by a black novelist, Amy Abugo Ongiri reminds us that Himes never really established his own bona fides in film: "He never achieved the financial success or artistic legitimacy he sought in his lifetime, though he would be courted by both major publishers and Hollywood studios,"[6] including producer Samuel Goldwyn, Jr. According to biographers Edward Margolies and Michael Fabre, their negotiations about turning *Cotton Comes to Harlem* into a screenplay ended with mixed results:

> Samuel Goldwyn, Jr. had bought the film rights to *Cotton Comes to Harlem* and wanted Himes to write the script. Chester advised him to try Claude Brown, but Goldwyn persisted. He suggested that Himes pare down the complex plot to sharpen the differences between the two detectives, perhaps even reduce his two heroes to one as way of adding

more suspense. As an inducement, he offered Himes $750 a week, a secretary, and expenses, hinting that he might drop the option unless Himes agreed. Himes thought he could do the work in a week, but whatever he submitted failed to satisfy Goldwyn.[7]

Himes's deference toward Claude Brown, a Harlem native and author of the autobiographical novel *Manchild in the Promised Land* (1965), signals his own appreciation of Brown's lived experience in urban spaces as a counterbalance to the fictional Harlem of the detective novels. After all, the original audience for Himes's detective fiction was not American but French, as Joseph McClaren points out.[8] Himes's portrayal of the mythical Harlem was not subject to verisimilitude because he was not writing to an audience of his peers, as he recalls in his autobiography: "I would sit in my room and become hysterical thinking about the wild, incredible story I was writing. But it was only for the French, I thought, and they would believe anything about Americans, black or white, if it was bad enough."[9]

Goldwyn's suggestion that Himes reconfigure the plot to accommodate one detective can be read not only as a breach of creative vision but also as evidence of his familiarity with the conventions of the hardboiled detective genre popularized by white authors, which privileged a single detective working alone. Peter J. Rabinowitz discusses Himes's deployment of the detective team as an innovation of the tried and true formula of previous (white) detective fiction and film in the mold of Raymond Chandler's detective Philip Marlowe: "Chandler's brand of individualistic heroism, that is the lonely detective's maintenance of his principles in the face of an intrinsically evil world, is impossible for Himes' black precinct detectives and, indeed, the fact that they always appear as a team is itself a clue that individualism of the Marlowe sort is not available on the streets of Harlem."[10] Extending the logic of Rabinowitz's argument, the kinds of problems that Marlowe and Grave Digger Jones and Coffin Ed face are fundamentally different in scope—individuals seeking extralegal assistance on private matters versus communities relying on the unfriendly intervention of law enforcement—and thus require entirely different sleuthing interventions. Novotny Lawrence argues that the duo differs not just from the loner white private eye but also from the stereotype of the ethnic detective because of the "double consciousness" they experience as black detectives in a white police force.[11] As the symbol of a racially marked "ghetto" space rather than a bustling metropolis, Harlem demands its own type of claims to a faithful translation to film.

For Davis, the opportunity to shoot the film on location was sufficient enticement to persuade him to accept Goldwyn's offer to direct the script he had rewritten. He recalls feeling that his "brand" was a known quantity there and describes such acceptance in transactional terms: "I was comfortable in Harlem; people knew me there as one of the homeboys. I wasn't white. I wasn't an outsider. People would be glad to see me working there because I was Ossie Davis, the man who had eulogized Malcolm X. The community would treat me as one of its own."[12] However, things did not go as smoothly as Davis had envisioned; the community's "welcoming" spirit did not extend to the film's white film crew, and a script supervisor was injured when a local threw a bottle that hit her on the head.[13] Davis found that his personal "homeboy" status did not overcome the fact that he was working *in* Harlem but was not himself *from* there, much like the two protagonists of the film, Coffin Ed Johnson and Grave Digger Jones. Though his past service to the community was well known, the people of Harlem demanded that he demonstrate his loyalty anew—by hiring black "apprentices" to bypass the virtual embargo that the unions had on jobs in New York and further honoring that commitment after founding Third World Cinema. While his primary rationale for opening his own studio was to bring his projects to fruition, Davis continued to provide opportunities for local youth of color to break into the film industry, thus earning the right to film in Harlem undisturbed.[14]

Even the nature of the conflict Davis faced during production attests to the Harlemites' response to him as an *artist* with the influence to share some of the Hollywood wealth with others, rather than as the community leader and activist he thought himself to be, "the man who had eulogized Malcolm X." Though neither Davis nor Himes was officially associated with the Black Arts movement, both men were politically engaged during the post-civil-rights era, which saw the cultural and political landscape change with the rise of black nationalism, Black Power, and the Black Arts movement. Though Ongiri explains that the rhetoric of Black Power advanced a notion of "hypermasculinity" and violence to solve social problems, while the Black Arts movement advocated "authentic" cultural production as a sufficient intervention, she points to the perception that urban poverty epitomized black culture as one of the few assumptions shared by both movements:

> The notion that the urban poor experience is definitional in the construction of African American identity is largely a result of the Black Arts/Black Power moment. The central questions first cogently posed by the Black Arts Movement continue to remain unanswered and mostly

unexplored. How would African American artists and intellectuals be accountable to the masses of African American people? How would the masses of African American people be integrated into the dominant culture? What stood to be lost and what stood to be gained for African American culture if the project of integration was a success?[15]

By juxtaposing this emphasis on artistic production with abundant references to shoot-outs, a high body count, and car chases, both the film and novel versions of *Cotton Comes to Harlem* likewise find common ground between the Black Arts aesthetic preoccupation and the Black Power agenda of self-empowerment through violence. While neither film nor novel directly answers the last question that Ongiri lists, both Davis's and Himes's fictive versions of Harlem take time out of the madcap detective plot to give some serious consideration to the role of the African American artist and "the masses." The titular bale of cotton thus functions as more than a MacGuffin—though it is the plot device that keeps audiences and characters guessing about the whereabouts of the $87,000 that O'Malley embezzled from his supporters, it also serves a cultural emblem and an unimpeachable test of rural literacy. As Lawrence points out, neither Grave Digger Jones nor Coffin Ed Johnson fully detects the significance of the cotton fibers: "the two detectives . . . are more concerned with solving their case rather than the value of the material."[16] Uncle Bud (Red Foxx), the oldest featured character and the only person in the narrative to have ever picked cotton in the fields, identifies not just the bale as an object but also its quality. Fittingly, he absconds with the loot and actually resettles in a rural African country, thus putting the lie to both Marcus Garvey's and Deke O'Malley's urban reverie of "going home" as an unproblematic solution to social ills such as institutional racism. Only someone used to farm labor truly knows what it takes to settle down and prosper in an agrarian society: money enough to hire others to work for you.

Though the male characters spend much ammunition fighting over ownership of the bale of cotton, only Billie strikes out directly against the cotton itself, incorporating physical violence into her choreography as she hits and punches the bale in time to George Tipton singing about "boot[ing] Cotton's butt."[17] Unlike the black detectives, who must be seen to collaborate in solving the crime, the dancer can appear alone onstage because the nature of her artistic performance is inherently collective and communal: her movements take place in time to the music recorded by another artist, and she engages with props and set design crafted by still more theater professionals. The biggest difference between how the detectives and the dancer define or experience the successful conclusion of their respective enterprises has to do with the stakes involved: since Grave Digger Jones and Coffin Ed broke the law by extorting money from a local white mobster, they then have to trick the back-to-Africa followers into believing their stolen $87,000 was returned to them, or else the detectives would be subject to punishment. They perform a version of justice that the film's audience knows to be inaccurate. In contrast, the interaction between dancer and audience at the Apollo is transparent and open: the audience conveys its approbation or disapproval by either cheering or booing the dance's revisionist history of slavery and its implied claim to have transcended the bonds that King Cotton imposed on previous generations of southern blacks. Since this is precisely the narrative arc that grounds the plot of the film—the rejection of an old southern legacy of exploitation in favor of embracing a new, urban, black self-sufficiency—Billie's dance at the Apollo stands in mimetic relation to the film's own revisionism.

Paula Massood advances a reading of Davis's film as a "black ghetto chronotope" because it combines visual references to multiple temporalities at once: the ahistorical past of an imagined African homeland, the urban activism of the Black Power movement, and tongue-in-cheek allusions to the rural past of slavery, which she terms "an antebellum idyll."[18] To this, I would counter that the only "idyll" present in the film is the neocolonial fantasy of Uncle Bud's African sojourn. The vignettes showing him surrounded by his nubile, native brides are an ironic send-up of the plantation society of Dixie. Massood's reading of the confluence between temporal and spatial dimensions of "ghetto" life is persuasive. Throughout her book, she argues that blaxploitation films "struggle to articulate a black aesthetic, one in which the city plays a central role."[19] By conducting a close reading of the scenes depicting transactional performances of masculinity and femininity in *Cotton Comes to Harlem*, I suggest that Davis's metacinematic meditation on a transactional black visual aesthetic has a different inflection from those of other blaxploitation films, one centered less on the city itself and more on the artist as its representative figure.

## BLACK AESTHETIC VERSUS BLACK IS BEAUTIFUL

Although the question "Is that black enough for you?" recurs throughout *Cotton Comes to Harlem*, only two primary characters test their own performance of blackness against the expectations of their audiences: the Reverend Deke O'Malley, whose goal is to defraud diasporic Harlemites dreaming of settling down in an African motherland, and Billie, the burlesque dancer who rejects the standard props of her trade—balloons, fans, and feathers—as assimilationist,

The Reverend Deke O'Malley preparing to speak to the crowd at his felonious back-to-Africa rally. (*Cotton Comes to Harlem* DVD, MGM Home Entertainment)

in favor of a politically charged choreography that more accurately reflects the audience's shared history of oppression and sense of community. Billie's stated disavowal of the visual rhetoric of striptease performances stems from her own dissatisfaction at the dissonance she perceives between her personal beliefs and her artistic conventions; instead, she opts to align the outward signs of her own body—dark skin, natural hair—with the aspirations she has for her art to better reflect her political views. Police detectives Coffin Ed and Grave Digger Jones, for their part, serve as the primary arbiters of O'Malley's false performance of a representative Afrocentrism. By highlighting the detectives' function as agents of surveillance and portraying the minister through the lens of their official gaze, which is informed by his rap sheet—as a former convict turned putative "race leader" weighed down by the bling of a showman—the film forecloses the possibility that the audience will be taken in by O'Malley's claim to be "black enough" for his followers. His elaborate costumes and jewelry stand in contradistinction to the detectives' sharp dress and calm, cool demeanor, which establish them as the paragons of virile black masculinity. Whereas O'Malley's criminal scheme gets derailed by conflicts between the women he beds, Grave Digger Jones and Coffin Ed acknowledge the appeal of the "stone cold fox" but also control their impulses until the time is right for action.

While Grave Digger Jones's and Coffin Ed's manly virtue is obvious to the filmgoer, Peter Freese remarks that these characters' interlocutors take a different view: "Himes' black policemen . . . are looked upon as traitors to their race, because, although their very color should put them among the oppressed, their badges make them representatives of the oppressive machinery of 'The Man.'"[20] Thus, their brand of black masculinity wins the day with film audiences, though their professional affiliation with the institutional racism of the police force renders them eternal outsiders to the very community they so zealously watch out for: Harlemites. O'Malley proves himself to be a charlatan, and both the people he conned and the audience members witness his very public fall from grace at the Apollo Theater, the same venue where Billie triumphantly performs her dance.

The conflict between manliness and posturing comes to a head early in the film and constitutes the text's first engagement with Black Power ideology. Like many key figures in the Black Arts movement, *Cotton Comes to Harlem* rejects the prevalent mantra that "blackness is [inherently] beautiful." This rejection takes place during a confrontation between the two detectives and a black militant group, the Black Berets, during the back-to-Africa rally that sets the plot in motion. As people rush to pay their $100 deposit on a voyage to Africa aboard the ship *Black Beauty*, the Black Berets leave their perch across the street and move toward Coffin Ed and Grave Digger Jones. A confrontation ensues that becomes a contest in which the self-declared agents of an autonomous black nationalism and the two detectives whom they dismiss as sellouts or compradors try to out-macho one another. When the militants insult the detectives by declaring that the only person more objectionable than a "honky pig cop is a nigger pig cop," Coffin Ed (Godfrey Cambridge) replies with a smart-aleck rejoinder: "What kind of talk is that, soul brother? Don't you know that black is beautiful?" The two sides fight until Coffin Ed and Grave Digger vault one of the Berets up into the air. After his peers catch him, the Black Berets beat a hasty retreat. By depicting the vanquished black militant as being airborne, the film deploys a visual metaphor that suggests the brash young man is full of nothing but "hot air," when compared to the grit and substance of Coffin Ed and Grave Digger Jones. Though the policemen and the black nationalists might be at loggerheads, both recognize O'Malley as a fraud who is targeting their unsuspecting neighbors.

Coffin Ed Johnson and Grave Digger Jones prevent the Black Berets from interfering with the back-to-Africa rally. (*Cotton Comes to Harlem* DVD, MGM Home Entertainment)

A similar dismissal of the "black is beautiful" mantra is evident in the following passage from Julian Mayfield's "You Touch My Black Aesthetic I'll Touch Yours": "Superficial appurtenances such as music, language, dress, and slogans, and other 'Black is Beautiful,' fads can so easily be chewed up, digested, and spat out by this vigorous, if sick, society, that no aesthetic is safe within its grinding teeth."[21] This is a wholesale dismissal of the outward Afrocentrism so central to Black Power visual rhetoric by comparing it to an illness. Like Mayfield, Coffin Ed and Grave Digger Jones reject the Black Berets as lightweights, posers following a "fad" but lacking the real authority to act.

While this scene is the only one in which the phrase "black is beautiful" is uttered, *Cotton Comes to Harlem* also includes O'Malley, his henchmen, and their hapless victims as partaking in the shared hysteria encapsulated by this idea. A less dismissive evaluation of the banality of the sentiment can be found in Black Arts author Hoyt W. Fuller's description: "Across this country, young black men and women have been infected with a fever of affirmation. They are saying, 'We are black and beautiful,' and the ghetto is reacting with a liberating shock of realization which transcends mere chauvinism. They are rediscovering their heritage and their history, seeing it with newly focused eyes, struck with the wonder of that strength which has enabled them to endure and, in spirit, to defeat the power of prolonged and calculated oppression."[22] Though Fuller also uses the language of disease and contagion here, he interprets the effect of the "black is beautiful" mantra as salutary for the inner-city community. He sees it acting as a catalyst to prompt a celebration of the African American urbanites' own agency rather than reinforcing stereotypical narratives of perpetual victimization. However, this newly zealous embrace of the past does not, in and of itself, constitute a black aesthetic because it lacks the rigor and consistency of an artistic undertaking.

The black aesthetic cannot be fully in effect, in Fuller's view, until the possibility of assessment and evaluation of its merits arises in the form of a black critic: "What the sponsors of this workshop most hope for in this delicate and dangerous experiment is the emergence of new black critics who will be able to articulate and expound the new aesthetic and eventually set in motion the long overdue assault against white critics."[23] This view of a black aesthetic is profoundly dynamic and transactional; it depends on intellectual exchange and debate to come into being as simultaneously a practice and a set of ideals. This is precisely the type of back-and-forth interaction between performers (O'Malley, Billie, and Davis as director) and critics (Grave Digger Jones and Coffin Ed, the audience at the Apollo, film reviewers) that *Cotton Comes to Harlem* contends is a constitutive part of a meaningful visual black aesthetic through its various paratexts (wardrobe, marquee, soundtrack, publicity materials, etc.).

Despite Fuller's and Massood's emphasis on the "ghetto" as a site where blackness is authenticated, Davis's directorial debut projected this discussion beyond the confines of both geography and temporality. As a cinematic text, *Cotton Comes to Harlem* presented an image of urban toughness (and humor) for the consumption and entertainment of spectators from across multiple class, race, gender, and temporal subject positions. We must also remember that Himes's Harlem was a transnational invention, drafted for the consumption of European audiences with a thirst for learning about American life through the lens of crime fiction. To locate the instances in which a black visual aesthetic is most clearly articulated and held up for review, it is important to pause on the scenes depicting black audiences' response to black artists' performances.

## DESTABILIZING INFLUENCE OF PERFORMANCE OF FEMININITY

Critics of Himes's novel and Davis's film alike have pointed out the relatively marginal role that female characters play within the respective narratives. Even as Joseph McClaren argued that Davis's film adaptation of *Cotton Comes to Harlem* was "dominated by the participation of African-Americans in significant roles" and that "the film was also primarily geared toward a black viewing audience," he acknowledges that in the source material, "Himes does not offer any introspective analysis of African-American women but paints them as stereotypes who are defined by physical attributes and, in certain cases, base motives."[24] McClaren's assessment of Himes's conception of black femininity is accurate on the larger points; however, it could just as easily be applied to his portrayal of the male characters as well, whose actions do not appear to be the result of very complex motivations either.

Female critics in particular have been quick to write off the significance of Billie's role within the narrative as just one more salacious episode that affirms the testosterone-fueled landscape across which our two detective protagonists make their way in pursuit of a criminal. Ongiri, for example, dismisses Himes's Billie as "a ribald dancer at Harlem's notorious Cotton Club writh[ing] obscenely against a bale of cotton," an example of how "Grave Digger Jones and Coffin Ed see 'democracy at work.'"[25] She does not remark on the movie's depiction of the same character. In contrast, Massood acknowledges that Billie's role in the film "is more politicized than most of the characters" and describes her motivation as a desire to put into practice her own vision of what a black aesthetic could be: "Billie explicitly states a desire to add a political dimension to her routines, thus referencing the Black Arts Movement, and self-reflexively commenting on the film's own aesthetic system."[26] I agree with this characterization but stress that the screenplay's insistent repetition of the question "Is that black enough for you?" is a constant reminder of the transactional nature of any successful performance of a black aesthetic. As Fuller remarked, someone must play the role of the "black critic" in order for a particular black aesthetic to be received and evaluated.

In both Himes's novel and Davis's film, Billie appears as a successful, independent woman with the power to alter the choreography and costuming of her show to suit her vision of a dance that her audience will recognize as authentically black. In the novel, Billie arrives at the idea of staging her dance as a revisionist retelling of the history of enslavement to King Cotton from bondage through sharecropping only after interacting with two southern men: Colonel

Calhoun, the leader of the reactionary "Back-to-the Southland" headquarters, which is trying to prevent black Harlemites from moving to Africa; and Uncle Bud, the junkman. Calhoun had placed an ad offering money for a bale of cotton, and Billie called the number to find out more. As she tells the detectives after her dance, the idea for the performance was "just a whim" prompted by the chance encounter with Uncle Bud: "His nappy white head made me think of cotton. I stopped and asked him if he could get me a bale of cotton for my cotton dance; I don't know why, just 'cause if he cut his hair it'd make a bale, I suppose, and he said, 'Gimme fifty dollars and I'll git you a bale of cotton Miss Billie,' and I gave him the fifty right then and there, knowing I'd get it back from the club. And sure enough, that same night he delivered it."[27] Unlike the gullible masses who eagerly give their money to O'Malley hoping he will solve their problems by sailing them to Africa, Billie here demonstrates her good financial instincts as well as her creativity. She reacts to the environment around her and incorporates the sudden vogue for southern cotton into her routine. By calling Calhoun, she piques his interest in attending her show, thereby attesting to Billie's skills as a successful promoter of her brand. When she decides to conduct a financial transaction with an independent contractor (Uncle Bud), she does so only because she knows she will be reimbursed by her employer (the Cotton Club). Finally, she succeeds in raising funds for her chosen charity—"the actors' benefit fund"—by auctioning the bale of cotton at the end of her performance, though this endeavor comes at the cost of her professional pride.[28] This is significant because it highlights her own hypocrisy as an artist: though she was willing to part with only $50 to purchase the bale of cotton, she expects the audience members to bid upward of $1,000 for it.

Himes's Billie miscalculates the influence of her sex appeal on her audience, much in the same way that Davis misjudged the Harlem community's willingness to welcome his white film crew just because the director had eulogized Malcolm X. Billie's suggestive dance turns on the audience members but not enough for them to blindly do her bidding and make a bid to support a group of anonymous "actors." Just as she had no use for a bale of cotton in her own residence, neither did anyone in the audience, except for Calhoun. Billie turns the tables on her audience once more, by verbally assessing their own performance of blackness in the face of the auction and finding it lacking because no person of color outbids the white southerner. As the "black critic," Billie vents her frustration by deriding the audience's personal memories of her risqué performance as mere simulacra of her dance: "'Cheapskates,' Billie sneered. 'You're going to close your eyes and imagine it's me, but it ain't going to be the same.'"[29] Speaking as critic, Billie points to the unwillingness of the black audience to compete with a white southerner on an equal financial basis as proof that they lack the very revolutionary Afrocentrism that fueled her dance performance. Because they cannot uphold this ideal and conduct themselves as equals to the whites, Billie suggests, the black audience members' private sexual fantasies and conjured memories of her body writhing suggestively on the bale of cotton will lack the same sexual charge that characterizes her own dance.

The black audience at the Cotton Club lets Billie down in a similar way to how Himes felt Americans reacted negatively to his literary aspirations. As he recalls in his autobiography, "Nothing in all my life hurt me as much as the American rejection of my thoughts."[30] Though his books sold well, they were not regarded as being literary in the same way as were the works of Richard Wright. Instead, his reputation as a writer stateside was refracted through the lens of a different cadre of peers, as Ongiri remarks: "Himes was often grouped with popular African American 'street realist' writers such as Donald Goines and Iceberg Slim (Robert Beck)."[31] These writers' output was considered "pulp fiction" in much the same way that Billie's choreographed burlesque performance has been dismissed as mere sexual titillation: "Billie performs striptease on the bale of cotton."[32] In both cases, their artwork has been reduced to mere sex appeal despite the visual imagery of power and mastery over the legacy of repression conveyed by Billie's choreography, which has her dancing *atop* the bale of cotton in an urban club rather than being weighed down by it as countless field slaves and sharecroppers were in the rural South. In *Pimping Fictions*, Justin Gifford sums up the impact that discussing black crime fiction alongside pulp fiction published for a black readership has had: "The constraints created by the pulp publishing industry have placed black crime novelists in a particularly vulnerable position in the literary marketplace."[33] It is of little wonder, then, that the film adaptation cuts out the auction scene altogether in order to maintain the transactions between dancer and audience more clearly in the realm of the artistic, rather than commercial.

Whereas the novel version of Billie ends with the failure of the artist and her audience to connect and recognize each other as equal partners in the production of a shared black aesthetic, the film version situates Billie as an icon squarely embraced by her community. As the camera follows O'Malley's malcontented girlfriend, Iris, as she makes her way to the Apollo Theater, the camera angle pans to show the marquee, which proudly announces the featured performer of the evening as "Harlem's Own Billie." As the scene transitions from the outside to the inside of the theater, the camera pauses on a life-size black-and-white

Billie dances atop the bale of cotton. (*Cotton Comes to Harlem* DVD, MGM Home Entertainment)

poster of Billie dressed in full performance regalia, adorned with necklaces and feathers. The next shot shows her in the middle of a dress rehearsal when she abruptly stops, removes her headdress, and exclaims in frustration, "Goddam it, none of these things are going to work." Despite cajoling from her male admirer, who warns her against "bust[ing] something between your assets and your liabilities," Billie continues undaunted: "Balloons, fans, feathers . . . I'm sick of them all! They are out of style and don't say a damn thing about my people." Her interlocutor interjects, "Forget them, forget them, cuz what you've got going for you, my, my, my, ain't never going out of style." Billie responds, "Uncle Tom is what they are. My dance has got to say something about my people, black people. We've got to set our people's mind to thinking. Get our own black thing together." Her admirer kisses her gently and then greets Iris, who walks in and starts rummaging through Billie's wardrobe, looking for a dress.

This film version depicts Billie as an artist who rejects the prevalent aesthetic in her artistic domain, the trappings that emphasize her gender and are meant to enhance her sex appeal to audiences. Billie's rejection of these props is in no way a disavowal of her own sexuality but a desire to shift the frame through which her blackness is showcased. Rather than incidental, she wants to make her black body central to a narrative that embraces a positive depiction of sexuality as empowerment. In this, her artistic vision may best be understood according to the black aesthetic theorized by Black Arts thinker Mayfield: "For those who must create, there is a Black Aesthetic which cannot be stolen from us, and it rests on something much more substantial than hip talk, African dress, natural hair and endless, fruitless discussions of 'soul.' It is in our own racial memory, and the unshakable knowledge of who we are, where we have been, and, springing from this, where we are going."[34] While the novel's Billie incorporates the cotton into her act "on a whim," the film's Billie "must create"; she is consumed by a desire to align her artistic vision and her political ideology, preferably through the medium of embodied performance. She deliberately sets out to look for props that will support her artistic goal of "set[ting] our people's mind to thinking" by "get[ting] our own black thing together."

Massood is one of the few critics to evaluate the significance of Billie's performance as a political act. Though I consider the plantation stage setting at its start to be satirical, Massood reads it as proof of her "antebellum idyll" theory, which holds that it is a romanticization of the agrarian past that continues to haunt the present:

> While an overt spectacle eliciting a double system of voyeuristic pleasure, Billie's performance defines the interconnections between the antebellum idyll and contemporary ghetto spaces by suggesting the legacy of the rural South in the modern northern city. At the same time, the routine indicates how sexuality and cinematic history are also implicated in these interconnections: the sexual ecstasy of King Cotton and its links to capitalism, the sexual repressed in the history of U.S. race relations, and the complicity of cinematic history in all of this.[35]

I read the cinematic and novelistic versions of this scene slightly differently, interpreting the film's depiction of a bale of cotton as an atavism, whereas the novel treats it as a relic. Thus, the auction, not the dance, at the end of Himes's novel supports Massood's interpretation because it literally reenacts for an audience "the sexual ecstasy of King Cotton and its links to capitalism," through the dehumanizing spectacle of the black female body as well as the bale of cotton being held up for sale. Davis's film, in contrast, does not depict the financial transaction of audience members purchasing tickets to view the performance.

Instead, the camera angles during Billie's dance change, from a central perspective, framing her dance moves onstage, to the reverse perspective, which focuses on the faces of the members of the mixed-gender and mixed-race audience, pausing to reflect on their reaction to what they see. The film shows Billie being subjected to both male and female gazes, which react positively to what they behold, thus validating the artist's black visual aesthetic. The longer the dance goes on, the more Billie strips, and as she lets go of the physical trappings of a plantation "racial memory" (the costume), the bolder her movements become, finally culminating in an exhaustive physical confrontation against the bale of cotton and all it represents. Davis lets Billie have the final say on what the black community should feel toward an agrarian past—fight against it and let it go—whereas Himes brings Billie's aspirations down to size by having the southern white Colonel buy his way into relevance in modern Harlem society. Though Billie is no Foxy Brown or Cleopatra Jones, she is willing to fight to get her vision of a liberated and libidinous black visual aesthetic accepted by the audience at the Apollo and in the movie theaters beyond predominantly black urban communities.

## NOTES

1. Ed Guerrero, *Framing Blackness: The African American Image in Film* (Philadelphia: Temple University Press, 2012), 81.
2. Ronald Gold, "Director Dared Use Race Humor: Soul as Lure for Cotton's B. O. Bale," *Variety*, September 30, 1970, 1, 62.
3. Ossie Davis and Ruby Dee, *With Ossie and Ruby: In This Life Together* (New York: William Morrow, 1998), 335.
4. Gold, "Director Dared," 1.
5. Ibid., 62.
6. Amy Abugo Ongiri, *Spectacular Blackness: The Cultural Politics of the Black Power Movement and the Search for a Black Aesthetic* (Charlottesville: University of Virginia Press, 2010), 4.
7. Edward Margolies and Michael Fabre, *The Several Lives of Chester Himes* (Jackson: University Press of Mississippi, 2008), 141–42.
8. Joseph McClaren, "*Cotton Comes to Harlem*: The Novel, the Film and the Critics," *Popular Culture Review* 5, no. 1 (1994): 45.
9. Chester Himes, *The Autobiography of Chester Himes: My Life of Absurdity*, vol. 2 (Garden City, NJ: Doubleday, 1976), 109.
10. Peter J. Rabinowitz, "Chandler Comes to Harlem: Racial Politics in the Thrillers of Chester Himes," in *The Sleuth and the Scholar: Origins, Evolution, and Current Trends in Detective Fiction*, ed. Barbara A. Rader and Howard G. Settler (Westport, CT: Greenwood, 1988), 21.

11. Novotny Lawrence, *Blaxploitation Films of the 1970s: Blackness and Genre* (New York: Routledge, 2008), 30.
12. Davis and Dee, *With Ossie and Ruby*, 336.
13. Ibid., 337.
14. Ibid.
15. Ongiri, *Spectacular Blackness*, 23.
16. Lawrence, *Blaxploitation Films of the 1970s*, 34.
17. Galt McDermott, "Cotton Comes to Harlem," on *The Cotton Comes to Harlem Soundtrack*, featuring George Tipton, vocals, United Artists, 1970.
18. Paula Massood, "Cotton in the City: The Black Ghetto, Blaxploitation, and Beyond," in *Black City Cinema: African American Urban Experiences in Film* (Philadelphia: Temple University Press, 2003), 93.
19. Ibid., 116.
20. Peter Freese, *The Ethnic Detective: Chester Himes, Harry Kemelman, Tony Hillerman* (Essen, Germany: Die Blaue Eule, 1992), 60.
21. Julian Mayfield, "You Touch My Black Aesthetic and I'll Touch Yours," in *The Black Aesthetic*, ed. Addison Gayle, Jr. (New York: Anchor Books, 1972), 27.
22. Hoyt W. Fuller, "Towards a Black Aesthetic," in Gayle, *Black Aesthetic*, 7–8.
23. Ibid., 8.
24. McClaren, "*Cotton Comes to Harlem*," 42–43.
25. Ongiri, *Spectacular Blackness*, 11.
26. Massood, *Black City Cinema*, 90.
27. Chester Himes, *Cotton Comes to Harlem* (1965; repr., New York: Vintage Books, 1988), 155.
28. Ibid., 148.
29. Ibid.
30. Himes, *My Life of Absurdity*, 110.
31. Ongiri, *Spectacular Blackness*, 14.
32. Lorna Fitzsimmons, "Adapting *Cotton Comes to Harlem*: From Inter- to Intraracial Conflict," *Afro-Americans in New York Life and History* 25, no. 2 (2001): 45.
33. Justin Gifford, *Pimping Fictions: African American Crime Literature and the Untold Story of Black Pulp Publishing* (Philadelphia: Temple University Press, 2013), 3.
34. Mayfield, "You Touch My Black Aesthetic," 26.
35. Massood, *Black City Cinema*, 90.

## WORKS CITED

Davis, Ossie, and Ruby Dee. *With Ossie and Ruby: In This Life Together*. New York: William Morrow, 1998.

Fitzsimmons, Lorna. "Adapting *Cotton Comes to Harlem*: From Inter- to Intraracial Conflict." *Afro-Americans in New York Life and History* 25, no. 2 (2001): 45–57.

Freese, Peter. *The Ethnic Detective: Chester Himes, Harry Kemelman, Tony Hillerman*. Essen, Germany: Die Blaue Eule, 1992.

Fuller, Hoyt W. "Towards a Black Aesthetic." In *The Black Aesthetic*, edited by Addison Gayle, Jr., 3–11. New York: Anchor Books, 1972.

Gifford, Justin. *Pimping Fictions: African American Crime Literature and the Untold Story of Black Pulp Publishing*. Philadelphia: Temple University Press, 2013.

Gold, Ronald. "Director Dared Use Race Humor: Soul as Lure for Cotton's B. O. Bale." *Variety*, September 30, 1970.

Guerrero, Ed. *Framing Blackness: The African American Image in Film*. Philadelphia: Temple University Press, 2012.

Himes, Chester. *The Autobiography of Chester Himes: My Life of Absurdity*. Vol. 2. Garden City, NJ: Doubleday, 1976.

———. *Cotton Comes to Harlem*. 1965. Reprint, New York: Vintage Books, 1988.

Lawrence, Novotny. *Blaxploitation Films of the 1970s: Blackness and Genre*. New York: Routledge, 2008.

Margolies, Edward, and Michael Fabre. *The Several Lives of Chester Himes*. Jackson: University Press of Mississippi, 2008.

Massood, Paula. *Black City Cinema: African American Urban Experiences in Film*. Philadelphia: Temple University Press, 2003.

Mayfield, Julian. "You Touch My Black Aesthetic and I'll Touch Yours." In *The Black Aesthetic*, edited by Addison Gayle, Jr., 24–31. New York: Anchor Books, 1972.

McClaren, Joseph. "*Cotton Comes to Harlem*: The Novel, the Film and the Critics." *Popular Culture Review* 5, no. 1 (1994): 37–46.

McDermott, Galt. "Cotton Comes to Harlem." On *The Cotton Comes to Harlem Soundtrack*, featuring George Tipton, vocals. United Artists, 1970. LP.

Ongiri, Amy Abugo. *Spectacular Blackness: The Cultural Politics of the Black Power Movement and the Search for a Black Aesthetic*. Charlottesville: University of Virginia Press, 2010.

Rabinowitz, Peter J. "Chandler Comes to Harlem: Racial Politics in the Thrillers of Chester Himes." In *The Sleuth and the Scholar: Origins, Evolution, and Current Trends in Detective Fiction*, edited by Barbara A. Rader and Howard G. Settler. Westport, CT: Greenwood, 1988.

# 2

# RACIAL EXPLOITATION IN *WATERMELON MAN*
## CONTEMPORARY APPLICATIONS

### CHARLES E. WILSON, JR.

Melvin Van Peebles's film *Watermelon Man* does not represent the blaxploitation movement in the strictest sense. It is not set in a decidedly urban space, where the black hero or heroine is tasked with confronting violent crime in a drug-infested area. The film does not feature characters sporting urban fashions such as brightly colored suits and platform shoes or wearing towering afros in celebration of their blackness. Instead, *Watermelon Man* uses blackness to infiltrate and challenge the mores and belief system of the supposedly idyllic and civilized suburbs. Further, like standard blaxploitation films, it "serve[s] as a window into the black experience during the 1970s coded by race, gender, and class."[1] The film does "feature a black hero or heroine who is both socially and politically conscious."[2] Instead of black culture and black identity being exploited, it is the assumed American culture and value system that are exploited/exposed. The hypocrisy underlying the social structure of suburbia is placed in sharp contrast to the urban social structure most often depicted in blaxploitation films. Blacks are not using violence as a means to defeat white villains; instead, they are using their minds to upend the power structure that creates and maintains white privilege. This perspective is consistent with blaxploitation characteristics wherein dramatic conflict "operates as a metaphor in which whites represent the oppressive establishment.... Their defeat at the hands of the African American protagonists is symbolic of blacks overcoming racism perpetuated by the machine."[3] With David Walker's expanded definition of blaxploitation, *Watermelon Man* is easily situated in the movement. According to Walker, "The reality is that blaxploitation is neither positive nor negative; it simply is what it is. And what it is, first and foremost, is a genre of film that includes action, comedy, drama, romance, and even documentary—made and marketed to a predominantly black audience—as well as the era in which these films were made."[4]

## CONTEMPORARY RELEVANCE

*Watermelon Man* depicts the nation's overall response to the "browning" of the population. From the late 1960s to the present day, demographers have anticipated a time when America would be a so-called minority-majority country, asserting that people of color (blacks, Hispanics, Asians) would outnumber those of European descent. In the latter part of the twentieth century, this transformation was to happen by 2000. As the twenty-first century dawned, the prediction was extended thirty more years, and more recently, the target has been extended to 2050, one might suggest, to allow the "majority" population more time to adjust to a notion that has already become a political reality. Wendy Roth notes, "predictions that within a few decades minority groups will be the majority of the population can produce a sense of racial group threat, a fear that rapidly growing groups like Latinos will challenge the privileges that others have long held."[5] And Ronald R. Sundstrom notes, "The demographic change that is sometimes called 'the browning of America' promises to transform not only the population of the United States but also the meaning of race and ethnicity with the nation."[6]

The 2008 election of a biracial president (Barack Obama identifies as African American, and the world follows suit) made clear the reality of the minority-majority status, and his reelection in 2012 confirmed the truth. Even so, some Americans remain shocked and even appalled at the presence of a black president. As social scientists Donald Kinder and Allison Dale-Riddle assert, "Race was deeply implicated in the 2008 contest. Obama's candidacy provoked a huge racial divide in the vote. Obama's support among black Americans was driven significantly by racial group solidarity. Opposition to Obama among white Americans was driven significantly by resentments rooted in race. All things considered, Barack Obama became president in spite of his race."[7]

Some politicians continue to recoil at the very idea of a black commander in chief, a thought that for them is akin to the nightmare experienced by *Watermelon Man*'s protagonist, Jeff Gerber. Suddenly, America has become black, and the shock is unbearable. This demographic shift is a disruption of the racialized binary, black inferior / white superior, that racist whites hold as some kind of celestial truth. Bryant Keith Alexander has maintained that "while racism is often felt as problematic and intellectually interpreted as specious, the historical repetition creates a social interaction that is always and already expected."[8] In other words, racism and racial inequality have always been intact; they maintain their power and primacy by virtue of their longevity (or repetitious existence). But the changing demography interrogates and disrupts that "reality." As a consequence, those who wish to maintain the status quo scurry to protect their long-held political and social power.

In November 2014, America endured one of the most hotly contested midterm elections in its history. Enjoying a conservative sweep in Congress and in most gubernatorial races, the new Republication majority threatened to repeal the Affordable Care Act—ACA (also known as Obamacare). The political Right argues that the ACA will ultimately cripple the U.S. economy, while the political Left counters that the ACA not only will provide the basic right of health-care coverage to hundreds of thousands of Americans but also will stabilize the lives of underprivileged (mostly black and brown) people. For these supporters of the ACA, access to health care is both a class and race-equality issue. They also contend that because the ACA is based on the policies adopted by the Commonwealth of Massachusetts during the Mitt Romney administration, the arguments levied against it are solely because President Obama is African American. Shortly after the 2012 election, a defeated Romney ironically stated that President Obama won because he had promised minority people certain entitlements. Race figures very prominently in America's current political debates, because once again, America is reeling from the shock of its new racial identity. When certain political figures state that they must reclaim America, they are parroting Jeff Gerber's "I want my whiteness back!" They want America to return to its heyday as a white-supremacist regime.

While the country continues its demographic shift, some factions still wish to regress. At a time when it has become more commonplace for blacks to assume leadership positions (president, secretary of state, attorney general, etc.), some cannot fathom this new reality, which includes interracial relationships and the children from those couplings. The media is replete with various images of biraciality. Yet early in 2013, a firestorm erupted when General Mills featured in a Cheerios commercial a biracial child with a black father and a white mother. That there was such a reactionary outburst underscores the shock that some people still feel about modern examples of human love and companionship. This astonishment is expertly drawn in *Watermelon Man*.

*Watermelon Man* offers a somewhat comedic lens through which to consider the United States' ongoing cultural transformations. As is often the case, demographic shifts challenge not only our self-perceptions but also our stereotypes about others. The challenge to self-perception is a challenge to privilege, a privilege that goes largely unnoticed by those who hold it until they are at risk of losing it. Just as Jeff Gerber is forced to decide how he will ultimately react to the transformation, so, too, must America adjust to change (reality) and also determine how it will not just survive but also thrive in its new (golden) skin. The film presents an uncomfortable truth about the long-term treatment of those whom Audrey Smedley refers as "the low-status races." She continues, "The great, often unspoken, dilemma for the low-status races in North America was, and still is, how to deal with the identities that the dominant society has imposed on them. Most minorities have had no option but to accept race as a reality and to function in American society knowing that most whites consider them intellectually and morally inferior. This is an enormous burden in an ostensibly free society, where individuals are supposedly judged on the basis of factors other than race status."[9] Jeff experiences the life of a "high-status race" and a "low-status race" within a matter of hours. The ways in which he manages his transformation and cultivates a new set of survival skills ultimately determines his humanity. Similarly, the ways in which the United States responds to its ongoing and rapidly increasing racial shift will determine its standing as either a real democracy or a country that continues to defer a dream that should by now be a reality.

## WATERMELON MAN

*Watermelon Man* employs blaxploitation features to execute its analysis of America's racial issues. The film recounts the story of middle-class, white bigot Jeff Gerber, who awakens in the middle of the night to discover that he has transformed into a black man. He must now cope with forms of prejudice that he previously meted out to blacks. Jeff is played by the veteran black actor and comedian Godfrey Cambridge, who opens the film in whiteface and wearing a strawberry-blond wig. The makeup looks contrived and artificial, suggesting that Gerber's white self is not his true identity. Even though he thinks he is most comfortable as a white man, the bizarre makeup invites the audience to question that very notion. Obviously, once Jeff transforms into a black man, he looks more authentic, more natural. Jeff's emerging (and natural) blackness affirms blackness as a normative condition for America in general.

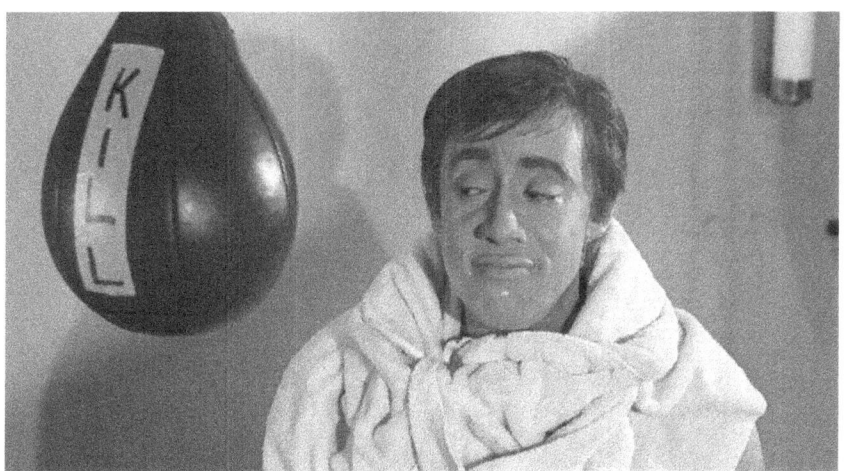

Black comedian Godfrey Cambridge in whiteface portraying Jeff Gerber. (*Watermelon Man* DVD, Columbia Tristar Home Entertainment)

Prior to the change, Jeff leads a charmed life as an insurance salesman, with a devoted wife, Althea (Estelle Parsons), and two children, Burton (Scott Garrett) and Janice (Erin Moran). Able to care for his family without financial strain, Jeff returns home from work each night to a home-cooked meal and children who are eager to see him. Other than his boorish demeanor and unrestrained arrogance (he constantly belittles blacks and women), he easily fits into his community. Jeff's obnoxious behavior does not prevent him from enjoying economic success and social standing. Because he is a white male, his actions are, by definition, right. Jeff's livelihood is not dependent on his calculated consideration of every simple decision or his every move. Even when walking through the secretarial pool at his office and referring to the women as "sluts" or belittling Joe, the older black man who serves him at a diner, Jeff does not fear reprisal for his actions, as the people he insults do not wield the same power that he does. With a complete lack of regard, he says whatever he wishes to whomever he wishes. In short, Jeff benefits from his white male privilege at every turn and is quick to remind women and African Americans that he is superior to them.

Jeff's arrogance is further established through his daily ritual, which involves racing the commuter bus that takes him to work for a part of its route prior to boarding the vehicle. Each day the other passengers cheer on the African American driver, hoping that he will beat Jeff to the stop where he will board the vehicle. However, while racing Jeff, the driver must also continue

Jeff Gerber sits waiting for the bus after having beaten it to the stop. (*Watermelon Man* DVD, Columbia Tristar Home Entertainment)

to make the scheduled stops, which puts him at a significant disadvantage, as his competitor does not have to stop and therefore consistently gets ahead. As a result, Jeff always emerges victorious. Although the race sequence seemingly represents a meaningless contest, it is a powerful metaphor about white privilege and the African American experience. Jeff's ability to race the bus unfettered demonstrates the privilege associated with his white, heteronormative masculinity. More specifically, the world is ruled by people who look like him, and as a result, he can acquire the American Dream more easily. In contrast, the bus driver, who works his job while racing Jeff, has to work twice as hard to overcome, a point that speaks to the social, political, and economic disenfranchisement of African Americans. Van Peebles returns to this theme throughout *Watermelon Man*, particularly, in Jeff's interactions with the African American elevator operator at his job and the black man who serves him at a diner that he frequents. Therefore, these characters' daily survival in the face of white persecution makes them victorious and heroic, and it pits their true integrity against Jeff's impropriety.

However, once Jeff turns black, the race between him and the bus driver takes on different connotations. His running is perceived by the whites along his route as threatening, as they believe that he has stolen something and is fleeing the scene of a crime. Similar to lynch mobs in the late 1800s and early 1900s, the whites encircle him, curse him, and accuse him of theft. As a black man, Jeff feels the immediate wrath of the white majority. The villainy of white privilege and authority is palpable, especially when the supposedly objective police officer makes it apparent that he too believes that Jeff is a criminal. White Jeff's running is a hobby (even part of his obsessive exercise regimen), but black Jeff's running is perceived as sinister. It cannot be normative; it must be aberrant. The very act of racing the bus becomes "racialized." Even Jeff responds to his son's query about whether he will race the bus (after Jeff's transformation) with "Don't bring up the *race* issue again" (my emphasis). Jeff links the simple act of racing the bus with the more charged notion that when race becomes an ethnic marker, even simple acts become complicated and potentially treacherous. When he is white, his running through the tree-lined streets of his peaceful neighborhood in a suit and white sneakers is considered charming, albeit a bit eccentric. But when he dons the similar outfit as a black man, he is treated as a perpetrator threatening the safety and security of an otherwise tranquil place. According to Baz Dreisinger, "Once Jeff looks black, he *is* black. The fact that he may possess a 'white self' within is irrelevant; his physical appearance is the sole determinant of racial identity."[10] Jeff is quickly becoming the classic hero-protagonist. Facing increased odds as he is immersed further into the black male experience, Jeff must learn coping mechanisms that militate against the dangerous privilege he once enjoyed in his white skin. Every action he takes from now on will be an act of rebellion against bigotry. In some ways, Jeff is in conflict with himself. The white Jeff and the black Jeff are at war, in much the same way that America is at war with itself during its most turbulent social transitions. The original social compact between blacks and whites (unequal though it was) has been rendered all the more unstable.

Rumbling in the background of Jeff's story is the television coverage of mounting racial tensions in the country. One is reminded that *Watermelon Man* was filmed and then released in the throes of and subsequent to one of the most racially charged periods in American history: the 1968 assassinations of Martin Luther King, Jr., and Robert Kennedy and the ensuing riots, along with the sacrificed presidency of Lyndon Johnson (sacrificed because of the civil rights gains that defined his administration). Change is afoot, and although white Jeff tries to ignore the inevitable, it will ultimately impact his own transformation. Jeff does not understand why the blacks are "rioting." To him, they should have no complaints to register about living in America. Althea believes that whites should take a greater interest in the civil rights movement. That Jeff vilifies the blacks while Althea validates the civil rights movement is quite telling. Althea legitimizes the fight for racial equality. However, Jeff believes any attempt to alter the racial dynamics in the country is an inherently violent act, when in fact the violence that erupted in the movement resulted generally from white mob opposition. Jeff does not want to think about the inequities because to think about them would require reconsideration of his own privileged state. Jeff dismisses any deep thought about the matter—in stereotypical fashion—by stating that whites are afraid of being bashed in the head with a watermelon and being the victims of theft.

Althea, on the other hand (at least initially), is more sensitive to the plight of blacks. She sees purpose in what they are doing, in part because she sees her own life as rather boring and passionless. Just as she admonishes whites to take interest in the movement and in societal progress, Althea would like to be involved in some way, to do something useful in the real world and to make real change. Her life has become mundane; even lovemaking is regimented (it occurs only on Wednesdays). At this point in life, Althea craves difference. When her children ask why their father races the bus, she responds by stating that different people engage in different activities, like stamp collecting, assembling model airplanes, drinking alcohol, or even smoking pot. Althea is willing to allow people their own identity and their own urges and desires. She does not believe they should be trapped by a trait as inconsequential as skin color.

While Althea desires more spontaneity, more freedom, and more flexibility, Jeff embraces rigidity. He refuses to make love more than once a week because he fears fathering a third child. He wants everything to remain the same. Althea believes that they have many more years of active life ahead of them and that they should welcome the possibilities of personal growth and fulfillment. Jeff only wants the status quo. If he allows any change, he believes the floodgates will open, and he will lose complete control over his life.

Jeff's color transformation comes in the middle of the night when he wanders into the bathroom. The bright light against his dark skin is at once shocking and traumatizing. He believes he has spent too much time under the sunlamp. That he has even used a sunlamp is ironic, when he considers white skin to be superior to dark. Yet his racist (illogical) assumptions about color render some coloring as acceptable, as long as he is in control of how much coloring and as long as the coloring is within the bounds of the (arbitrary) societal standard. Jeff is horrified at what he sees. The camera keeps angling on his (big and dark) hips so as to enhance the crude and monstrous nature of the surprise. He stares at himself, hoping that somehow his rightful white color will be restored. Returning to bed, he says that when he awakes from this obvious nightmare, his skin will once again be "lovely and white." But deep down knowing that some new reality has taken shape, lying next to his wife, he also states that if Althea stays asleep, he will not be forced to wake up to the harsh "reality" of being black.

Jeff Gerber discovers that he has turned into a black man. (*Watermelon Man* DVD, Columbia Tristar Home Entertainment)

Unfortunately for Jeff, the dream/nightmare does not end. In the full light of day, his blackness remains. Suddenly becoming religious, he tries to bargain with God, stating that he will accept twenty more pounds of weight if God will grant him whiteness. Then, in a typically arrogant posture, he curses God, stating that God "doesn't give a damn." When Althea sees him for the first time, she screams, threatens to call the police, and asks if she should hide the money. She then accuses Jeff of using the sunlamp too much, instead of spending time with her, making love, and producing more children. In retaliation, Jeff accuses Althea's mother of looking Chinese. By making this accusation, Jeff insinuates that Althea's bloodline is somehow to blame for his current predicament. That Jeff has observed "other" ethnic traits in his mother-in-law underscores the fact that racial purity is a myth. The natural human condition is one of diversity, instead. Still, Althea smarts at Jeff's accusation, responding that her mother's eyes are merely "almond shaped." Such a trait is allowable; there is just a hint of the exotic to make it acceptable. And when Althea peeks under Jeff's towel, hoping that Jeff's manhood has been enhanced, Jeff responds, "That's an old wives' tale." Obviously, however, it represents one myth that Althea had hoped would be true. And it is one that Jeff had desired. He too surveyed his lower torso upon discovering his blackness, hoping for "masculine" growth. Jeff will accept the one asset of being black as long as he is not required to relinquish all whiteness.

Jeff's most desperate attempt to remedy his new condition is subjecting his skin to a plaster mold. That he would suffer resembling a disfigured lab experiment instead of embracing his darker skin is indicative of the racist indoctrination he has suffered and also perpetuated. He almost asphyxiates himself in the process of trying to whiten up. Death seems more appealing than blackness. Upon realizing that the cast has had no effect on his color, Jeff runs through the house yelling, in puerile fashion, "I want my whiteness back!" Jeff believes that he has been victimized and that he deserves to possess the one trait that society deems acceptable and that society rewards with its constant approval. He needs the security blanket of whiteness. Jeff feels trapped in his own house, isolated from a world that was formerly his own. Even though he has yet to be objectified by the outside world, he has already begun to internalize such objectification. This self-persecution is a veiled attempt to prepare for what he knows will be a mean-spirited onslaught from his former peers.

Jeff's hypersensitivity is revealed when he is startled by the sound of the doorbell. Althea reminds him that "the Ku Klux Klan never rings the bell." Even still, Jeff feels guilty for being black, he feels guilty for hiding out in a white neighborhood, and he feels guilty and ashamed about a future that he knows will now be fraught with the kind of compromise he has never been forced to make. His attack on the white deliveryman (who has come to replace the sunlamp) is an attack on the very principles he has held so dear. The deliveryman represents the commerce that has defined Jeff's previous success, a commerce that shores up white men, historically at the expense of black men. Without being able to fight the white establishment, Jeff lashes out at its representative. And when Althea secures a stool in an attempt to contain Jeff, he is immediately transformed into the crazed/caged animal that society will now define him to be. Sadly, Althea has participated in the objectification of her husband when she emerges as animal tamer.

And such objectification has just begun. For the first time in Jeff's life, he is confronted with overt racism when he attempts to enter the country club to meet a client for lunch. The country club is not just a social venue; it is the place where high-stakes business deals are made. Those who are at the center of the economic and political power structure have access to such clubs. Jeff is refused entrance by the doorman, who informs him that his client has been called away on an emergency. Jeff understands that this is a mere ruse and that he is really being denied entry because he is black. In the past, Jeff has probably participated in such a ruse, so he certainly knows the rules of so-called polite society. When he is denied entry at the club, Jeff is denied the access to financial fulfillment and stability. It is the final blow to his former identity. Jeff Gerber, the businessman, can no longer conduct business.

With Jeff's professional standing now diminished, he will need to re-create himself and pursue another path toward self-actualization. His boss, Mr. Townsend (Howard Caine), offers Jeff one possibility—breaking into a new market and selling insurance to blacks. Returning to his office, Jeff, somewhat mocking his new identity, extends an open invitation to his coworkers to consult him on all matters related to gospel singing, tap dancing, and boxing, while exhorting them to "beware the black scourge." Comedic and somewhat self-deprecating, black Jeff appropriates the stereotypes that white Jeff would have freely spewed forth and empowers himself before such stereotypes can be used against him. Jeff's behavior here confirms the assertion that *Watermelon Man* is "ultimately transform[ed] . . . from a nonthreatening racial farce to a tale of one man's conversion from bigot to revolutionary."[11]

Finally deciding to consult a medical professional, Jeff visits Dr. Wainwright (Kay E. Kuter), who believes that "something in [Jeff's] family lineage" may be the culprit. He is even more intrigued when he discovers that Jeff's full name is Jefferson Washington Gerber, reminding Jeff that ex-slaves often bestowed on themselves the names of former presidents. In this way, Dr. Wainwright suggests that Jeff is really of mixed heritage and that the black strain/stain is just now presenting itself. Simplistic though the explanation is, the doctor's assessment provides Jeff a basis for rebuilding his identity, thus rebuilding his life. The fact is, no matter the cause of the transformation, Jeff must equip himself with emotional fortitude to withstand the micro- and macroaggressions that he is bound to suffer in a racially hostile world. And even still, Dr. Wainwright's explanation does remind one that given the sexual transgressions practiced in America's past, racial purity is at best a myth.

Jeff as representative black man is no new phenomenon. Like those former slaves from the mid-1860s, as noted by Dr. Wainwright, who chose to rename themselves, to the victims of post-Reconstruction tactics of disenfranchisement, to the victims of early twentieth-century lynch mobs, to the pre-civil-rights-era activists, to Jeff's modern-day 1960s, black presence in American society is nothing new. It did not just suddenly appear. While it seems that Jeff's blackness (with its overnight "arrival") is new, it, in fact, is only new and shocking to white Jeff. The growing minority population in America is nothing new. It has been emerging over a very long period of time, since America's inception. And even racial backlash cannot prevent the continued "browning" process. Just as Jeff's blackness is made permanent, so, too, is America's racial transformation. The one-hundred-year history that predates Jeff's contemporary moment is a history fraught with advancement and regression, with promise and disappointment.

And those same civil rights activists from Jeff's 1960s moment did not suddenly appear out of nothingness; they are the progeny of a people who have long suffered in the fight for social, political, and economic equality. Some people may see them as an unnecessary disturbance; instead, they represent the hope for America's ultimate fulfillment of its potential. They are not being impatient; they have been patient for a very long time. It is their duty to aid America in honoring its stated creed.

In the forty-plus years since the premiere of *Watermelon Man*, America is still suffering bouts of the advancement/regression paradigm. Inasmuch as progress has been made, a new slave system has also emerged, called the prison industrial complex. With unfair sentencing laws skewed against black and brown men, America has revitalized the prison convict system from the post-Reconstruction and turn-of-the-twentieth-century period. Such a system reminds the audience that the past battles for equality and social justice are still being waged. Jeff's sudden emergence into blackness thrusts him into the realities of minority life that he has so easily dismissed in the past. Being judged, and also persecuted, for one's color/ethnicity is appalling when one must experience such intrusions firsthand. When Jeff is removed from the country club, he could have been accused of inciting a riot just because he was trying to assert his rights as a human being. The law might find him guilty. But if he were still white and tried to asset his personhood, he would more than likely be supported in that effort. He would, in fact, be seen as patriotic for demanding that his constitutionally mandated rights be protected and applied. At any moment, in his black skin, however, Jeff could be accused of a trumped-up crime and hauled off to jail. And without the appropriate financial and legal support, he would lose. As quickly as he once threatened to expose the diner as a "homosexual hangout," he now could be subjected to the whimsical threats of any white person he might have the misfortune of encountering. The longer that he lives in his black skin, the more susceptible he becomes to such an atrocity. And one hundred years of social progress will do nothing to prevent the potential tragedy.

Ultimately unable to detect a scientific cause, Dr. Wainwright refers Jeff to a black physician, Dr. John L. Catlin, who confirms dispassionately, and very simply, that Jeff is black. Captions appear on the screen that read "put your best foot forward"; "be a credit to your race"; "you're a negro!"; and lastly, "yessiree, facts are facts." In this transitional moment in the film, Jeff can no longer deny his new existence, and he becomes more resigned to his transformation. He must now decide what to do with this new self-knowledge and determine how he is to function in the world. Now that Negro is no longer the "other" to him, he must seek his own agency, his own subject self. Eschewing the stereotypes about blacks that he has held true for so long, Jeff has to recalculate his status. In the same way that former slaves attempted agency by naming themselves from the American white power structure (former presidents), Jeff, too, must embrace this historical practice of self-actualization. In so doing, he appropriates the power of the oppressor and reassigns this authority to the oppressed, not just to himself but to what will be his new community.

By the time he arrives home, he is emotionally and intellectually armed to face the neighbors who have come to banish him from the community. Initially offering him $50,000 for a $37,000 house, Jeff determines that a $13,000 profit is still too modest, claiming that he could make just as much or more from his watermelon patch and the admission fees to his planned revival meetings. A tough negotiator, Jeff eventually garners a $100,000 offer, telling the four neighbors, "I think the neighborhood is a bit too Jewish anyway." For the moment, assuming the role of capitalist bigot, Jeff drives a hard bargain. He knows he is the one in power, because he has something these neighbors want so desperately—his immediate departure. Jeff has everything to gain. Whatever profit he makes above $37,000 rewards him for his blackness. And even if negotiations had failed, Jeff would have enjoyed the pleasure of torturing his neighbors with his presence. The fact that these men have already secured from a bank an amount more than double the value of Jeff's house highlights the economic power they wield. Under normal circumstances, a black man like Jeff could not begin to compete against such financial heavyweights. But because they desire a community free of racial "stain," Jeff forces them to purchase their "freedom." And in a perverse twist, they purchase Jeff's freedom, too. He can now start his own business and better control his own destiny.

And Jeff's neighbors are left to confront their collective conscience. To their credit, the men understand that their actions are abhorrent. As they leave, the spokesperson apologetically hopes that maybe the offer will help them "seem less villainous." However, their villainy has already been confirmed by the fact that at least one of them has been telephoning the Gerber house and harassing both Jeff and Althea: "Jeff Gerber? Move out, Nigger!" So even though they come calmly and with what seems a reasonable offer (from a market-driven, real estate perspective), their politeness has already been tainted by their uncivilized and intrusive behavior. In this way, they *are* the Ku Klux Klan who have rung the doorbell, because their mission is the same—to root out any form of difference or perceived inferiority. At least, in this case, Jeff has advanced as a result of his encounter with the Klan.

After the neighbors' departure, Althea becomes unhinged, asking Jeff, "Why do you insist on being Negro?" And when Jeff seeks affection from her, she demurs, "It won't be Wednesday, until, until I get my bearings," indicating to Jeff that she will never make love to him again, because she will never regain her comfort level with him. Instead, she joins her children, whom she has already sent away to Indianapolis. She admits, "I'm still liberal but only to a point." Althea could afford to be open-minded when she was merely a spectator to the civil unrest and when the civil unrest was "locked" inside the television screen, far removed from her everyday existence. Her sense of noblesse oblige gave her license to be sensitive to the plight of blacks and even to cheer their efforts. But now that she is faced with racial tension inside her home, in a situation in which she is called on to make a real sacrifice, she finds herself ill equipped to compromise. Her privilege has defined her, and she is unwilling to relinquish it. Her reminder, "Everyone liked me!" is indicative of the kind of social capital she has enjoyed and even celebrated. The very notion that she should be despised and ostracized is untenable. And now that she no longer has the lofty position of spectator in this racial drama, Althea questions the validity of the black activists on television. While she had once championed their cause (at least in comments to white Jeff), she now questions their objectives: "Why must they be so pushy?" In an almost sudden transposition of beliefs, Althea voices Jeff's former opinion. With her comfort zone breached, Althea eschews the black freedom struggle. She wants the activists to adopt a more measured approach, one that does not disrupt her life or question her right to enjoy such a life. Whereas before, she seemed to embrace the notion of extending rights to others, to enhance the humanity of whites by doing so, she now believes that such an extension of rights would come at the expense of her own. Rights come in a limited quantity. In a zero-sum game, when blacks gain rights, whites lose them. Althea reveals her latent racism, because she has believed (deep in the recesses of her being) that her identity exists because the identity of another group is somehow inferior. If blacks are now "pushy," they are fighting for something they obviously do not deserve. On the other hand, she deserves all of the amenities that she has come to expect and to enjoy. Not being able to remove the "stain" from her home, she chooses instead to remove herself. Her departure is a protective posture not just for herself or her children but also for any future children. The latter protection is even more ironic given the fact that she had once wanted more children with Jeff.

Jeff, abandoned by his wife and feeling the need for physical contact, visits Erica, a blonde from the secretarial pool who has flirted with him ever since his transformation. They make passionate love, whereupon she becomes almost obsessed with his color and his musculature. She determines that she never again wants to sleep with a white man. Realizing that their relationship would be superficial only, Jeff calls her "a bigot" and explains to her that she cares for him not as a human being but rather as a specimen. She responds by calling him a "black bastard" and ultimately "a nigger." She even screams out "rape" as he leaves her apartment. When she cannot control Jeff and objectify him, she assumes the only power she thinks she can wield over him: as victimized white woman suffering the brutality of a black man. By accusing him of rape, she attempts to absolve herself of any responsibility for the sexual act that she only moments ago enjoyed. Since she cannot objectify him, she accuses him of objectifying (raping) her.

One of the women abandons Jeff because he is black, while the other one wants him only because he is black. In both situations, Jeff's humanity is assailed. Neither woman is concerned with his personhood, his aspirations, even his frailties. His color is all that matters; it either repels or attracts. Even though Jeff might not want the color to define him, society uses it to define him. Now that Jeff has used his color to provide some economic freedom, he must determine how to further empower himself and his newfound community. With his transformation, *Watermelon Man* has achieved what William Lyne suggests black films must: "They should work toward the decolonization of black minds and reclaiming black spirit."[12]

Uncomfortable selling insurance to black people when many of them do not really need the product, Jeff sees these black people, instead, as human beings and not as consumers. He wants to offer this community sound financial advice that fulfills their individual needs and circumstances. He is treating them as human beings rather than as customers from whom he is to make a profit. Jeff's own humanity is restored when he thinks selflessly of others. With feelings of solidarity come feelings of responsibility and protection. Jeff has been transformed from one who believes in an individualistic, competitive model of existence to one who believes in a community, shared model. Instead of maintaining that success as a businessman (and as a human being) is predicated on his ability to defeat others (by taking advantage of them financially and selling them needless insurance), Jeff has adopted the philosophy that his membership in this community is dependent on his serving as an ally and advocate. To do so, he must not seek advantage. Rather, he must promote the success and stability of his community. In so doing, his success and reward are made even better. When the lives of his new community members improve, his life improves. The competitive model certainly did not work for him ultimately, because once his new trait is revealed, members of his former society (whose rules he had adopted) abandon him. They see his defeat as their success. But in this new community, he stands the chance of his kindness and concern being reciprocated.

Jeff's redemptive behavior is best described as a transformation of traditional American individualism (with its competitive model) into what scholar Jack Turner terms an African American individualism, a concept that is shaped by four specific concepts: socioeconomic realism, sensitivity to dialectics of identity and difference, historical consciousness, and relinquishment as a virtuous act.[13] Embracing socioeconomic realism is to understand that economic assets are not distributed equitably in society and that a privileged status results in greater control of such assets. With regard to identity and difference, it is the difference or "otherness" of a person that shapes her or his identity and gives her or him a unique perspective on how well or how unfairly society is functioning. The "othered" individual also understands that her or his condition is not innate but is shaped by the need of the majority to feel superior. Historical consciousness provides the broader context for understanding the current condition. When individuals or groups risk succumbing to notions of inferiority, they must engage in analysis and reflection to understand the roots of such beliefs. Relinquishment as virtue simply refers to transferring a socially provided advantage to others who are less fortunate in the interest of true democracy. With Jeff having experienced privilege and power when he was white, he is in the best position to comprehend these concepts now that he has witnessed the potential social and economic burdens of being black. And his understanding enhances his humanity.

Before Jeff establishes his own business but after he has contemplated his departure from Mr. Townsend's company, he applies with an employment agency. Even with all of his professional experience, he is offered only a garbage man position. And while one of his coworkers insists that he will acclimate to the odor, Jeff determines that he never wants to accept the "smell" of defeat. Self-determination is the only option for him, and it will be rooted in this newly acquired African American individualism.

This reclamation of self is highlighted in the film's final scene, which shows a liberated Jeff participating in an African-themed martial arts class. This scene "affirms [the] equation of black power and black consciousness with black masculinity."[14] Jeff and the other black men—with their homemade, spear-like weapons and their bare-chested bravado, move about in unison, forming a community of strength and protection for each other. When they yell and posture synchronously, they emerge as a powerful, perhaps even intimidating, force. Rather than being a lone black voice struggling to be heard in the majority world, Jeff is surrounded by men of similar language, culture, and history. That the film ends with a focus on African cultural practice and with Jeff and his cohorts in a warrior pose might suggest that the battle for racial, cultural, and artistic expression is still being waged, as the country continues to adjust to its ever-changing political, social, cultural, and racial identity. In choosing this ending, Van Peebles "avoided a narrative that presented blackness as a nightmare and provided instead a story about the path to racial enlightenment and eventual revolution."[15]

Jeff's journey highlights America's ever-changing demographic landscape, with its multitude of identities; his ultimate acceptance of self gives hope to a similar adjustment more broadly writ. The film anticipates this self-acceptance as it reminds the audience that social change is inevitable and resistance is futile. True freedom, as Jeff Gerber learns, is the embrace of progressive transformation. *Watermelon Man* challenges rigid perceptions while liberating those who are poised to move forward.

## NOTES

1. Ashley Sauers, "'Can You Dig It?': The Politics of Race, Gender, and Class in Blaxploitation Cinema," *Film Matters* 3 (2012): 15.
2. Novotny Lawrence, *Blaxploitation Films of the 1970s: Blackness and Genre* (New York: Routledge, 2008), 18.
3. Ibid., 19.
4. David Walker, introduction to *Reflections on Blaxploitation: Actors and Directors Speak*, by David Walker, Andrew J. Rausch, and Chris Watson (Lanham, MD: Scarecrow, 2009), viii.
5. Wendy Roth, *Race Migrations: Latinos and the Cultural Transformation of Race* (Stanford, CA: Stanford University Press, 2012), 6.
6. Ronald R. Sundstrom, *The Browning of America and the Evasion of Social Justice* (Albany: State University of New York Press, 2008), 1.
7. Donald R. Kinder and Allison Dale-Riddle, *The End of Race? Obama, 2008, and Racial Politics in America* (New Haven, CT: Yale University Press, 2012), 4.
8. Bryant Keith Alexander, *The Performative Sustainability of Race: Reflections on Black Culture and the Politics of Identity* (New York: Peter Lang, 2012), 9.
9. Audrey Smedley, *Race in North America: Origin and Evolution of a Worldview*, 3rd ed. (Boulder, CO: Westview, 2007), 339.
10. Baz Dreisinger, *Near Black: White-to-Black Passing in American Culture* (Amherst: University of Massachusetts Press, 2008), 64.
11. Racquel Gates, "Subverting Hollywood from the Inside Out: Melvin Van Peebles's *Watermelon Man*," *Film Quarterly* 38, no. 1 (2014): 9.
12. William Lyne, "No Accident: From Black Power to Black Box Office," *African American Review* 43, no. 1 (2000): 45.
13. Jack Turner, *Awakening to Race: Individualism and Social Consciousness in America* (Chicago: University of Chicago Press, 2012), 112–15.
14. Dreisinger, *Near Black*, 65.
15. Gates, "Subverting Hollywood," 14.

# WORKS CITED

Alexander, Bryant Keith. *The Performative Sustainability of Race: Reflections on Black Culture and the Politics of Identity*. New York: Peter Lang, 2012.

Dreisinger, Baz. *Near Black: White-to-Black Passing in American Culture*. Amherst: University of Massachusetts Press, 2008.

Gates, Racquel. "Subverting Hollywood from the Inside Out: Melvin Van Peebles's *Watermelon Man*." *Film Quarterly* 38, no. 1 (2014): 9–21.

Kinder, Donald R., and Allison Dale-Riddle. *The End of Race? Obama, 2008, and Racial Politics in America*. New Haven, CT: Yale University Press, 2012.

Lawrence, Novotny. *Blaxploitation Films of the 1970s: Blackness and Genre*. New York: Routledge, 2008.

Lyne, William. "No Accident: From Black Power to Black Box Office." *African American Review* 43, no. 1 (2000): 39–59.

Roth, Wendy. *Race Migrations: Latinos and the Cultural Transformation of Race*. Stanford, CA: Stanford University Press, 2012.

Sauers, Ashley. "'Can You Dig It?': The Politics of Race, Gender, and Class in Blaxploitation Cinema." *Film Matters* 3 (2012): 14–19.

Smedley, Audrey. *Race in North America: Origin and Evolution of a Worldview*. 3rd ed. Boulder, CO: Westview, 2007.

Sundstrom, Ronald R. *The Browning of America and the Evasion of Social Justice*. Albany: State University of New York Press, 2008.

Turner, Jack. *Awakening to Race: Individualism and Social Consciousness in America*. Chicago: University of Chicago Press, 2012.

Walker, David. Introduction to *Reflections on Blaxploitation: Actors and Directors Speak*, by David Walker, Andrew J. Rausch, and Chris Watson, vii–x. Lanham, MD: Scarecrow, 2009.

*Watermelon Man*. Directed by Melvin Van Peebles. Columbia Pictures, 1970. Film.

# 3

## *SWEETBACK* IN CHICAGO

### GERALD R. BUTTERS, JR.

*SWEET SWEETBACK'S BAADASSSSS SONG* IS ONE OF THE SEMINAL FILMS IN black independent filmmaking. Deemed "revolutionary," "pornographic," "reactionary," "landmark," and "trash," *Sweetback* is often considered to be the film that triggered the explosion of blaxploitation films in the period 1971–75. *Sweetback* was considered to be an example of grass-roots Black Power, displayed in artistic form. The stellar success of the film at the box office inspired independent film producers and made the struggling Hollywood studio system aware of the economic power of the large, oft-ignored African American film audience. *Sweetback*'s low production costs and staggering box-office take proved to producers that there was substantial revenue to be made off the African American moviegoing community. This narrative is well known among scholars examining black cinema. However, the impact that the revolutionary film had on localized audiences and moviegoing venues has rarely been discussed. As thousands of young African Americans began flocking to downtown theaters to see *Sweetback*, theater managers took notice, immediately recognizing the potential profit from black-themed films. This meant that *Sweet Sweetback's Baadasssss Song* had a tremendous impact on the racialized nature of moviegoing in urban areas. This chapter considers the impact of *Sweetback* on the city of Chicago in regard to racial politics, the filmmaking industry, and racial spatial patterns. While *Sweetback* premiered in Atlanta and Detroit, it had a tremendous impact on the geographic nature of filmgoing in Chicago. Black spectatorship in Chicago can often be classified as Before Sweetback (BS) and After Sweetback (AS). This film's enormous box-office gross and widespread controversy, which brought thousands of black Chicagoans into the Loop (the downtown district) to see the film, forever changed the nature of filmgoing in the city's center.

*Sweet Sweetback's Baadasssss Song* starred and was directed, written, produced, scored, edited, and composed by Melvin Van Peebles. Prior to bringing *Sweetback* to silver screens, Van Peebles had risen to prominence with the success of his film that he shot while living in France, *The Story of a Three-Day Pass* (1968). He had initially attempted to break into filmmaking in the United States. However, because he was a black man, his dream was deferred, as he quickly learned that such opportunities were largely reserved for white men. As a result of Hollywood's institutionalized racism, Van Peebles began his directing career abroad, where he eventually made *The Story of a Three-Day Pass*. The film was based on his novel *La Permission*, the story of a black army man on a three-day pass in France who spends an amorous weekend with a white French shopgirl. Directed in French New Wave style, the film was acclaimed by French critics. The success of *Three-Day Pass* earned Van Peebles a three-picture deal with Columbia.

The comedy *Watermelon Man* (1970) was Van Peebles's first film with the studio. The film tells the story of a white man, Jeff Gerber, who wakes up one morning to discover he has turned black overnight. As film scholar Racquel Gates explains, Gerber "learns what it means to live as a black man, lose his family, experience racial discrimination, and become the object of sexual fetishism by white women."[1] Columbia wanted *Watermelon Man* to have the veneer of being authentically black yet with a safe ideological message. Van Peebles battled with Columbia over the script, the casting, and even the title of the film.[2] After frustration with completion of the film, Van Peebles chose to finance and control his own production—*Sweetback*.

*Sweetback* centers on a sex performer (played as an adult by Van Peebles) on the run from the law. In the film's opening scenes, Sweetback's childhood is alternately depicted with his attempted escape from law enforcement. In a graphic, controversial scene, an adolescent Sweetback is seduced by a much-older prostitute who introduces him to sex and seemingly initiates him into adulthood. As she is climaxing, she yells out, "Ooh, you gotta sweet sweet back," implying that he is a sexual stud and thus giving him his nickname. As an adult, Sweetback works as a sex performer in a picaresque sex show. Apolitical in the film's beginning (and almost entirely silent and nonemotional), Sweetback witnesses police brutality toward a young black radical, Mu-Mu (Herbert Scales), and he (Sweetback) murders two racist cops. Jeopardizing his life, he breaks out of his social passivity and becomes a political outlaw. He goes on the lam for the rest of the film, slowly progressing from his South Central Los Angeles environs in the attempt to cross over into Mexico. A black antihero, Sweetback does what is necessary to survive along the way, including engaging in sex with a black woman so that she will free him from his handcuffs, defeating a white female motorcycle-gang leader in a sex duel, stabbing white cops, and biting the head off a lizard for nourishment. In the film's final scenes, Sweetback eludes the police by killing the hunting dogs that they are using to track him and crosses the Mexican border. Van Peebles discussed his inspiration for making *Sweetback*, explaining, "I wanted a victorious film,"[3] a point that is driven home in a title card that appears onscreen at the end of the film, which reads, "a baadasssss nigger is coming back to collect some dues." Thus, not only does Sweetback get away, but the title card implies that that at an undisclosed time, the title character will return in search of revenge against the oppressive establishment.

In bringing *Sweetback* to fruition, Van Peebles utilized an unconventional style of filmmaking. Enmeshed with late-1960s psychedelia, *Sweetback* used gospel-tinged Greek choruses to comment on the action, color solarizations, multiple superimpositions, image manipulation, and other phantasmagoric tools. Film scholar Gladstone Yearwood has argued that "Van Peebles' creative use of film language immediately set him up in opposition to the dominant ideologies of the cinema."[4] Van Peebles's use of experimental editing, sound, and color demonstrated that he was not interested in reproducing the cinematic grammar of most Hollywood films but wanted in cinema to forge a new back aesthetic. This small independent film, which only opened in two theaters in Detroit and Atlanta in April 1971, had an astounding impact. Not only did audiences react strongly to the film, deeming it both a positive and a negative force in black culture, but it became a cause célèbre among black and white intellectuals, journalists, and political activists. Black Panther leader Huey P. Newton declared that Sweetback was "the first truly revolutionary Black film made," and it became required viewing for Black Panther Party members.[5] The black moviegoing public also went wild over the film for a multiplicity of reasons.

Because of the film's theme, political message, onscreen performers, and production, *Sweet Sweetback's Baadasssss Song* was immediately categorized as a "black film." Van Peebles claimed, "to attract the masses we have to produce work that not only instructs but entertains."[6] *Sweetback* was a film by black people for black people, a mode of filmmaking that had not really been replicated since the demise of "race films" in the 1940s. David E. James has claimed that "black aesthetics . . . were radical, not because they invoked ironic inversions, stylistic switches undetectable from the outside, subversive adaptations of hegemonic forms or other form qualities that reflected ghetto life . . . but because they stressed a populist functionalism."⁷ *Sweetback* spoke to young black Chicago in the spring and summer of 1971, and there is no denying that Van Peebles showcased his interpretation of a black aesthetic. While there are no clearly defined rules for such an aesthetic, Van Peebles created a narrative that entertained while also speaking to black audiences on ideological, political, and symbolic levels. Leopold Senghor has argued that black art "must be functional, collective and committing. . . . Black art must expose the enemy, praise the people and support the revolution."⁸ *Sweetback* fulfilled Senghor's tenets in a messy, dystopian, and hyper-realistic way.

*Sweetback* opened the first full week of May 1971 at the Oriental Theatre, located in the Chicago Loop. The Oriental, which was an independent theater, sat at 24 West Randolph in the middle of the Loop, in close proximity to other motion picture theaters. Over the course of 1970–71, the management had screened a combination of mainstream Hollywood hits and sexploitation films like *Vixen* (1969) and *Threesome* (1970). During *Sweetback*'s opening week, the film earned $77,000 at the Oriental.⁹ The previous week's film at the Oriental, the Sidney Poitier feature *Brother John* (1971), earned $15,000 (but in its fifth week of release).

The first advertisement for *Sweetback* in the *Chicago Tribune* on May 7 was a prime example of true irony. A large photo of the antihero with a black hat is framed over an often-repeated line from the film: "you bled my momma—you bled my poppa—but you won't bleed me."¹⁰ Immediately underneath the image was a smaller ad for the Clark Theater's reissue of D. W. Griffith's *The Birth of a Nation* (1915), which proclaimed, "Still the Greatest Picture of All Time." *Birth*, of course, had the reputation of being one of the most racist American motion pictures of all time, so this juxtaposition illustrated that times had indeed changed—sort of.¹¹

*Sweetback* was undeniably a commercial success in its first week of release. This was particularly amazing considering the fact that *Sweetback* was rated X—which technically prohibited anyone under the age of eighteen from seeing the film. In 1971, filmmakers seeking a rating from the Motion Picture Association of America (MPAA) had to submit their film to its jury. If they did not submit the film, it was given an automatic X rating. Van Peebles chose not to submit his film and then used this fact to acquire racial loyalty. One of the taglines for the film read, "Rated X by an all-white jury." Jack Valenti, the president of the MPAA, told Van Peebles that he could not use that language to advertise *Sweetback*. Van Peebles quickly put Valenti on the spot by asking him, "Your jury is all white, isn't it?" Of course, the membership of the rating's board was indeed all white, which served as further evidence of the manner in which blacks had been marginalized by Hollywood. In the end, the controversy surrounding *Sweetback*'s X rating helped fuel the box office, as audiences turned out in droves to view the film.¹²

*SWEETBACK* IN CHICAGO

The Oriental Theatre, located in the Chicago Loop. (Classic Images)

*Sweetback* gave viewers, specifically black Chicagoans, an experience—an urban racialized experience—that was both communal and personal. While watching *Sweetback*, African Americans could voice frustration, hope, anxiety, and glee in the Oriental Theatre in a collective way. Word of mouth increased the overall box office of the film the second week of release, with the film earning a sizzling $94,000. Loop theaters had not done this well since the release of *Love Story* (at the end of 1970), a mainstream Hollywood film. This illustrates the significance of *Sweetback*'s gross.[13] The film's postscript, "A Baadasssss Nigger Is Coming Back to Collect Some Dues," resonated with the urban Chicago audience. The fact that a black man met violence with violence and was overtly sexual (in comparison with the characters Sidney Poitier was playing) was landmark.

In the film's third week of release, it earned $92,000.[14] Despite the fact that the film was in its third week of release, it outperformed every movie in the Loop at the beginning of the summer season.[15] *Sweetback* continued to pull in huge numbers well into June. It was reported that "thousands of stomping Black teens cheered 'Sweetback' on to 'victory.'"[16] In the end, *Sweetback* played at the Oriental for two months and became one of the Loop's most successful releases of the year.

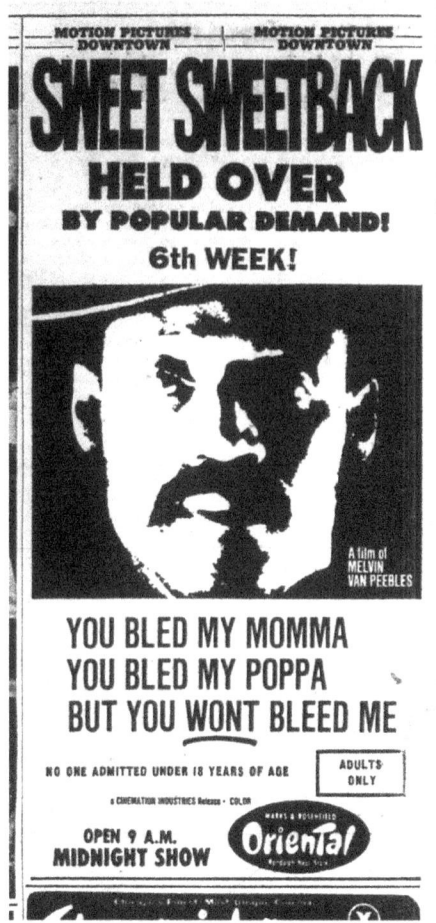

An advertisement promoting *Sweet Sweetback's Baadasssss Song* at the Oriental Theatre. (*Chicago Tribune*)

*Sweetback* was also a turning point in the history of the Oriental Theatre, which in the late 1960s and 1970s was one of the most popular movie palaces. As an example of the Oriental's status, in 1970 it was home to the Chicago premiere of *Airport*, a widely popular mainstream Hollywood film that played in the theater for almost three months. Because many younger African American moviegoers spurred *Sweetback* to financial success, the film changed the reputation of the Oriental. As John Sanchez reports on the Cinema Treasures website, "the theater got the stigma of playing solely to African American audiences, and whites stayed away in droves."[17] Hence, in a short amount of time, the Oriental gained the reputation of being a "black space," and white audience members stayed away from the theater.

Word of mouth among younger African American moviegoers, precipitated by a firestorm of controversy, led to tremendous financial gain for the Oriental.

But not all black Chicagoans were pleased with the success of the film. Criticism of *Sweetback* first began as filmgoers and parents initially began discussing the politics of the film among themselves before sending damning commentary and letters to newspaper editors and the press, more broadly. A critic of the film in the Nation of Islam's newspaper, *Muhammad Speaks*, acknowledged, "I was horrified by the film and surprised at the response of the students. What to me was a racist and exploitive piece of egomania, seemed to have great appeal to them. I believe that the Black youth of this country are so starved for Black heroes . . . that they willingly sacrifice intelligent and revolutionary ideology for the 'accomplishment' of seeing Black people on the screen."[18] One unhappy patron reported to a journalist that she had just returned from the Oriental Theatre, where the film was playing, and that she found it a "filthy, dirty movie" that was a "disgrace to the Negro people": "I have never been so embarrassed and humiliated in my life." The author, Joonie Jones, was thirty-nine years old, and her comments illustrate the radical generational divide that became apparent in discussions of the film. Black *Chicago Sun-Times* critic Sam Worthington criticized the film's "shallow characterizations" but argued, "*Sweet Sweetback's Baadasssss Song* is a grotesque, violent and beautifully honest film that takes no crap from Whitey and his overcivilized hang-ups while it deals with some specifics of the black experience." He claimed that "for the first time in cinematic history in America, a movie speaks out of an undeniable black consciousness."[19]

Interestingly, *Sweetback* was almost completely ignored by Chicago's black press until the backlash against the film began. The *Chicago Defender* did not initially run any articles on the groundbreaking film despite the huge box-office attendance. *Muhammad Speaks* was the lone black newspaper that did pay attention to *Sweetback*. A lengthy letter to the editor by Ogan Tayo set the tone and was the catalyst for criticism that would ensue for several weeks. Tayo wrote, "Why would the most Vile and Filthy Movie ever to play movie theatre screens Be Shown in Black Communities throughout North America? The film is called 'Sweet Sweetback' . . . By Melvin Van Peebles. Never has such a bold attempt been made by Black People to discredit and 'drag' Black People by the lowest degree of Civilization."[20] Tayo went on to explain that *Sweetback* did not represent "our Strong Positive Points."[21]

The relationship between the black press and *Sweetback* is problematic. Yearwood argues that "a middle-class heroic type is generally advocated as an exemplary black film hero."[22] Sweetback, as a sex performer and outlaw, did not adhere to the privileged black characters often portrayed by Sidney Poitier in the years preceding the emergence of blaxploitation cinema. Yearwood indicates that the primary objection to the film came from the black middle class, who "saw the intrusion of folk styles and black working class urban cultural expression as coercive, destructive elements."[23] Yet this argument is complicated when one considers those who critiqued and condemned the film in Chicago. In particular, many members of the Nation of Islam were working-class black activists, community organizers, and those who had been involved in the civil rights movement.

The Kuumba Workshop, a South Side Black Arts organization founded in 1968, took the lead in condemning *Sweetback*. Kuumba was a leading player in the Black Arts movement and was "dedicated to contributing to the Black liberation struggle through creative expression."[24] The Workshop attempted to create an all-inclusive arts organization with a wide range of activities focusing primarily on the production of live theater. Kuumba became the primary black organization in Chicago to take on black-themed motion pictures that it perceived were racially offensive. Kuumba took a grass-roots approach to fighting what it believed were exploitive motion pictures, often by picketing and protesting in front of theaters that showed such movies. But the group also drafted sophisticated political position papers that laid out its objections to certain motion pictures. These papers are important cultural documents of the time because they demonstrate that black support for films like *Sweetback* was not universal. The Board of Directors for Kuumba included historian Lerone Bennett, Jr., poet Gwendolyn Brooks, and editor and theoretician of the Black Arts movement Hoyt Fuller. But the position papers were largely drawn up by the husband-and-wife team Francis and Val Gray Ward, who ran the Workshop's day-to-day activities. Francis was a well-known journalist, and Val was an accomplished actress (they are both still active and well regarded in their fields).

Kuumba began working in tandem with the *Chicago Defender*, as the newspaper decided to give the organization extensive coverage beginning in mid-July 1971. In a July 12 front-page article focusing on *Sweetback*, the newspaper reported that "Kuumba has vowed to keep the film from entering the black community and will fight to keep others like it from being produced."[25] The *Defender* reported on Kuumba's position paper on *Sweetback* and finally acknowledged the widespread popularity of the film and the positive press that it was receiving. The article briefly commented on Kuumba's criticism of *Sweetback* but was largely a call to action for the black community. Val Gray Ward stated, "What we hope we can establish is an atmosphere in which we—black people become the critics. We must stop accepting and supporting movies, TV shows etc., simply because black folks are involved in them. We must begin to analyze critically whether this new rage for black images is the product of concern for black people's liberation or merely the product of 'black skin, white masks' in which the black image-maker—become the critics."²⁶ After this initial article, the *Chicago Defender* allowed Kuumba to utilize the paper as its platform in a four-part series of articles written in editorial style and published over the next week. Ward attempted to incorporate Black Nationalist philosophy for the *Defender*'s readership. The use of the phrase "black skin, white masks" was an obvious reference to the famous tome by Frantz Fanon. Fanon's intellectualism was more in the vein of black activists, confounding Yearwood's argument that primarily the black middle class critiqued the film.

The Kuumba Workshop asserted that *Sweetback* "is destructive to Black people because of its images, messages and absolute lack of positive portrayal of either Black characters or community."²⁷ Kuumba members recognized that the primary audience for films like *Sweetback* was African American youth. They were afraid that impressionable teens would make poor judgments based on the film's narrative. They claimed, "The minds of these young Blacks are our most priceless resource and yet we sit by seemingly helpless while these minds are being deluded, brainwashed and coopted by a deluge of fantasies fronted off as 'victories?' over the 'man.' How deceptively dangerous it is for these young brothers and sisters who packed into the Oriental . . . to believe that victory over the white man is really that simple."²⁸

The Kuumba Workshop paper on *Sweetback* is significant because it was one of the first attempts in the early 1970s of Black Arts or civil rights organizations to mediate what was being represented on the screen in regard to African American imagery. The following is a summary of Kuumba's arguments against the film:

1. The film presents the worst, most negative images of black women.
2. It glorifies the hustler/stud as a hero in the black community, presenting an image especially damaging to highly impressionable young blacks.
3. It exploits and misuses sex for the sake of titillating and lust instead of showing sex as an act of love and spiritual devotion between two people.
4. It fails to show the social, political, economic, and cultural contexts of the black realism it reveals. Without such perspective, the viewer is left with impressions of black people that tend to conform to the worst racial stereotypes of blacks as a lower-level, immoral, and inferior people.
5. It presents a deceptively degenerate and oversimplified view of what it takes to "win" in the struggle for black liberation. Victory over the forces of racist oppression will take much more than the ability to outrun police and dogs from Los Angeles to the Mexican border.²⁹

Kuumba denounced the film explicitly. Arguing that it did not have "a single positive image," the Workshop took a relatively conservative view of *Sweetback*, particularly regarding the film's overt sexual content. Kuumba claimed that Van Peebles "pictures sexual freakishness as an essential and unmistakable part of black reality" and that "all of the women [in the film] are whores from start to finish." This line of thought was later expanded on by a members of Kuumba's Board of Directors, Lerone Bennett, Jr. Kuumba also reacted negatively to the explicit violence in the movie, arguing that Van Peebles had an "obsessive preoccupation with spilling, dripping blood." Perhaps the Workshop's greatest fear was that the overwhelming success of *Sweetback* would lead to a succession of clones that would warp the minds of young African Americans. It argued that "Hollywood has seen the moneymaking potential . . . of *Sweetback* . . . [and they] have become convinced that the only elements needed to sell movies to blacks are sex (lots and lots of it), black folks on screen, and violence." In essence, Kuumba was determined to stop the evolution of the blaxploitation movement before it began.[30]

The *Defender* reported on Kuumba's activities, particularly when its activism against *Sweetback* began. Val Gray Ward, the director of the organization, argued, "We are being congratulated by people who felt the film was negative yet had no way of registering their grievances."[31] Kuumba organized a campaign against the film, gaining support from other prominent black Chicagoans in the process. Peter Bailey, associate editor of *Ebony*, claimed that *Sweetback* "uses sexual gimmicks that are very destructive to blacks to titillate the audience." Poet Gwendolyn Brooks claimed that *Sweetback* "was a collection of dangerous images for young people," but this did not keep the public from the film.[32] A public forum, organized to rally public sentiment against the exhibition of the film, was held at Holy Angels Church on July 23, 1971.

One important strain of criticism against *Sweetback* by Chicago critics was its frank sexuality. Kuumba stressed this in its position paper, as did other local activists and journalists. *Chicago Tribune* columnist Vernon Jarrett titled one of his editorials "Sex, Not Liberation, Was Movie's Theme" in his takedown of the film. Jarrett argued that "titillating sex, crude sex, and grossly perverted sex" were the "big themes" in *Sweetback* and that "conspicuously absent was the traditional manner in which blacks have viewed sex."[33] Moreover, he described *Sweetback* as pornography and claimed that a few social messages did not redeem the film. In and August 6, 1971, column, he argued that the new depictions of black male sexuality on-screen "were not human sex but uncontrollable, violent 'animal' sex" and that they needed to be publicly castigated.[34]

The struggle against so-called blaxploitation films and pornography would often be combined in the argument against screen trends by critics, both black and white. Lerone Bennett, Jr., penned an influential *Ebony* article on the *Sweetback* controversy titled "The Emancipation Orgasm: Sweetback in Wonderland." Bennett has often been given credit for starting the discussion on *Sweetback* and "blaxploitation" film. But Bennett's *Ebony* article emerged in September 1971, and the Kuumba position paper on *Sweetback* was published in July. Bennett, an active member of Kuumba, must have been influenced by the discussions taking place within the arts organization over the merits and demerits of the film. He elevated the discussion to a national platform, arguing that "the reasons for the movie's appeal, apart from the sex and violence, . . . was that it shows a black man thumbing his nose at society and getting away with it." He claimed that *Sweetback* was "a trivial and tasteless negative classic" and that it was "neither revolutionary nor black." Criticizing Sweetback's reliance on sex in his eventual escape to Mexico, Bennett boldly proclaimed, "nobody ever fucked his way to freedom."[35]

Melvin Van Peebles took on the establishment with *Sweetback* and met resistance from both white- and black-owned media outlets. This took place on both the local and national levels. *Variety* is a prime example of a nationally distributed publication's resistance to the film's popularity. The show-business trade Bible reported box-office grosses for *Sweetback* in Chicago but only once validated the remarkable success of the film in its headlines. One such example is from the May 26, 1971, issue, which touted *Escape from the Planet of the Apes* grossing $40,000 and *They Might Be Giants* making $11,000, while the fact that *Sweetback* had earned $92,000 in the same week of release was neglected in the headlines.

The popularity of *Sweetback* was striking, but so was the black Chicago press's failure to report on its impact. The controversy over *Sweetback* was not even mentioned by the *Chicago Defender* until July 13, 1971, long after the film had stopped playing on the big screen at the Oriental. As Jon Hartmann has argued in *Film History*, "the Black press was reluctant to offer an opinion on the work and its exploitation-film trappings." Hartmann claimed that "following the legal victories achieved since the outset of the Civil Rights movement, the newspapers tended to uphold a conservative, unstated Black aesthetic that demanded unambiguously pristine Black images."[36] This certainly seemed the case with the black press in Chicago. Throughout the black film boom of 1970–75, newspapers like the *Defender* gave scattershot coverage to African American–themed films that were wildly popular in the black community. A quote from Bennett explains this situation:

> Nothing shows this more clearly than the fact that black media do not give serious attention to television and movies, two of the most powerful media developed by man. Not a single black newspaper, not a single black magazine, not a single black radio station gives serious and sustained coverage to television and motion pictures. Not a single black newspaper, not a single mass-circulation black magazine, not a single black radio station has a resident film or movie critic. To make matters worse, black intellectuals and writers—including the author—rarely descend from the Olympian heights of the theater and the novel to the grubby terrain of the popular arts.[37]

Earl Calloway contributed film editorials to the *Chicago Defender*, but they were infrequent and usually tended to denigrate a film that he felt was intellectually or racially insulting. Overall, the black press in Chicago ignored the phenomenon of black crowds attending films like *Sweetback* in the Loop. When the *Defender* did comment on motion pictures, it was often simply a reproduction of promotional materials from the studios or reports on black organizational efforts to protest certain films.

Through the rest of 1971, *Sweetback* moved to smaller neighborhood theaters. The film played at the Bel Air in October and at the Jeffrey and Hamm on the South Side of Chicago in the fall. *Sweet Sweetback's Baadasssss Song* was a turning point in the history of film exhibition and reception in the city of Chicago. The enormous popularity of the film, with its stupendous box-office take, encouraged theater management in the Loop to book other black-themed motion pictures. This was most pronounced at the Roosevelt Theater, which had a legacy of catering to African American audiences. Following the popularity of *Sweetback*, other theaters ignored black Chicago audiences at their own economic peril. An explosion of black-themed films ensued in 1971–72, and many theaters that had not played such films in the past now screened black-cast films. Following the success of *Sweetback*, African American youth now considered the Loop a moviegoing destination. Thousands of African American teenagers and twenty-somethings frequented the Loop on weekends to see African American heroes and heroines on the screen. *Sweetback* also began a period of activism against the crop of new blaxploitation movies that premiered as a result of the film's popularity. Kuumba continued its campaign against what it considered to be exploitive films that were teaching black youth negative values.

Seminal motion pictures such as *Sweet Sweetback's Baadasssss Song* had an impact on motion picture production, exhibition, and reception that was both national and local in scope. While it is rare that a motion picture can have such an impact, there are times in American film history when a singular motion picture can cause repercussions that impact local markets.

*Sweetback*'s enormous commercial success in Chicago, its radical black politics, and the controversy it courted demonstrated that African American moviegoing in the Loop had consequences that went beyond the economic. Black-themed motion pictures could be a catalyst for political and demographic change.

## NOTES

1. Racquel Gates, "Subverting Hollywood from the Inside Out: Melvin Van Peebles' *Watermelon Man*," *Film Quarterly* 68, no. 1 (2014): 9.
2. Ibid., 14.
3. Melvin Van Peebles, *Sweet Sweetback's Baadasssss Song* (Ann Arbor, MI: Neo, 1972), 9.
4. Gladstone Yearwood, *Black Film as Signifying Practice: Cinema, Narration and the African American Aesthetic Tradition* (Trenton, NJ: Africa World, 1999), 187.
5. Huey Newton, *To Die for the People* (New York: Random House, 1972), 113.
6. Melvin Van Peebles and James Surowiecki, "Making It," *Transition* 79 (1999): 180.
7. David E. James, *Allegories of Cinema: American Film in the Sixties* (Princeton, NJ: Princeton University Press, 1989), 177.
8. Ron Karenga, "Black Cultural Nationalism," in *The Black Aesthetic*, ed. Addison Gayle, Jr. (New York: Anchor, 1972), 3.
9. "'Sweetback' Syrupy $77,000," *Variety*, May 15, 1971, 12. Van Peebles had not always been as successful at the Chicago box office. His first major Hollywood release, *Watermelon Man*, with Godfrey Cambridge, opened at the Chicago Theater on September 11, 1970. While it made $50,000 in its opening week, attendance quickly fell off.
10. Advertisement, *Chicago Tribune*, May 7, 1971, 15.
11. Advertisements for *Sweet Sweetback's Baadasssss Song* and *The Birth of a Nation*, *Chicago Tribune*, May 7, 1971, sec. 2, p. 15.
12. Van Peebles and Surowiecki, "Making It," 183.
13. Gene Siskel, "Great White Hope," *Chicago Tribune*, December 30, 1970, A7.
14. *Variety*, May 21, 1971, 10.
15. *Variety*, May 26, 1971, 10.
16. Francis Ward, *Superfly: A Political and Cultural Condemnation* (Chicago: Institute of Positive Education, 1972), 3.
17. John Sanchez, comment on "Ford Center for the Performing Arts Oriental Theatre," Cinema Treasures, February 23, 2005, http://cinematreasures.org/comments?page=7&theater_id=254. Black-themed motion pictures had rarely played at the Oriental before *Sweetback*.

18. Sharon Tarr, "Black Cultural Imperative: Tell Our Story with Dignity," *Muhammad Speaks*, July 23, 1971, 10.
19. Quoted in Lerone Bennett, "The Emancipation Orgasm: Sweetback in Wonderland," *Ebony*, September 1971, 112.
20. Ogan Tayo, "Reader Says 'Sweet Sweetback . . .' Is 'Filth That Produces Filth,'" *Muhammad Speaks*, July 16, 1971, 10.
21. Ibid.
22. Yearwood, *Black Film as Signifying Practice*, 188.
23. Ibid.
24. Ward, *Superfly*, 16.
25. "Artists Here Attack 'Sweetback,'" *Chicago Daily Defender*, July 12, 1971, 3.
26. Ibid.
27. Ibid., 2.
28. Ibid., 4.
29. Kuumba Workshop, "Sweet Sweetback's Baadasssss Song: A Kuumba Workshop Critique," Box 2, Folder 3, p. 1, Kuumba Workshop Papers, Special Collections, Harold Washington Library, Chicago, IL.
30. Ibid., 5, 10, 12.
31. Tony Griffs, "Anti-'Sweetback' Movement Grows," *Chicago Defender*, July 13, 1971, 2, 19.
32. Ibid.
33. Vernon Jarrett, "Sex, Not Liberation, Was Movie's Theme," *Chicago Tribune*, July 18, 1971, 5.
34. Vernon Jarrett, "Now He Is a Baaaaaad Dude," *Chicago Tribune*, August 6, 1971, 13.
35. Bennett, "Emancipation Orgasm," 112, 118.
36. Jon Hartmann, "The Trope of Blaxploitation in Critical Responses to Sweetback," *Film History* 6 (1994): 393.
37. Bennett, "Emancipation Orgasm," 106.

## WORKS CITED

"Artists Here Attack 'Sweetback.'" *Chicago Daily Defender*, July 12, 1971.
Bennett, Lerone, Jr. "The Emancipation Orgasm: Sweetback in Wonderland." *Ebony*, September 1971, 106–18.
Gates, Racquel. "Subverting Hollywood from the Inside Out: Melvin Van Peebles' *Watermelon Man*." *Film Quarterly* 68, no. 1 (2014): 9–21.
Griffs, Tony. "Anti-'Sweetback' Movement Grows." *Chicago Defender*, July 13, 1971.
Hartmann, Jon. "The Trope of Blaxploitation in Critical Responses to Sweetback." *Film History* 6 (1994): 382–404.
James, David E. *Allegories of Cinema: American Film in the Sixties*. Princeton, NJ: Princeton University Press, 1989.
Jarrett, Vernon. "Now He Is a Baaaaaad Dude." *Chicago Tribune*, August 6, 1971, 13.
———. "Sex, Not Liberation, Was Movie's Theme." *Chicago Tribune*, July 18, 1971.

Karenga, Ron. "Black Cultural Nationalism." In *The Black Aesthetic*, ed. Addison Gayle, Jr., 32–38. New York: Anchor, 1972.

Kuumba Workshop. "Sweet Sweetback's Baadasss Song: A Kuumba Workshop Critique." Box 2, Folder 3, Kuumba Workshop Papers, Special Collections, Harold Washington Library, Chicago, IL.

Newton, Huey. *To Die for the People*. New York: Random House, 1972.

Siskel, Gene. "Great White Hope." *Chicago Tribune*, December 30, 1970.

"'Sweetback' Syrupy $77,000." *Variety*, May 15, 1971.

Tarr, Sharon. "Black Cultural Imperative: Tell Our Story with Dignity." *Muhammad Speaks*, July 23, 1971.

Tayo, Ogan. "Reader Says 'Sweet Sweetback . . .' Is 'Filth That Produces Filth.'" *Muhammad Speaks*, July 16, 1971.

Van Peebles, Melvin. *Sweet Sweetback's Baadasssss Song*. Ann Arbor, MI: Neo, 1972.

Van Peebles, Melvin, and James Surowiecki. "Making It." *Transition* 79 (1999): 176–92.

Ward, Francis. *Superfly: A Political and Cultural Condemnation*. Chicago: Institute of Positive Education, 1972.

Yearwood, Gladstone. *Black Film as Signifying Practice: Cinema, Narration and the African American Aesthetic Tradition*. Trenton, NJ: Africa World, 1999.

PART II

# THE CANON AND THE NOT SO CANON

# 4

## IN THE BEGINNING THERE WAS *SHAFT*

### ERIC PIERSON

The years have not always been kind to blaxploitation. It has been maligned, mocked, and misunderstood. As both a genre and an era, blaxploitation spawned well over 200 movies, grossed millions of dollars, launched many careers, and changed the face of pop culture forever. But somehow it has been largely ignored in the history books.

—David Walker

IN THE BEGINNING THERE WAS *SHAFT* (1971), OR WAS IT *SWEET SWEETback's Baadasssss Song* (1971) or perhaps *Cotton Comes to Harlem* (1970) that marks the official beginning of the film movement of the 1970s that is most commonly referred to as blaxploitation? Some scholars contend that the movement came to an end in 1973, others opt for 1975, while another segment of the academic population argues that 1977 marks the era's official demise.

Regardless of the exact film that served as the catalyst for the blaxploitation movement or when this cycle of motion pictures came to an end, the interest in and the impact of the period remains strong some forty years later. For instance, Netflix includes in its library a number of popular and lesser-known blaxploitation titles such as *Detroit 9000* (1973), *The Black Godfather* (1974), and *The Monkey Hustle* (1976). Similarly, presented on Amazon under an array of catchy packaging like "Soul Cinema," "Black Gold," or "The Best of," scholars and fans can purchase pristine copies of *Dolemite* (1973), *Black Belt Jones* (1974), *Three the Hard*

*Way* (1974), and *Cleopatra Jones and the Casino of Gold* (1975). Moreover, the resurgence of these films has given movies that garnered limited distribution when originally produced new life. Examples include relatively obscure films such as *Black Shampoo* (1976), *Black Vengeance* (1975), and *Black Brothers* (1977).

Not only do the films of the blaxploitation era remain visible, but some of their most notable icons such as John Shaft continue to occupy a prominent space in the popular imagination. In 2000, John Singleton directed a contemporary reimagining of *Shaft*, and in 2001, Disney's *The Princess Dairies* referenced the film in describing the wardrobe of one of its characters.[1] John Shaft is also being resurrected in literary form, as Ernest Tidyman's seven original novels centering on the detective have been scheduled for reprint, and the new publisher plans "to release new prose and original graphic novels featuring the character in addition to new editions of the original novels."[2] In this series of books, John Shaft will be resurrected from the dead, because Tidyman killed the character off in the last installment of the original series, appropriately titled *The Last Shaft*. Furthermore, in February 2015, New Line Cinema announced its plan to reboot *Shaft*, meaning that forty-plus years after the film's initial release, the studio executives feel strongly that the slick, black private detective maintains the cultural capital to draw audiences to theaters.[3] Finally, it is also important to highlight that blaxploitation continues to influence the work of directors like Quentin Tarantino as well as hip hop artists. Thus, the oft-disregarded movement has left an indelible imprint on cinema and on media more broadly.

Despite blaxploitation's sustained influence, the movies did not receive a great deal of attention from film scholars either during the movement or in the years immediately following its demise. Fortunately, a new generation of film scholars has begun revisiting the movement, highlighting its impact on black representation and film history, among other topics. This chapter expands the ongoing discourse, contributing new information on *Shaft*'s creative history. In particular, this piece focuses less on the images created by Gordon Parks and more on the institutional mechanism that shaped and influenced those images. Finally, it outlines the process that MGM underwent in turning an unpublished novel centered on a black detective into a major motion picture.

*Shaft* presents a protagonist unlike the black characters that had appeared in 1960s films. While the characters that the actors Jim Brown and Sidney Poitier played in films like *Rio Conchos* (1964) and *Guess Who's Coming to Dinner?* (1967) were important alterations of Hollywood's traditional shucking and jiving coons and loyal toms, their agency was limited, making them safe for white mass audiences, which at the time constituted the largest segment of the moviegoing population. In contrast, Shaft was not created to suit or allay whites' fears, and as a result, he was constructed as violent, anti-Semitic, overtly sexual, and culturally centered. This new yet problematic construction of black masculinity connected with audiences when adapted for the screen, providing a wealth of data in the mainstream press, materials that I incorporate into this chapter. However, the majority of the research used in this analysis comes from the Joel Freeman Collection, which is housed in the Margaret Herrick Library at the Academy of Motion Pictures Arts and Sciences, in Beverly Hills, California.[4]

## *SHAFT* THE NOVEL

> Shaft has no prejudice, he'll kill anyone—black or white.
> —cover of *Shaft*, by Ernest Tidyman

The John Shaft character initially appeared in Ernest Tidyman's novel *Shaft*, which was released in 1970. Tidyman, a white Cleveland native, seemed an unlikely source for the character that so effectively captured the vibe, language, and experiences of an African American. His novel focuses on the title character, a tough New York private detective who is hired to find a Harlem gangster's recently kidnapped daughter. Shaft is a man of the streets who operates under a set of rules that often put him at odds with the New York City police, who clearly function as a metaphor for the racist, oppressive establishment. As a result, his life is further complicated by the fact that he operates within a racist world. Thus, "in blaxploitation cinema, characters like John Shaft at times work for and within the system; however, they do so on their own terms and for the betterment of the black community."[5]

Detective novels have a long tradition of featuring characters that live by a set of rules that place them outside societal norms, yet even as outsiders, they still have a code under which they operate. Readers' enjoyment of these characters is often tied to the writer's ability to get them to also accept the code. The code for killing is often a fairly simple one; characters kill only when they have to, and it is never something that they enjoy. The rules that John Shaft follows are very different from those of other fictional detectives. Early in the novel, he kills two men out of what appears to be an uncontrollable murderous impulse. In the passage, two strangers enter Shaft's office, words are exchanged, and a fistfight ensues. He easily disarms both men during the scuffle, and then, suddenly,

> Shaft reached over with his left hand to the skinny one, crumpling the grotesquely wide lapels of the double-breasted brown suit in his fist. He moved back, raising the gangling form with him, staying in a crouch, keeping the gun steady and aimed. Then he spun and whipped. Every taut muscle of Shaft's body went into the twist and turn, the wrench of his arm and the lash of his wrist. The limp, bent form in brown danced, skated and angled crazily through the open space between the desk and the window. The glass exploded against the head and shoulders of the projectile. It crashed and clattered and tinkled as the body went hurtling through and out into the bright, breezy, sunny day.[6]

Next, Shaft begins to question the second man at gunpoint and finds that he and his companion work for a local gangster, Bumpy Jonas, who sent them to hire him for a job. This information further infuriates Shaft. "Shaft was insulted. Send a boy to fetch a boy. He heard a commotion developing in the corridor outside the offices and he considered pulling the trigger. Squeeze it off right into the middle of the furrows of fright that covered the wet, ugly face. But he would never get the wall clean and he hated the sinus-corroding fumes of fresh paint."[7] This passage immediately establishes Shaft as a violent private detective who is quick to kill. He had already thrown one man from a window, and had it not been for his disdain for the smell of fresh paint, he would have brutally executed the other simply because he was insulted that Bumpy Jonas had sent him.

Another prominent theme running throughout the novel is an overt denunciation of homosexuality. Shaft and other characters express extreme disdain for gay communities, a viewpoint emphasized during several passages in which characters demean and insult gay people and, in one case, create a scenario in which a gay man who finds Shaft attractive is bashed.

> Shaft leaned over the counter to whisper.
>
> "You know where the boathouse is in Central Park?"
>
> The fag nodded eagerly. Shaft looked at his watch.
>
> "I'll be there about twelve-forty five. No, make that one A.M. sharp. Okay?"
>
> "Do we have to meet in the park?"
>
> "Well, if you don't want to . . ."

"Oh, all right."

"*Ciao.*"

"*Ciao.*"

The muggers and that one deserved each other. He hoped the little fart was a karate champion; he would last about ten minutes longer that way. Until somebody stuffed his brown belt in one ear and pulled it out the other. Knotted.[8]

The characters' aggressive actions toward gay characters occur throughout the novel yet have no real function in moving the story forward. That Tidyman neither explains nor has characters comment on Shaft's homophobia further complicates the character that readers are asked to view as a hero. Moreover, the protagonist's other motivations remain a mystery, as readers never receive answers to seminal questions such as, What makes Shaft tick? What are his politics? Where do his loyalties lie? Rather than answering such pressing queries, Tidyman simply glorifies Shaft's violent acts of aggression, inadvertently implying that his behavior is innate. Because Tidyman's construction of Shaft had limitations, a number of changes had to be made before the character could be brought to the big screen. Among the traits that were exorcised were his murderous impulses and his homophobia. The screenwriters would also have to create a character with clearer motives and loyalties if audiences were to accept him as a hero.

*Shaft* officially began its journey to the big screen on April 7, 1970, when Tidyman signed a distribution deal with independent producers Stirling Silliphant and Roger Lewis. With the success of *Cotton Comes to Harlem* (1970), there was a great deal of interest in black detective novels, even one like *Shaft* that had yet to be published. According to the original agreement, Silliphant and Lewis would pay Tidyman $50,000 for the rights to the character, and Tidyman would write the screenplay for the motion picture. This was an extremely lucrative deal for Tidyman, who at the time he signed the agreement was an unknown writer whose most impressive accomplishment up to that point was penning an unpublished manuscript.

In contrast, Silliphant and Lewis were both laudable Hollywood producers who used their industry status to secure financing from MGM to produce *Shaft*. Prior to working on the seminal blaxploitation picture, Silliphant had enjoyed great success as a writer and film and television producer. He created the series *Route 66* (1960–64) and *Naked City* (1958–63) and wrote the screenplay for the cult classic *Village of the Damned* (1960). Perhaps Silliphant's most notable accomplishment was his screen adaptation of the race-themed film *In the Heat of the Night* (1967), for which he earned Academy Awards for Best Writing and for Screenplay Based on Material from Another Medium. This forever solidified him as the man who penned the iconic line, "They call me Mr. Tibbs." Similarly, Lewis was an established Hollywood producer. His most prominent films before working on *Shaft* included two critically acclaimed dramas, *The Pawnbroker* (1964) and *The Swimmer* (1968).

Because Tidyman had neither published a novel nor written a screenplay when he signed the deal with Silliphant and Lewis, it is curious that he was given such a significant role in *Shaft*'s production. Given Silliphant's vast experience and substantial résumé, why did he not draft the script? The answer may lie in the rumors regarding the lineage of the manuscript. After the deal was signed, there was speculation regarding the Shaft character's true creator. Unsubstantiated rumors that a young African American man had actually created the title character once again surfaced after *Shaft* became a box-office success. In an era of heightened suspicion of whites by African Americans, it is hard to say if the allegation holds any merit. In the interviews that I conducted with Joel Freeman, *Shaft*'s producer, he stated that he was unaware of any such issue.[9] Gordon Parks, *Shaft*'s director, was aware of the controversy but distanced himself from the accusations when asked about them, explaining that whatever occurred with the acquisition of the rights to *Shaft* "happened within the studio."[10]

*Shaft* was Gordon Parks's follow-up to *The Learning Tree* (1969), a marginally successful film based on his autobiographical novel of the same title.[11] Parks, who at the time he shot *The Learning Tree* had directed two documentaries, was primarily known for his groundbreaking work as a photographer. Though proud of those accomplishments, he was motivated to expand beyond his work in still images and nonnarrative cinema and demonstrate that he could direct a narrative feature. In the attempt to ensure that *The Learning Tree* would accurately reflect his vision and display his directorial ability, Parks filled a number of critical roles during the film's production. He adapted the screenplay from his book, directed the project, wrote the musical score, and edited the final cut of the film. Parks's efforts paid off, as *The Learning Tree* received a number of excellent notices, most of which complimented him on his direction.[12]

Parks's first foray into narrative cinema made him a sought-after commodity, especially given his standing as Hollywood's lone African American director. In late 1969, he was considering four films in search of his next project before he settled on *Shaft*.[13] In August 1970, he officially signed on to the project for a sum of $50,000 and 5 percent of the film's profits.[14] Further, Parks's contract required that he supervise the film through the completion of postproduction and included a clause stipulating that he would lose one percentage point of his profit sharing for every $10,000 the film went over budget.[15] The deal was questionable given that when Parks signed his contract, MGM had yet to provide him with a budget, a cast, a line producer, a shooting schedule, or production permits. Still, he accepted the terms and immediately began working under immense pressure to bring John Shaft to the silver screen.

After signing to direct *Shaft*, Parks recruited Freeman to produce the film. In a personal interview, Freeman recalled how a chance meeting years earlier actually led to his hiring.

> I had very casually met Gordon once before when he was a *Life* magazine photographer.... Gordon is now on the lot [Warner Bros.], and he is going to do the *Learning Tree*. And he is walking down the street, and I run into him. I said, "Look, if you need any help at all, 'cause I do know the way around here, just pick up the phone and call me." He was very happy. He never forgot that. Now along comes *Shaft*. And Roger Lewis and Sterling Silliphant were partners with Ernie Tidyman, a trio, and they're not producers in that sense. Gordon says to Jim Aubrey [president at MGM] and some others, "Let's get Joel Freeman." And I get this phone call, and it's from Gordon. And he says, "How would like to do *Shaft*?" I said, "You're kidding?" He said, "No." So I go over, and just like that [*snap*] we made a deal. That's how it came about.[16]

Freeman's seemingly innocuous meeting with Parks may have helped him land the job as producer, but he was more than qualified to handle the project, as he had amassed an impressive résumé in the film industry. Freeman had held a number of positions including editor, assistant director, production manager, production supervisor, executive producer, producer, and company executive on over twenty-five films. The most notable include *Bad Day at Black Rock* (1955), *The Blackboard Jungle* (1955), *The Farmer's Daughter* (1947), *Camelot* (1967), and *The Heart Is a Lonely Hunter* (1968). Working on *Shaft*, Freeman served as producer and facilitated the tense relationship that, as a result of creative differences and the execs' unrealistic demands, emerged between Parks and the MGM bosses. For his work, Freeman was paid $50,000 and 3 percent of the profits;[17] however, unlike Parks's, his contract did not include a penalty if *Shaft* came in over budget.

Freeman and Parks's first major task was to ensure that the film's shooting script was acceptable. Tidyman wrote the original version, which closely followed the novel's story line and depiction of the character. However, neither Parks nor Freeman found it acceptable. The director recalled that the initial screenplay lacked pizzazz and that it neither captured New York's feel nor the Shaft character.[18] Additionally, the original script ended with Shaft being wounded by gangsters, and it was unclear whether he prevailed over his adversaries.

Unhappy with Tidyman's initial screenplay, in October 1970, Freeman hired accomplished Hollywood writer John D. F. Black and paid him $10,000 to draft a new version of the *Shaft* script. Like the original screenplay, Black's first draft opened with Shaft having sex with his girlfriend, Elle, and ended with the couple having sex on a pile of money. This script marked the beginning of what Freeman describes as "problems with the studio." MGM had to approve the screenplay before shooting could begin, and several internal office memos made it clear that the studio heads did not think highly of Black, despite the fact that he had worked on over twenty-five films and television series before *Shaft*. For example, MGM's vice president of production, Herbert Solow, sent a memo to the production team inquiring, "Is there anyone else besides John Black that can write this script?"[19]

It is also important to note that Freeman and Parks also shared the studio executives' concerns about Black's screenplay. Freeman thought the script was "just awful,"[20] while Parks was so disappointed with the writer's initial work that he sent Black a memo demanding the following changes/revisions: "Fix the dialogue which is tasteless and perhaps cruel. Shaft should walk off into infinity at the end of the film. Shaft utters too many obscenities. Change the name of Knocks Person to Bumpy Jonas."[21] Black revised the screenplay per Parks's instructions and delivered the second draft on January 4, 1971. That did not mark the end of the writer's work, as he was instructed to revise it two more times. Black completed the final shooting script on January 13, 1971, just one week before the film was scheduled to go into production.

While finalizing a strong script was obviously critical to *Shaft*'s success, casting the right actor to play the cool, slick title character was perhaps the most crucial element of the preproduction process. Working closely together, Parks and Freeman waded through photos and résumés of almost every African American male actor in Hollywood in search of the perfect actor to portray Shaft. A memo from the William Morris Agency to Gordon Parks listed the following actors as possible candidates for the seminal role: Rupert Crosse, Bernie Casey, Terry Carter, and Billy Dee Williams. Of those actors, Freeman recalls being very impressed with Bernie Casey, who early on emerged as the front-runner for the role. On November 2, 1970, the *Hollywood Reporter* announced that Fred Williamson and Jim Brown were also being considered for the part. Though Freeman explains that Brown was never in contention to play Shaft, he verified that Williamson did in fact test for the iconic role. "Freddie at that time was a terrible actor. I mean, let's face it—don't quote me 'cause he will come beat me up, and I want to play golf with him, so you know—but he was not a good actor. He came in with the character totally wrong, totally erroneous, as far as his interpretation was concerned—the gold cigarette, the whole thing, attitude was just not right."[22]

After auditioning a number of actors in Hollywood to no avail, Freeman and Parks traveled to New York, where they continued their search.[23] Richard Roundtree was among the actors who read for the part in a series of cattle calls designed to attract both well-established and unknown performers. Up to that point, Roundtree had appeared in small parts in two films, *Parachute to Paradise* (1969) and *What Do You Say to a Naked Lady?* (1970). His most prominent work was as a model in black magazines, where he appeared in ads for hair-care products. When he auditioned for Shaft, he was earning $60 a week playing the lead role in *The Great White Hope* onstage in Philadelphia.[24] The minute that Freeman and Parks laid eyes on the up-and-coming actor, they knew that he was perfect for the role. Freeman explained, "Shaft had to walk and stand with certain jauntiness, a swagger, an insouciance which Roundtree came by readily and naturally."[25] Parks was equally impressed with the actor. "I wanted Shaft to emerge as an original, rather than someone who would more or less take the role and mold it to his own way of acting. We want to create Shaft through some brilliant young actor. And Richard Roundtree is, I feel, 'the man.'"[26]

Though Freeman and Parks immediately fell in love with Roundtree, the studio execs initially wanted to cast a high-profile actor as John Shaft. However, they conceded to the producer's and director's insistence that Roundtree was right for the part and agreed to pay the actor $25,000 to play the role that was to make him a popular-culture icon. After reaching the agreement with Roundtree, Freeman and Parks started grooming the young actor to play John Shaft. First, they required him to quit *The Great White Hope*, as they wanted him fully committed to the film. Next, they asked Roundtree to grow a mustache and longer sideburns, much to the dismay of Solow, who issued one of his infamous memos, contending that Roundtree's sideburns and wardrobe looked "too faggy."[27] Parks and Freeman ignored the disparaging remarks and moved forward, selecting Shaft's wardrobe and hiring Roundtree's personal barber, who remained on the set for the entire shooting period to ensure that the look they had worked hard to create was maintained.

In addition to helping prepare Roundtree to play Shaft, Parks concurrently began assembling the film's crew. His primary mission in doing so was to provide African Americans the opportunity to work in the motion picture industry, a goal that he was able to accomplish. He spoke with a sense of pride when talking about the hiring of African American crewmembers:

> Hugh Robertson was the editor, and some of my assistants were black. I got as many as I possibly could. I wouldn't hire anybody who was not capable of doing what they were to do, no matter what color they were. So the same as I did in *The Learning Tree*, I shot it. They told me, "We don't have blacks that do that particular job," and I said, "Well, try." They come and said, "Well, we did find a guy." Fine, great. I just felt that blacks haven't been given the chance that they should have had in Hollywood, and they should search for as many as they possibly could.[28]

While Parks and Freeman were in New York completing preproduction, back in Hollywood, MGM was addressing budget-related issues. The original budget dated September 8, 1970, was $1,756,724 over a forty-seven-day shooting schedule that was slated to begin on November 9, 1970. The plan was to shoot all of the exterior scenes first and then move indoors before the New York winter descended upon the city. However, after missing the initial production date, on December 9, 1970, the studio presented a revised budget of $2,093,905 with shooting set to occur over fifty days starting on January 20, 1971. The increase in the budget factored in the potential need to add several days to the shooting schedule due to bad weather, yet when the budget was finalized the following day, the time for the shoot was reduced back to forty-seven days.

Though minimal by today's standards, in 1970, a $2 million budget for a black-themed picture starring an unknown actor was a major risk for the studio execs, who were uncertain whether *Shaft* would draw large audiences. Among the other items listed in the final budget was Freeman's $50,000 salary and Parks's $50,000 fee for directing the film. Tidyman's $50,000 writing fee was also included in the budget and proved to be a great bargain given that less than a year after *Shaft* began shooting, the writer won the Academy Award for his adaptation of *The French Connection* (1971). Had Silliphant and Lewis struck the deal later, they would have had to pay Tidyman a much-higher salary.

Much to Freeman and Parks's surprise, the MGM bosses reduced *Shaft*'s budget to $1,800,279 over a forty-two-day shoot, shortly before the film went into production. Gone were the insurance days that were initially added to account for the cold New York winter. As if that were not bad enough, MGM eventually further reduced the budget to $1.5 million. Yet Freeman was unfazed by the changes: "They wanted the picture, and they said, "We can't budget for more than $1.5 million." And we said, 'Okay, if that's what you want to do, go ahead and budget it. I'll tell you right now, I know what the picture is going to cost.' So we came in at $1,240,000, and that was it. So you know, the studio, I mean, they were in profit immediately."[29]

One day before *Shaft* was set to begin filming, Parks and Freeman experienced their first real crisis when they received a series of phone calls from James Aubrey, MGM's president. Parks recounted, "Jim Aubrey called up, told me to fire everybody but Roundtree and close your office and come out to California and do it [the film] out there. I didn't fire everybody. I didn't close the studio."[30] Rather than shut the production down, Parks and Freeman flew to California to meet with Aubrey's lieutenants. Parks continued, "I asked them if they felt the film could really be done as well in California as New York. They said no. I said, 'Well, why don't you tell Jim that.' They said, 'Well, you don't tell Jim things like that.'"[31] Parks and Freeman insisted on a face-to-face meeting with Aubrey so they could hear his objections firsthand. Parks recalled,

> We had a meeting, and I sat next to Jim. I said, "Why do you want us to bring the film to California?" He said, "Well, I'm afraid you're going to run into a lot of bad weather and production problems out there, and it's going to cost a lot of money." So that's when I told my noble lie, which everybody smiled at. I said, "I have a lens that can turn summer into winter and winter into summer [*laughs*]. Jim looked at me as if I was crazy. He said, "You're kidding." I said, "No, I'm not kidding." And he said, "Well, let me think it over." I went back to my office. He called up and said, "Well, you got it, okay." And so I said, "Well, Jim, if I hadn't have gotten it and it came to shooting it here, you'd had to get another director, 'cause I wouldn't try to shoot it in California." So he said, "Okay." But once given the green light, the studio backed me all the way. They didn't give me any problems."[32]

With the battle over the film's location won, Freeman and Parks returned to New York, where shooting began in Times Square on January 18, 1971. There,

Richard Roundtree as John Shaft. (*Shaft* DVD, MGM Home Entertainment)

Shaft crosses the busy New York City street during the film's opening sequence. (*Shaft* DVD, MGM Home Entertainment

they shot the now-iconic sequence of Roundtree ascending from the subway before coolly walking through the New York streets to Isaac Hayes's Academy Award–winning "Theme from *Shaft*." Because permits to block traffic and stunt drivers and cars cost money that the production team did not have, Parks filmed the scene without such safeguards in place. Discussing the sequence, Freeman explained, "The moment the film started, I was directing from about five stories up over Broadway, talking direct to Richard via telephone. I told him to walk across Broadway and Forty-Second Street against the traffic. He said, 'Are you trying to kill me?' 'You're Shaft, man, you can do anything.' He said, 'Okay, get the ambulance already,' and he went on and did it. Marvelous thing—he believed in himself, and he believed he was Shaft."[33] Roundtree has a somewhat different recollection of the iconic sequence and his decision to participate in it. "I didn't have sense enough to be afraid. I just plowed across the street. I guess I thought, since this was a movie and cameras were turning I'd be protected. Nothing so gross as instant death."[34]

There were very few luxuries allowed during the filming of *Shaft*. The crew did not have trailers, crafts services, or dressing rooms, and most of the filming was done out of the cinema-mobile.[35] Freeman spoke with energy as he described how they braved the elements and kept the Teamsters happy while completing the film.

> We made it all union—New York Teamsters, everybody. And they were the happiest guys in the world, you know. I said to David [Golden, the production supervisor], "Let the Teamsters take the cars home at night. What the hell's the difference?" And they'd come in the morning, and they'd be happy [they] didn't have to change trains, cars, whatever. They'd pick us up. They were happy as a lark. It was tough. It was cold. We worked out of the cinema-mobile. You can't go into New York with dressing rooms and that other crap. I've done that, I hated it, but this was a real tight kind of operation.[36]

The cinema-mobile provided the production crew with flexibility and spontaneity in filming.[37] One such moment occurred when Roundtree found himself in the middle of a gay-rights protest. Parks stopped the cinema-mobile as they were driving around Times Square, shooting footage for the opening of the film, when he saw the rally. He then found a place across the street and instructed Roundtree to walk through the group and react to them. The protestors were unaware that they were in the film, which was a distinct advantage of shooting

Gordon Parks speaks with Shaft during his cameo appearance in the film. (*Shaft* DVD, MGM Home Entertainment)

a film during that period, as moviemakers enjoyed more freedom to shoot just about anywhere and were not required to have people who happened to be captured in the shots sign permission waivers. Thus, the city belonged to them, and its citizens became unpaid extras that helped add to *Shaft*'s authenticity.

The cast and crew fought the cold throughout the first month of filming, which took place entirely outdoors. The crew eventually moved indoors, completing the film's principal photography on March 12, 1971. According to Freeman, the shooting proceeded very well. The only problem was the physical demand that the project placed on Roundtree, who was in almost every scene of the film. The actor had to wear layers of thermal underwear to make it through hours-long stretches in the cold weather, and he performed a number of his own stunts, including the famous shot of him crashing through a widow with his gun blazing during the film's final, climactic sequence. While completing the stunt, Roundtree sustained a back injury that he still suffers from to this day.

A standing deal between Stax Records and MGM was instrumental in the creation of the *Shaft* soundtrack. Prior to shooting, Isaac Hayes had been contacted regarding the possibility of writing a score for the film. As a result, the opening sequence of the film was sent to Hayes in an effort to provide him with insight about the "flavor of the film."[38] He was eventually signed to compose the soundtrack, which functions as the perfect aural accompaniment to the visual image. Freeman described the meeting when Hayes first played the music for the opening sequence: "Ike arrives. It was hysterical: he was wearing leopard skin down to his ankles, with a leopard-skin crown hat, you know. I just went like this [*shocked expression*], and I was really impressed with him. He sat down and played a tape for us that was unbelievable. And it was a tempo track. It was just so incredible, like—what's the expression—right on! Hit it on the button! Couldn't have done any better."[39]

The studio paid Hayes $20,000 to write the score, but because he had never scored a film, the MGM execs worried that the colorful artist might not be the best fit for the project. To allay their concerns, the powers that be created a space for Hayes on the MGM lot and hired the Bar-Kays to work alongside him in the scoring process. After approximately four weeks of rehearsal, Hayes went into the studio to begin work on the soundtrack. Freeman recounted, "So we're on the recording stage, and the music is just, I mean, it's unbelievable, it's so great. We're all just—we're feeling impressed, excited."[40] On the second day of recording, Freeman made a small suggestion to Hayes that had a profound impact on the direction of the soundtrack, which up until that point had been primarily instrumental. "I called Ike over, and I said, 'Ike, I'm going say something to you. If you came in with lyrics tomorrow for the title music, okay, I think we could be nominated for an Academy Award.' And he said, 'Okay' [*in a deep voice*], like he does, you know. Like Ike, this was him."[41] Hayes agreed, and the following day, he came to the studio holding an envelope on which he had written the lyrics to "Theme from *Shaft*," which indeed earned Hayes an Oscar on its way to selling two million copies. Further, the song helped establish the sound of the 1970s and still resonates loudly in popular culture, as it has been used numerous times on television and in film in the years since *Shaft*'s release.

With the score complete, MGM worked with Freeman to develop *Shaft*'s marketing campaign. He and Parks have always contended that their goal was to make a crossover film that just happened to feature a black hero. No matter how committed they both were to making a mainstream film that would appeal to a large cross-section of the moviegoing audience, it became clear early on that MGM had a different agenda. Among the items in Freeman's production files were notes sent to the production supervisor, David Golden, regarding a meeting that took place between Freeman, Jim Aubrey, Doug Netter, and William Singleton three days after the film began shooting. The meeting notes reflect a clear strategy on the part of the studio to exploit the African American audience. One section reads,

> They spoke of the importance of exploitation and felt it more strongly, now more than ever before, that this picture will be a damned good shot for the studio if handled correctly. Doug is working on the publicity aspects and everything should be handled correctly by the blacks with the black press including disc jockeys and magazines. Doug talked of Al Bell of Stax Records and stated he was a very bright guy. Doug also said that Stax was sending their Vice President in charge of exploitation and advertising to see Doug tomorrow. They have a network of blacks to push records throughout the country and all of those people will be at our disposal. Jim said we would be very impressed with Bell.[42]

In February 1971, the studio hired Communiplex, a coalition of African American marketing firms, to provide national exploitation and market counseling for *Shaft*.[43] The studio's desire to emphatically gear the film to the African American audience was in conflict with the picture that Freeman and Parks felt they were making. In fact, among Freeman's production notes was a reminder to himself that stated that he wanted to discuss with Silliphant *Shaft*'s crossover appeal. Highlighted in the memo under item 1 was "Too Black" and under 2 "Too preoccupied with it." Discussing the memo, Freeman contended, "We knew that this was a film which all kinds of people could enjoy, not just black people."[44] After the film was released, Freeman reiterated, "The white audience enjoyed it, and the black audience enjoyed it. And that was really great, and that was what we were hoping for. That picture is not made just for the black audience, no way. That picture was made for everybody."[45]

The promotional materials that MGM sent out to theaters focused on *Shaft*'s action sequences and called attention to the film's black hero. The only posters that MGM's marketing team gave theater owners featured the shot of John Shaft breaking through the window while firing his gun. Theaters received a note with the posters that read, "Cool slick, smart, and dangerous. A hard and handsome breed of Black man spawned amongst the violence and danger of the innards of Harlem in which he now moves with self-assured ease. He's also a cat whom moves [sic] easily in 'Whitey's' trough. A kind of Black man too many know too little about."[46]

MGM also conducted test screenings as a part of its marketing strategy. The first test audience was invited to view the film on May 23, 1971, at the Academy Theater in Inglewood, California. Freeman remarked, "If you had been at the preview which we did in Inglewood, California, out near the race track, they were screaming and up in their seats at the end of the picture, when [Shaft] goes through the window, that whole thing—I mean, literally screaming. I tell you it was so exciting. It was just something totally new."[47] Of the 166 people who completed surveys after the first screening, 84 considered the film excellent and 62 checked good, while 13 rated the film fair and 3 thought it was poor. When asked if they would recommend the film to their friends, 130 of the respondents said yes. When the participants were asked to cite the reasons they enjoyed the film, their answers revealed that there were a number of reasons that *Shaft* appealed to them. Some actual excerpts from the respondents are as follows:

> Because it was the way New York is. I lived back there and I saw so many things that made the movie so together. Gordon Parks outdid himself.

> Because I'm black and extremely proud to see a film that has toughness in it. I'm not a militant or want to frighten anyone, but I love the honesty of this.

> Because I feel that "Shaft" is a very together film that lets the people of this world know how black people are and what they can do.

> It was a real movie about black people. We are not all dumb, foot shuffling and head moving people.

> Superbly done—plot, photography, filming, music.[48]

Though the majority of the attendees appreciated *Shaft*, there were some audience members who disliked the film. When asked why *Shaft* did not appeal to them, they responded,

> Excessive Profanity. Do most people really use that muck.

> Stereotyped black James Bond. Dialogue at times unintelligible. Maybe just as well.

> The profanity and mixed bed scene.

> Love making with the white girl.[49]

Women provided the majority of the negative comments about *Shaft*. Though their perspectives were important, the women represented a small segment of the audience. Hence, according to Freeman, the audience responses from the screenings were so overwhelmingly positive that they did not feel the need to change anything.

Though there was talk of the crossover appeal, it was clear that MGM execs believed that *Shaft*'s success hinged on the African American audience. Their perspective became more apparent when they started commissioning screenings of *Shaft* at fundraisers for the African American community. One of the most visible of these screenings was the First Annual Benefit for the Foundation for Families or Beneficiaries of Deceased Policemen Killed in the Line of Duty, which was held on June 29, 1971, at the DeMille Theater in New York City. A selection of New York's prominent black media members, the *New York Amsterdam News*, and the radio station WLIB sponsored the exclusive event, and a similar fundraiser was held for the Echo House, a self-help community project, in Baltimore the following month.

## *SHAFT* OPENS

*Shaft*'s distribution pattern was not unusual at the time of its release. The film opened in first-run theaters on a week-by-week basis until it played in cities across most of the United States. During the 1970s, theater owners booked a film for a set period of time, but there were no restrictions on the number of showings a theater could have in a given day. Without such restriction, *Shaft* was able to generate huge per-screen revenues even though it never ascended to number one at the box office. Chicago's Roosevelt Theater, where *Shaft* did phenomenal business after opening on June 23, 1971, serves as a prime example. Its run was so successful at the Roosevelt (the only place in town showing *Shaft*) that the theater had to add midnight shows during the week to meet the demand for tickets. The first showing of *Shaft* was at 9:00 a.m., and the last show was at midnight, for a total of fourteen showings of the film per day. The Roosevelt reported in its advertising for the film that *Shaft* had broken all existing box-office records for the theater.

Understandably, Parks was thrilled that *Shaft* performed so well at the box office. He recalled the moment that he was initially informed that the film was on its way to becoming a hit:

| Week Ending | Dollars this Week | Rank | Total Number of Cities | Total Number of Theaters | Weeks on Chart | Total Dollars to Date |
|---|---|---|---|---|---|---|
| 6/30/71 | 87,000 | 21 | 4 | 4 | 1 | 87,000 |
| 7/7/71 | 310,000 | 6 | 7 | 8 | 2 | 395,000 |
| 7/14/71 | 452,000 | 4 | 10 | 29 | 3 | 863,214 |
| 7/21/71 | 349,500 | 4 | 11 | 13 | 4 | 1,242,658 |
| 7/28/71 | 359,200 | 4 | 12 | 24 | 5 | 1,557,166 |
| 8/4/71 | 310,000 | 7 | 11 | 18 | 6 | 1,899,498 |
| 8/11/71 | 319,700 | 7 | 10 | 13 | 7 | 2,234,811 |
| 8/18/71 | 227,050 | 9 | 9 | 10 | 8 | 2,462,918 |
| 8/25/71 | 305,000 | 5 | 10 | 10 | 9 | 2,799,635 |
| 9/1/71 | 154,700 | 13 | 7 | 9 | 10 | 2,953,956 |
| 9/8/71 | 174,000 | 12 | 7 | 9 | 11 | 3,129,488 |
| 9/15/71 | 170,998 | 7 | 7 | 10 | 12 | 3,300,840 |
| 9/22/71 | 100,550 | 8 | 7 | 8 | 13 | 3,395,115 |
| 9/29/71 | 79,350 | 16 | 6 | 7 | 14 | 3,474,171 |
| 10/6/71 | 77,000 | 14 | 7 | 8 | 15 | 3,550,243 |
| 10/13/71 | 73,350 | 23 | 6 | 7 | 16 | 3,624,901 |
| 10/20/71 | 66,700 | 22 | 7 | 8 | 17 | 3,692,591 |
| 10/27/71 | 35,000 | 34 | 4 | 5 | 18 | 3,727,391 |
| 11/3/71 | 35,000 | 31 | 4 | 5 | 19 | 3,763,091 |
| 11/10/71 | 21,200 | 33 | 5 | 6 | 20 | 3,783,591 |
| 11/17/71 | 23,250 | 39 | 6 | 7 | 21 | 3,808,371 |

Box-office date for *Shaft*. (*Variety*, July 1, 1971–November 18, 1971)

I had a feeling that it was a good film, but I didn't know it was going to explode. I was asleep when the film opened on Broadway. My son David called me about three o'clock in the morning and said, "Dad you gotta get up." I said, "Get up for what? Do you realize it's three o'clock?" He said, "You want to get up for what's going on on Broadway. You'll want to see this." So I went up there, and there was a line around the block. And they couldn't close the show down for three days. People kept coming.[50]

While audiences flocked to see *Shaft*, critics debated the value of the new type of black hero featured in the movie. Clayton Riley, a black film critic for the *New York Times*, penned a review that warned audiences planning to see the film.

Amusement is a cheap high; being entertained means never having to face the truth. We lie to each other in order to keep reality's terrors at arm's length. One can hope that things will get better before the world gets wise. Meanwhile we con each other with harmless (we think) pretensions. . . . Films like *Shaft* will be well received in this city because they provide Whites with a comfortable image of Blacks as noncompetitors, as people whose essential concern in life is making Mr. Charlie happy. Black history's delicious breast of Mammy being stuffed into the collective mouth of America's White Kids of All Ages. It's about Saturday night diversions being provided by the darkies, the plantation boss striding through the cabin to check out some of those plump and dusty belles.[51]

Riley's warning cries failed to drown out *Shaft*'s positive reviews. Vincent Canby, also a film critic for the *New York Times*, described the film as "the first good Saturday night movie I've seen in years."[52] Canby's statement became part of the advertising campaign as the film played across the country. The black press was also very supportive of the film. Maurice Peterson of *Essence* magazine wrote, "Never have we been allowed to go to the movies just to enjoy ourselves—that is, not until *Shaft*. . . . *Shaft* is the first picture to show a black man who leads a life free of racial torment. He is black and proud of it, but not obsessed with it."[53] *Ebony* and *Black Stars* ran celebrity pieces on Richard Roundtree that both provided his newly found fan base with more insight about the actor and praised *Shaft*.

The film also received support from the NAACP at its annual Image Awards ceremony, which recognizes achievement in black filmmaking. Joel Freeman received Producer of the Year honors for his work on *Shaft*, while Gordon Parks was named Director of the Year. The awards were important stamps of approval from the African American community's premier civil rights organization.

Although *Shaft* will more than likely always be considered a canon blaxploitation film, Freeman and Parks rejected the label. Freeman became very animated when defining *Shaft* and how it is different from other films belonging to the movement.

> I want to straighten something out which I firmly believe and so does Gordon. *Shaft*, the first one, was *not*—no, it was the first, it was the beginning of an era, and that era was the first black hero image that everyone could identify with. That was what *Shaft* was. *Shaft* was an action film, but it was not—it wasn't full of drugs, it wasn't full of any of that stuff. But following that, along comes *Across 110th Street* and the

other bunches of porns, down and dirty, raunchy. We were not the same thing. I mean, *Shaft* had some class to it, let's face it. Even though the subject matter was kind of simplified, it still had some . . . some—oh, what's the word—the word I was thinking was "dignity," and it did. *Shaft* had some dignity. I mean, sure, the language in it, the characters, they were real. . . . Listen, I have written letters to *Variety* and every place else, you know, and every time somebody lumps it with the other pictures saying it was, my answer is, "It is not, and stop calling it that, because that is not what it was."[54]

Though Parks viewed *Shaft* as a film featuring a black hero, he acknowledged, "People sometimes mix it up with black exploitation films—just breaks me to my heart. Who was exploiting who? I had black crews behind the camera doing things that they had never done before and at certain positions, and it was very important."[55]

In spite of Freeman and Parks's disappointment, *Shaft* will always be linked to blaxploitation because it did in fact help create the model that subsequent black-themed action films followed. In some instances, *Shaft*'s positive attributes were co-opted by filmmakers seeking to capitalize on the black audience, and prior to their deaths Freeman and Parks spent past forty-plus years trying to reclaim them. A definition of blaxploitation would be useful in examining how *Shaft* compares with other films of the period. Blaxploitation was a series of films made between 1970 and 1975 that were designed primarily for the African American inner-city audience. The films usually had urban settings, and the primary conflict was between a black protagonist and a white villain. Protracted scenes of sex and violence often connected the narratives in these films. For some critics and scholars, the films were exploitive, because they frequently lacked African American input but generated profits for white-owned studios.[56]

In many ways, *Shaft* was fundamentally different from the other films. First of all, working with a predominantly black crew, an African American directed the feature. Most of the ensuing films did not. Parks understood the power of the visual form and was careful and meticulous in crafting *Shaft*. For him, *Shaft* was not just another job; it was a labor of love. Furthermore, the budget for *Shaft*, though low by Hollywood standards, was significantly higher than the average blaxploitation film, a factor that led to its higher-quality production values than other films in the movement. *Shaft* also made Hollywood aware of the black audience, and the films that came after ratcheted up the sex and violence as a means of exploiting that market.

One of the positive aspects of the blaxploitation movement was that it served as a catalyst for studios to begin producing a more diverse body of films geared toward African American moviegoing audiences. Unfortunately, many black films of the era that do not belong to the movement are often overshadowed by it. For example, dramas such as *Sounder* (1972) and *Lady Sings the Blues* (1972) featured alternative representations of African Americans and, in conjunction with blaxploitation films, work to demonstrate that blacks are not monolithic. It is unlikely that those films would have been made had it not been for blaxploitation films' popularity. In addition to narrative films, two documentaries, *Soul to Soul* (1972) and *Wattstax* (1973), which celebrate African American music, were also distributed during the period. Finally, films focusing on the contemporary African American family, including *Claudine* (1974) and *Cooley High* (1975), were also released during the blaxploitation movement.

At the end of the blaxploitation era, black filmmaking in Hollywood did not sustain. Some critics have viewed the period as a phase that black filmmakers would have evolved out of in the subsequent years. Unfortunately, the new crop of filmmakers were never provided the opportunity do so, and black filmmaking was stunted as a result. Perhaps it was naïve to believe that Hollywood would suddenly shift focus and treat African American directors, performers, and audiences in a serious manner once the profits from blaxploitation fare dried up. Yet, given that *Shaft* helped create a lucrative formula, I believe that it was a realistic expectation. That Hollywood moved on so easily from highlighting black experiences when there was clearly a demand for them demonstrates that for that institution, and countless others, it is money and not black lives that matter most.

## NOTES

The epigraph is from David Walker, introduction to *Reflections on Blaxploitation: Actors and Directors Speak*, by David Walker, Andrew J. Rausch, and Chris Watson (Lanham, MD: Scarecrow, 2009), x.

1. In *The Princess Diaries*, when the character Joe appears in a full-length leather coat comments are made regarding how much he looks like Shaft. The resemblance of this white character to Shaft becomes a running gag throughput the film.
2. Graeme McMillan, "Dynamite to Resurrect Blaxploitation Hero John Shaft," *Hollywood Reporter*, May 29, 2014.
3. Dave McNary, "'Shaft' Reboot in the Works at New Line," *Variety*, February 18, 2015.
4. Out of a desire to aid in recounting a more robust history of *Shaft*, Freemen granted me access to all the materials related to the film, which include his personal

documents that were not part of the library's collection. In addition to those resources, I interviewed Freeman for several hours about *Shaft* and its production. The documents and interviews provide insight into the inner workings of MGM and a creative team negotiating the filmmaking process. They highlight the inherent tensions in the creative process, which were heightened by the nature of the project and the changing structure of inner-city movie audiences.

5. Novotny Lawrence, *Blaxploitation Films of the 1970s: Blackness and Genre* (New York: Routledge, 2008), 18.
6. Ernest Tidyman, *Shaft* (New York: Macmillan, 1970), 21.
7. Ibid., 22.
8. Ibid., 29.
9. Joel Freeman, interview by Eric Pierson, July 7, 1999.
10. Gordon Parks, interview by Eric Pierson, July 14, 1999.
11. In bringing *The Learning Tree* to the silver screen, Parks became the first African American to direct a Hollywood film.
12. "Gordon Parks: Soul of an Artist," *Soul Illustrated*, June 1969, 29–35.
13. Ibid., 35.
14. Signing for a percentage of the profits proved to be a very wise business decision for Parks, as he continued to receive royalty checks for this work on *Shaft* up until his death in early 2006.
15. Director's contract, Joel Freeman Collection, Margaret Herrick Library, Academy of Motion Picture Arts and Sciences, Beverly Hills, CA.
16. Freeman, interview.
17. Producer's contract, Joel Freeman Collection.
18. Parks, interview.
19. Memo from Herbert Solow to production team, Joel Freeman Collection.
20. Freeman, interview.
21. Memo from Gordon Parks to John Black, Joel Freeman Collection.
22. Freeman, interview.
23. Casting notes, Joel Freeman Collection. Bill Cosby's name was among the notes in Freeman's casting file, but when questioned about it, Freeman laughed and said that Cosby was never a serious contender for the role. Freeman, interview.
24. Walter Price Burrell, "Richard Roundtree: A Year after Shaft," *Black Stars*, July 1972.
25. Production memo from Herbert Solow, November 24, 1970, Joel Freeman Collection.
26. Ibid.
27. Ibid.
28. Parks, interview.
29. Freeman, interview.
30. Parks, interview.
31. Ibid.
32. Ibid. Freeman explained that the fight to keep the film in New York was part of the vision that he and Parks had for the film. "The studio fought us, and we said, 'No,

this is a New York guy. He can't be a California guy. It doesn't work. He's got to be a New York guy.'" Freeman, interview.
33. Parks, interview.
34. *Shaft* press release, Joel Freeman Collection.
35. Parks, interview.
36. Freeman, interview.
37. The cinema-mobile was a production studio on wheels. This gave the production team the flexibility to move quickly through the streets of New York.
38. Freeman, interview.
39. Ibid.
40. Ibid.
41. Ibid.
42. Meeting notes, production memo from Herbert Solow to David Golden, November 24, 1970, Joel Freeman Collection.
43. *Variety*, February 24, 1971.
44. Freeman, interview.
45. Ibid.
46. Promotional materials, Joel Freeman Collection.
47. Freeman, interview.
48. Promotional materials, Joel Freeman Collection.
49. Ibid.
50. Parks, interview.
51. Clayton Riley, "A Black Critics View of *Shaft*: A Black Movie for White Audiences," *New York Times*, July 25, 1971.
52. Vincent Camby, "Film Review of *Shaft*," *New York Times*, July 19, 1971.
53. Maurice Peterson, review of *Shaft*, *Essence*, July 1971.
54. Freeman, interview.
55. Parks, interview.
56. Lawrence, *Blaxploitation Films*, 97.

## WORKS CITED

Burrell, Walter Price. "Richard Roundtree: A Year after Shaft." *Black Stars*, July 1972.
Camby, Vincent. "Film Review of *Shaft*." *New York Times*, July 19, 1971.
Freeman, Joel. Interview by Eric Pierson. July 7, 1999.
"Gordon Parks: Soul of an Artist." *Soul Illustrated*, June 1969.
Lawrence, Novotny. *Blaxploitation Films of the 1970s: Blackness and Genre*. New York: Routledge, 2008.
McMillan, Graeme. "Dynamite to Resurrect Blaxploitation Hero John Shaft." *Hollywood Reporter*, May 29, 2014.
McNary, Dave. "'Shaft' Reboot in the Works at New Line." *Variety*, February 18, 2015.
Parks, Gordon. Interview by Eric Pierson. July 14, 1999.

Peterson, Maurice. Review of *Shaft*. *Essence*, July 1971.
*Princess Diaries, The*. Directed by Garry Marshall. Burbank, CA: Walt Disney Pictures. 2001. Film.
Riley, Clayton. "A Black Critic's View of *Shaft*: A Black Movie for White Audiences." *New York Times*, July 25, 1971.
Tidyman, Ernest. *Shaft*. New York: Macmillan, 1970.
Walker, David. Introduction to *Reflections on Blaxploitation: Actors and Directors Speak*, by David Walker, Andrew J. Rausch, and Chris Watson, vii–x. Lanham, MD: Scarecrow, 2009.

# 5

## THE BLOOD OF THE THING (IS THE TRUTH OF THE THING)

### VIRAL PATHOGENS AND UNCANNY ONTOLOGIES IN *GANJA AND HESS*

**HARRISON M. J. SHERROD**

What is the prognosis?
—Frantz Fanon, *Black Skin, White Masks*

This is a *psychic epidemic*, not a lesser germ like typhoid fever or syphilis. We can handle those. This belongs under some ancient Demonic Theory of Disease.
—Ishmael Reed, *Mumbo Jumbo*

Stoker's *Dracula* is no vampire novel, but rather the written account of our bureaucratization. Anyone is free to call this a horror novel as well.
—Friedrich Kittler, *Dracula's Legacy*

IN 1896, THE YEAR FRENCH MEDICAL STUDENT ERNEST DUCHESNE stumbled upon the antibiotic power of penicillin (later rediscovered by Alexander Fleming), the United States Supreme Court made a landmark ruling in the case of *Plessy v. Ferguson*. To the naked eye, Homer A. Plessy was a white man with no discernible black features. In response to the recent segregation of Louisiana railway cars, he argued that because his racial makeup included only a minute fraction of African ancestry, he should be awarded the status of white citizenship. However, Plessy's lawsuit was swiftly struck down by an eight-to-one vote, thereby justifying the "separate but (un)equal" partitioning of public facilities.

*Plessy v. Ferguson* laid the groundwork for the notion of hypodescent, otherwise known as the one-drop rule, which prescribed that any individual with even an iota of African blood must be classified as black.[1] The implications of the ruling were clear: race was no longer synonymous with skin color—in the era of modern microbiology, it could now be conceptualized at the molecular level, leading stereotypical black shortcomings (lethargy, violence, prurience) to be attributed to hereditary disease.[2] By the standards of the late nineteenth century, blackness was tantamount to a dangerous pathogen and thus required the proper prophylaxis: diagnosis, isolation, and in extreme cases, sterilization.[3] Indeed, throughout history, pundits and politicians have deployed germ rhetoric to circumscribe black identity and rationalize catastrophic social phenomena that have unjustly been attributed to the black populace, such as the AIDS virus, the crack-cocaine epidemic, and urban warfare (note that the latter two of these ills feature prominently in many blaxploitation films).[4]

A year after Duchesne's medical breakthrough and Plessy's defeat, a relatively unknown British author explored similar themes of contamination and foreign invasion. Written in response to "the late-Victorian nightmare of reverse colonization,"[5] Bram Stoker's *Dracula* has become an allegory for the obsessive-compulsive xenophobia of racial otherness (the same strain of fear that prompted the *Plessy* verdict). However, the novel could have just as easily been set in the antebellum South (needless to say, the black vampire is otherness squared). Indeed, these seemingly disparate coordinates share more than chronological symmetry. In Bill Gunn's 1973 avant-garde horror masterpiece *Ganja and Hess*, the vampire becomes a fecund metaphor for the plight of the black subject defined by viral prejudices, transgressing biological, cultural, and ontological boundaries.

Gunn was a prominent playwright in the New York theater scene, while also appearing in a handful of minor television roles. In 1970, he adapted the screenplay for Hal Ashby's *The Landlord*, a send-up of gentrification in Park Slope, and directed his first feature film, *Stop*, a Pinteresque psychodrama. Keen to capitalize on the popularity of William Crain's *Blacula* (1972), which had achieved massive success the year prior, executive producers Kelly-Jordan enlisted Gunn to make a black vampire film. Despite his aversion to working in the blaxploitation idiom, Gunn saw an opportunity to articulate his own idiosyncratic vision at the expense of a Hollywood studio. The final cut largely departed from the script approved by Kelly-Jordan (note that the word "vampire" is never explicitly uttered), and though *Ganja and Hess* won the Critics Prize at the 1973 Cannes Film Festival, the rights to the film were sold to Heritage Enterprises after an abysmal box-office stint. In an attempt to salvage a commercially palatable product, the film was reedited (from 113 to 78 minutes) and released under a handful of hackneyed alternate titles (*Blood Couple*, *Double Possession*, etc.), prompting Gunn, producer Chiz Shultz, and editor Victor Kanefsky to disown the project. Aside from occasional repertory screenings, the undoctored version of the film was unavailable for several decades, but thankfully the original 35 mm negative from the Museum of Modern Art archives recently underwent a restoration process and is now widely accessible. Despite its underground status, *Ganja and Hess* was championed by film critics and scholars. In *American Film Now*, James Monaco called it "an underground classic, . . . the most complicated, intriguing, subtle, sophisticated, and passionate Black film of the Seventies."[6] The digest *Video Watchdog* ran a lengthy piece on the "savaging and salvaging" of the film as part of its "Special Lost & Found" issue.[7] Manthia Diawara and Phyllis Klotman have undertaken the most comprehensive study of *Ganja and Hess*, offering a formal/quasi-psychoanalytic reading of the film that encompasses its religious motifs and feminist undercurrents.[8]

*Ganja and Hess*'s freeform plot owes more to the elliptical dream logic of the avant-garde than the tropes of psychotronic cinema.[9] According to Kanefsky, when Gunn was asked about the symbolism of the film, he would often quote Ingmar Bergman on the open-ended nature of his work. It follows that a careful reading of the bare-bones story line is a fruitless exercise in speculation and disregards the plurality of Gunn's visual language. The film centers on Dr. Hess Green (played by Duane Jones, who also appeared in George Romero's 1968 zombie cult classic *Night of the Living Dead*), an urbane anthropology professor who is stabbed by his schizophrenic assistant, George Meda (played by Gunn himself), with a diseased dagger from the ancient African civilization of Myrthia, thereby contaminating him with vampiric bloodlust.[10] Lost in delirium, Meda commits suicide, prompting the arrival of his wife, Ganja, whom Hess seduces and infects. However, this sequence of events is preceded by a series of shots juxtaposing artworks from the Brooklyn Museum and footage of a black congregation led in worship by Rev. Luther Williams, who also doubles as Hess's chauffeur. That Gunn opted to interpolate this seemingly inapposite prelude may initially seem odd, yet the stark contrast between the inanimate objects and the fervor of the parishioners gestures toward a dichotomy that underpins the film's entire premise: the struggle between person and thing.[11]

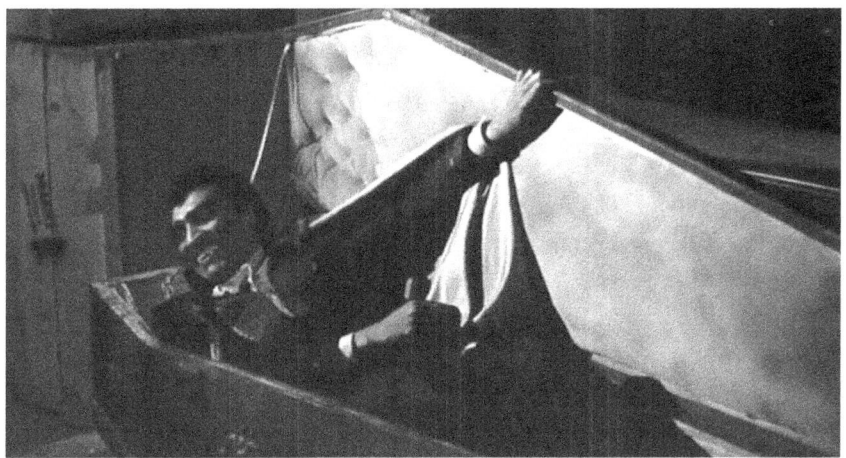

William Marshall as Blacula. (*Blacula* DVD, MGM Home Entertainment)

The vampire is almost always cast as the antagonist, a shadowy force to be vanquished, a bogeyman onto whom all cultural anxieties are projected. Gunn upends this convention by emphasizing the tragic perspective of vampirism mythology, thereby wielding it as an exemplum for African American history.[12] In the voice-over narration that opens the film, Rev. Williams describes Hess: "He's not a criminal; he's a victim. He's addicted to blood." Though the vampiric virus ostensibly lends the host immortality, Hess is ultimately portrayed as sickly and enervated, a far cry from Dracula, who is endowed with robust vitality, in addition to fantastic abilities such as superhuman strength and a controlling gaze. Therefore, the victimization precipitated by the vampiric germ correlates with the objectification of blacks fueled by pathological thinking. Prior to Meda's killing himself, he writes a scattershot credo that reads, "To the black male children, philosophy is a prison. It disregards the uncustomary things about you." This declaration provides an opportune entryway into the metaphysical quagmire implicit in black ways of being, especially the categorical paradox that legitimates slavery. As Bill Brown has suggested, the subhuman status of the African American slave presents an ontological conundrum, occupying a liminal space between subject and object, person and commodity.[13] Slaves were understood to possess free will (for the purposes of criminal punishment) but could be simultaneously bought and sold in auctions alongside inanimate pieces of furniture. This "ontological scandal" was no doubt perpetuated by the a priori assumption that slaves were intrinsically diseased and therefore less than human.

Indeed, illness is still associated with the loss of subjectivity in our contemporary lexicon: sick individuals will often report feeling as if they are not themselves, that is, temporarily devoid of an ego or identity.

This categorical breakdown finds an analog in the interstitial nature of monsters. Noël Carroll notes in his seminal survey of the horror genre that the "fantastic biologies" of such creatures are often characterized by an aberrant composite of heterogeneous species (recall the biraciality of Plessy). Describing these monsters, he writes, "They are un-natural relative to a culture's conceptual scheme of nature. They do not fit the scheme; they violate it."[14] It is no coincidence that Carroll's theory of art-horror hinges on a combination of fear and disgust—that is, monsters are perceived not as merely frightening or threatening but also as impure, that is, synonymous with "sickness, disease, and the plague."[15] Similarly, in differentiating between Kant's negative and indefinite judgment, Slavoj Žižek writes, "In the texts of popular culture, the uncanny creatures which are neither alive nor dead, the 'living dead' (vampires, etc.) are referred to as 'the undead'—although they are not dead, they are clearly not alive like us, ordinary mortals."[16] This is precisely the method of self-deception (termed "disavowal" in psychoanalytic nomenclature) that underpins the mechanics of slavery, the one-drop rule, and other manifestations of systemized racial discrimination. One can imagine a paranoid plantation owner thinking to himself, "I know very well that this slave is merely a thing, but nevertheless . . ." Slaves are not dead, lifeless objects, but neither are they human beings "like us." Put simply, if the vampire is classified as undead, then the black subject is inhuman. The lyrics of composer Sam Waymon's theme for the film echo this thesis succinctly: "Thousands of slaves were buried today, but murdered in such a way the slaves could not die."

Of course, it is fitting that Hess is a professor of archeology, a discipline concerned with resurrecting the past, and the necromantic dimension of excavation takes a literal turn when he is possessed by the history of his *objet trouvé*. Prior to Meda's outburst, Hess experiences a fever dream while examining the Myrthian dagger, which looks to be fashioned out of bone (a substitute for the vampire's fangs). His hallucinatory vision, accompanied by hypnotic incantations on the soundtrack, consists of an African matriarch (credited as the Queen of Myrthia) adorned in tribal regalia beckoning him with an outstretched hand. This (flash)back-to-Africa imagery is the result of the dagger becoming disenthralled from its status as anachronistic fetish object and converted into a reanimator of history. According to Arata, "In *Dracula* vampirism designates a kind of colonization of the body. Horror arises not because Dracula destroys bodies, but because he appropriates and transforms them. Having yielded to his assault, one literally 'goes native' by becoming a vampire oneself."[17] Hess "goes native" by becoming conscious of a moment that predates slavery, accessing the "long historical past" (to borrow a phrase from Frantz Fanon) that has always eluded the African American psyche. However, the progression from nostalgic dream state to vampiric metamorphosis mirrors the movement from freedom to bondage enacted in the Middle Passage. In *Ganja and Hess*, vampirism *is* slavery; it designates a viral colonization of the body and a denial of one's ontological status as human, that is, a realization of the demagogic germ rhetoric wielded against blacks throughout history.

Throughout the film, Gunn deliberately includes images that, if unmoored from their narrative context, become explicit signifiers of the horrors perpetrated against the black race. For example, after Hess awakes from his dream, he finds an inebriated Meda perched in a tree with a noose suspended from its branch. The composition of the shot is such that the viewer cannot see Meda's head, generating the impression that he has already been lynched and is speaking from the grave. A comparable effect is produced by the profusion of blood in the film.[18] In the documentary *The Blood of the Thing*, producer Chiz Schultz claims that Gunn wanted to divest blood of its grotesque connotations so that it could be viewed as any other habit-forming substance. Indeed, it is easy to interpret the vampiric motif in *Ganja and Hess* as a metaphor for drug addiction, a topic addressed (albeit ambivalently) in many blaxploitation films (see *Super Fly*, *Youngblood*, et al.). Indeed, this was the era of the FBI flooding Harlem with heroin in an attempt to nullify the Black Power movement. On the other hand, as Ganja's seduction of a dinner guest shifts from sex to cannibalism, the bloodied back of her victim is filmed in close-up, calling to mind the bodies of slaves postflagellation. Similarly, the shot of her guest's discarded body bag in a nearby field could easily double as a *Life* magazine photograph from the battlegrounds of Vietnam, a conflict fought primarily by young black men. Describing the taboo topic of black death, Sharon Patricia Holland writes, "Although some would argue that the United States is now a 'kinder, gentler nation,' we cannot escape the raw fact that our boundary is filled with the blood from five hundred years of slavery, removal, and conquest and that our border is a constant space of death and terror."[19] Such is the scope of Gunn's historical framework. The point is not that *Ganja and Hess* is a reductive metaphor for any one atrocity; rather, the film is haunted by ghosts from over a century of African American suffering.

Yet death also operates on an oblique, figurative level. To return to Brown's argument, the thingification of blacks ended with neither the abolishment of slavery nor the disintegration of Jim Crow laws. In his analysis of Spike Lee's

*Bamboozled* (2000), which concerns a black television writer who inadvertently amasses a collection of racist mechanical banks, Brown argues that negative black stereotypes (initially attributed to microbiologic flaws) have become reified in symbols of pop culture such as Sambo art, Negro collectibles, and minstrel shows (blaxploitation performs a similar semiotic function), thus perpetuating the literal and figurative objectification of black identity. Put differently, for the better part of the twentieth century, complex portraits of black subjectivity were largely absent from forms of mass media, which traded in one-dimensional racist caricatures. Drawing on Ernst Jentsch's concept of the uncanny, which is characterized by intellectual uncertainty in regard to animate versus inanimate objects such as lifelike automata, Brown contends that the conceptual paradox of the slave is the source of acute anxiety: "I simply want to reassert the specificity of Jentsch's interest in the ambiguously animate object and to imagine that uncanniness can be precipitated by cultural history precisely because law, politics, and ideology so patently contribute to untoward and ambiguous ontologies, to the riddle of person or thing."[20] For Brown, the continuous objectification of blacks is symptomatic of a cultural uncanny. If the specter of slavery is the latent content trapped in America's psyche, then every time blackness is reified, the repressed comes bubbling forth, because by Brown's estimation, "despite change over time, there's been no change."[21]

The practice of collecting is at the forefront of *Ganja and Hess*. The Hess mansion, where the vast majority of the film takes place, is a makeshift Wunderkammer filled with African statuettes, jazz records, and paintings. It is possible to treat this assemblage of objects as a postmodern protest against the hegemony of the Western canon—that is, a Nina Simone LP is of greater or equal value than Salvatore Albano's sculpture *The Fallen Angels* (both of which can be spotted early in the film). However, Gunn does not seem to favor one artifact over another, and if these objects are temporarily treated as ahistorical vessels devoid of any ethnic symbolism, another contrast comes into focus: the interplay between kineticism and inertia. Shot in close-up, Gunn's catalogue of relics resembles a series of still photographs—that is, the ontology of the objects is reiterated in their method of capture. These split-second images are interpolated throughout the film, creating brief fissures of narrative suspension that short-circuit cinematic time. Though they occasionally function as Eisensteinian visual metaphors, their ultimate effect is an uncanny contrast between person and thing. Diawara and Klotman allude to this slippage, describing the eye of a statue as possessing a "lifelike quality."[22] This reading is illuminated by Theodor Adorno's famous supposition that the phonic parallel between "museum" and "mausoleum" is not a mere coincidence. Put simply, the museum is where things go to die.

These images appear countless times, though I would like to focus on one particular example: soon after Ganja discovers her husband's frozen cadaver in the wine cellar, she slips into a trance-like state and delivers a surreal monologue. The sequence begins with a carving shot in profile against the void of a black background. As Ganja begins to speak, the camera slowly pans left to reveal her in an identical pose on the opposite side of the screen, showing only her dismembered head. This simple movement creates a sleight-of-hand effect, underscoring the porous barrier between person and thing. Of course, the uncanny force of this moment is emphasized by Ganja's choice of words: "It was as though I was a disease." In this single shot, the auditory and the visual mobilize different metaphors, but both allude to the ghostly subtext of the film: illness begets objectification—something blacks have known for over a century. Ganja's exchange with Archie the butler is a wry wink at this ontological ambiguity. When Archie is asked how long he has worked for Hess, he replies, "Madame, I came with the house," to which she jokes, "You mean the plumbers came in to put in the plumbing, and then they put you in it?" Additionally, Brown's reworking of the uncanny elucidates Ganja's shock at having murdered their dinner guest: her anxiety over becoming undead is compounded by the realization that she has reduced a fellow human being to a lifeless commodity—she is simultaneously objectified and objectifier. Thus, imbricated within the visual syntax of the film is the fear of becoming a thing in the most literal sense of the word: monster *and* object.

*Ganja and Hess* concludes with a return to its point of origin: the church. Deprived of blood, the couple eventually falls ill, and Hess seeks absolution from Rev. Williams, after which he effectively commits suicide by submitting himself to the shadow of a cross. If vampirism (a bedfellow of witchcraft, voodoo, etc.) is aligned with slavery, not to mention the sin of desire, then it seems logical to suppose that Christianity represents an escape. Cornell West has suggested that the church has historically functioned as a safe haven from persecution because it condemned the evils that white patriarchy feared most, namely, black sexuality and violence, that is, the same defects attributed to vampires and virology.[23] Sontag describes the cancer patient as "the object of practices of decontamination," a phrase that equally applies to the black subject cleansed by the rituals of the church.[24] However, the church was complicit in proselytizing germ rhetoric by providing an antidote for its "symptoms," and in a teleological twist, disease and undeath can only be vanquished through martyrdom, making it unclear whether

Hess's conversion from vampire to Christian disciple signifies salvation. This ambiguity is exemplified during the final images of the film, in which Ganja witnesses the nude, Christ-like body of her dinner-guest-cum-vampiric-victim resurrected from a swimming pool. As he sprints across the field, he hurdles over the dead body of Archie, a shot captured in freeze frame. Is this a return to the primitivist utopia of the dream sequence, or does the inertia of the image imply objectification in perpetuity? Has the vampiric germ been vanquished, or does Archie's corpse suggest a lifetime of illness? In this sequence, the ontological enigmas that buttress the film are entwined together to form a double helix: the vampire/slave binary becomes trapped in the fatal frame of the inanimate object world.

The history of blaxploitation cinema is also a vampire story. The pervasive discourse surrounding the movement has hinged on a contentious debate over precisely who was getting exploited or, put differently, who was getting the life sucked out of them. Despite the radical visual style and insurrectionary political import of *Sweet Sweetback's Baadasssss Song* (Huey P. Newton assigned it as mandatory viewing for all Black Panthers), critics such as bell hooks and others contend that the film's director, Melvin Van Peebles, was less preoccupied with achieving aesthetic iconoclasm or provoking revolutionary activity than he was with turning a profit. Unlike Gunn, Van Peebles privileged the bottom line over artistic integrity, a stance confirmed by his subsequent career as a stockbroker. Once producers observed the marketability of *Sweetback*, they rushed to imitate its formula in an attempt to capitalize (a polite synonym for prey) on a burgeoning black middle class, in addition to liberal white audiences. Another chapter in the long history of Sambo art, blaxploitation reified the African American struggle and nullified the militant outrage of the countercultural era with narrative bromides, leading black activists Jesse Jackson and the Kuumba Workshop to denounce the movement en masse. In the popular imagination, blaxploitation films have become even further unmoored from their historical context, functioning as empty signifiers of nostalgia. For example, Quentin Tarantino's *Jackie Brown* exemplifies a synchronic blank parody of blaxploitation culture bereft of any sociopolitical consciousness.

Academics have wrestled with the Faustian pact implicit in the consumption of these films: depictions of black bravado and empowerment on the big screen, but at what cost? There has been an attempt to recuperate the blaxploitation canon under the aegis of genre studies, feminist theory, and historiography with a focus on audience reception. Though these readings contain value, they betray an almost paranoiac urge to justify the significance of a movement that widely amounted to yet another iteration of blackness-turned-object. For an era of filmmaking so preoccupied with subverting the authority of "the Man," there remains too little scholarship on blaxploitation titles that were subject to extensive censorship or distribution troubles such as *Ganja and Hess* (Sun Ra's *Space Is the Place* [1974], Ivan Dixon's *The Spook Who Sat by the Door* [1973], and Christopher St. John's *Top of the Heap* [1972] come to mind). The lack of research on Gunn's oeuvre is likewise distressing (this is largely because his other feature films, *Stop* (1970) and *Personal Problems* (1980), are unavailable). Though he was not as militant or incendiary as his contemporary Van Peebles, Gunn was concerned with the psychological and philosophical ramifications of the political injustices that blaxploitation cinema dealt with only on a superficial level. Let this chapter be an invocation for the resurrection of more work on Gunn and sui generis films of the blaxploitation era.

## NOTES

I am indebted to Matthew Sims, a PhD candidate at the University of Chicago, for providing me with a treasure trove of research on germ theory.

1. Thadious M. Davis provides an excellent history of the *Plessy* case in her introduction to Nella Larsen's *Passing* (New York: Penguin, 1997). For an exhaustive chronicle of the history of blood, see Lawrence Hill's *Blood: The Stuff of Life* (Toronto: Anansi, 2013).
2. See David Raney, "Encroaching Dark: Germs and Race in Twentieth-Century American Literature and Culture," *Interdisciplinary Literary Studies* 6, no. 2 (2005): 1–23.
3. Blacks have been subjected to disease in the form of perverse government experiments like the Tuskegee Syphilis Study, in which several hundred men were unwittingly exposed to syphilis, spending years without medical care for the purposes of observation and research.
4. Of course, as Susan Sontag points out, illness metaphors have historically been used to demonize myriad ethnic groups that are deemed to pose a threat: "Throughout the nineteenth century, disease metaphors become more virulent, preposterous, demagogic. And there is an increasing tendency to call any situation one disapproves of a disease." Susan Sontag, *"Illness as Metaphor" and "AIDS and Its Metaphors"* (New York: Doubleday, 1990), 74.
5. Stephen D. Arata, "The Occidental Tourist: *Dracula* and the Anxiety of Reverse Colonization," in *Dracula*, ed. Nina Auerbach and David J. Skal (New York: Norton, 1997), 465.
6. James Monaco, *American Film Now* (New York: Oxford University Press, 1979), 205.
7. See David Walker and Tim Lucas, "Ganja & Hess," *Video Watchdog* 3 (1991). This essay is included on the Kino-Lorber DVD and Blu-ray.

8. Manthia Diawara and Phyllis Klotman, "*Ganja and Hess*: Vampires, Sex, and Addictions," *Jump Cut* 35 (1990): 30–36.
9. "Psychotronic" is a neologism coined by film critic Michael Weldon referring to low-budget sci-fi, horror, and exploitation movies. (For more, see Weldon, *The Encyclopedia for Psychotronic Film* [New York: Ballantine Books, 1987].)
10. By all accounts, Myrthia is a fictional civilization. Despite the etymological overlap, it is unlikely that Gunn intended to reference the Roman religious cult of Mithraism.
11. In this context, "thing" encapsulates a double meaning, referring to both inanimate object and alien creature.
12. For more on this topic, see Novotny Lawrence, "Fear of a Blaxploitation Monster: Blackness as a Generic Revision in *Blacula*," *Film International* 7, no. 3 (2009): 14–26.
13. See Bill Brown, "Reification, Reanimation, and the American Uncanny," *Critical Inquiry* 32 (2006): 175–207.
14. Noël Carroll, *The Philosophy of Horror, or Paradoxes of the Heart* (New York: Routledge, 1990), 34.
15. Ibid., 28.
16. Slavoj Žižek, "Kant as a Theoretician of Vampirism," in *The Gothic*, ed. Gilda Williams (London and Cambridge, MA: Whitechapel and MIT Press, 2007), 143. Originally published in *Lacanian Ink* 8 (1994).
17. Arata, "Occidental Tourist," 465.
18. Blood, the life force of the vampire, is conceived of in the popular imagination as a substance that transcends racial barriers (recall Shylock's monologue from the *Merchant of Venice*), yet historically its symbolic capital has been co-opted to ostracize black people. For example, during World War II, the blood used in transfusions was designated as either "white" or "colored" to maintain racial purity.
19. Sharon Patricia Holland, *Raising the Dead: Readings of Death and (Black) Subjectivity* (Durham, NC: Duke University Press, 2000), 4.
20. Brown, "Reification, Reanimation, and the American Uncanny," 199.
21. Ibid., 204.
22. Diawara and Klotman, "*Ganja and Hess*," 34.
23. I owe this connection to David Raney's "Encroaching Dark."
24. Susan Sontag, *Illness as Metaphor* (New York: Farrar, Straus and Giroux, 1978), 6.

# WORKS CITED

Arata, Stephen D. "The Occidental Tourist: *Dracula* and the Anxiety of Reverse Colonization." In *Dracula*, edited by Nina Auerbach and David J. Skal, 462–69. New York: Norton, 1997.

Brown, Bill. "Reification, Reanimation, and the American Uncanny." *Critical Inquiry* 32 (2006): 175–207.

Carroll, Noël. *The Philosophy of Horror, or Paradoxes of the Heart*. New York: Routledge, 1990.

Davis, Thadious M. Introduction to *Passing*, by Nella Larsen. New York: Penguin, 1997.

Diawara, Manthia, and Phyllis Klotman. "*Ganja and Hess*: Vampires, Sex, and Addictions." *Jump Cut* 35 (1990): 30–36.

*Ganja and Hess*. Directed by Bill Gunn. 1973. New York: Kino Lorber, 2012. Blu-ray.

Hill, Lawrence. *Blood: The Stuff of Life*. Toronto: Anansi, 2013.

Holland, Sharon Patricia. *Raising the Dead: Readings of Death and (Black) Subjectivity*. Durham, NC: Duke University Press, 2000.

Lawrence, Novotny. "Fear of a Blaxploitation Monster: Blackness as a Generic Revision in *Blacula*." *Film International* 7, no. 3 (2009): 14–26.

Monaco, James. *American Film Now*. New York: Oxford University Press, 1979.

Raney, David. "Encroaching Dark: Germs and Race in Twentieth-Century American Literature and Culture." *Interdisciplinary Literary Studies* 6, no. 2 (2005): 1–23.

Sontag, Susan. *Illness as Metaphor*. New York: Farrar, Straus and Giroux, 1978.

Walker, David, and Tim Lucas. "Ganja & Hess." *Video Watchdog* 3 (1991). This essay is included on the Kino Lorber *Ganja and Hess* DVD and Blu-ray.

Weldon, Michael. *The Encyclopedia for Psychotronic Film*. New York: Ballantine Books, 1987.

Žižek, Slavoj. "Kant as a Theoretician of Vampirism." In *The Gothic*, edited by Gilda Williams. London and Cambridge, MA: Whitechapel and MIT Press, 2007. Originally published in *Lacanian Ink* 8 (1994): 19–34.

# 6

## A WHITE FILM FOR A BLAXPLOITATION AUDIENCE?

### THE MAKING AND MARKETING OF *DETROIT 9000*

NOVOTNY LAWRENCE

By 1973, the black movie boom commonly referred to as blaxploitation had reached its apex as a result of the box-office performances of films such as *Cotton Comes to Harlem* (1970), *Sweet Sweetback's Baadasssss Song* (1971), *Shaft* (1971), and *Super Fly* (1972). Although these films did much to challenge and counter the stereotypical images that had circumscribed black performers in motion pictures since their emergence as a popular form of entertainment, they were not without their detractors. In particular, black critics such as Clayton Riley and Lerone Bennet, Jr., and activists such as former president of the Beverly Hill branch of the NAACP Junius Griffin viewed the films' reliance on violence and sex as a detriment to the struggle for black equality. In fact, expressing disdain for *Super Fly*, Griffin coined the term "blaxploitation" as a critique of the film and others like it, asserting, "Black exploitation in films has reached devastating proportions.... We must tell both white and black movie producers that we will not tolerate the continued warping of our black children's minds with the filth, violence, and cultural lies that are all pervasive in current productions of so-called black movies."[1] Though intended as a critique, in the aftermath of Griffin's diatribe, critics appropriated the term "blaxploitation" and began using it as a classification for the African American–themed pictures that dominated the box office until Hollywood stopped producing them in the ensuing years.

Since the demise of blaxploitation, the term has sustained, with fans, critics, and scholars continuing to use it with little regard for its meanings. From my perspective, going beyond blaxploitation warrants a deeper evaluation of the moniker, which for many people brings to mind pimps, dope pushers, and outrageous clothing. Much as iconic blaxploitation films constitute a great deal more than such superficial elements, the term is also complex because it begs the question, Who, if anyone, or what did the films exploit? With that in mind, this chapter uses *Detroit 9000* as a case study to address that query. The film is consistently classified as blaxploitation as a result of its inclusion of several of the conventions that characterize the movement—a black protagonist, a predominantly black urban setting, a display of black sexuality, violence, and a funky rhythm-and-blues soundtrack. On the surface, then, *9000* looks, sounds, and feels like a blaxploitation film; however, in this chapter, I deeply examine the film's conception, narrative, protagonists, and the marketing campaign to demonstrate how a white film came to be recognized as a film for black audiences, and as such I detail exactly who and what *9000* exploits.

## *DETROIT 9000*

*Detroit 9000* was initially conceived as a collaboration between iconic record label Motown and the General Film Corporation under the title *Motown 9000*.[2] Guided by founder Berry Gordy, Jr., by the time of the partnership, Motown had become a successful and reputable label, producing artists such as Smokey Robinson and the Miracles, The Supremes, and Marvin Gaye, among countless others. Though the company had achieved great respectability as a result of its artists' crossover hits, the same cannot be said for the General Film Corporation, whose origin and history remains largely obscure. However, in "Dimension Pictures: Portrait of a 1970s Independent," Ed Lowry discusses a collaboration between Dimension and the General Film Corporation, which he characterizes as "a small film company owned by Don Gottlieb and Arthur Marks, a former television producer-director who had turned to the production of R-rated exploitation films."[3]

Indeed, Marks confirms that the General Film Corporation specialized in lurid pictures, explaining he modeled the company after American International Pictures (AIP), which by releasing low-budget, titillating films such as *Girls in Prison* (1956), *Reform School Girl* (1957), and *Naked Paradise* (1957) had become *the* quintessential exploitation-picture producer. I discuss AIP later in this chapter to further highlight its influence on the General Film Corporation. At this point, however, it is simply important to note that given that Marks patterned his company after AIP, it is unsurprising that the General Film Corporation's releases included violent and erotic films with similarly suggestive titles, notably *Sugar Cookies* (1973), *Wonder Women* (1974), *The Centerfold Girls* (1974), and *Linda Lovelace for President* (1975).

While Motown Records and the General Film Corporation were strange bedfellows, they initially shared the common goal of bringing what came to be regarded as the first black-themed motion picture shot in, and focusing on, Detroit to the silver screen. However, that changed when Motown abruptly withdrew from the picture, citing its desire to keep its name synonymous with music. Undeterred by Motown's withdrawal, Marks and General Film Corporation executives continued production on the film with plans to release it under the original title.

After learning that *9000* was moving forward as initially planned, Gordy filed a multimillion-dollar copyright lawsuit against the General Film Corporation over its use of the word "Motown," alleging that the company had "infringed upon Motown's trademark, service mark, and trade name by producing and distributing a film titled *Motown 9000*."[4] General Film Corporation executives disagreed with Gordy and fought the lawsuit, explaining that the term "Motown" featured prominently in Detroit's collective vernacular long before the record label had adopted it for its moniker. "There are Motown cleaners, Motown gas stations and Motown drug stores. The word has been used commonly in Detroit since the 1930s and 1940s."[5] Perhaps seeking to avoid years of litigation, the two sides eventually settled the suit out of court, with the General Film Corporation agreeing to change the title of the film to *Detroit 9000* while Motown agreed to release the soundtrack.[6] Specifically, Brian Holland, Lamont Dozier, and Eddie Holland, the trio responsible for writing and producing many of the label's most popular tracks, would create the film's music. This was a favorable agreement for the record label, because it would only be responsible for the music rather than the filmic images that it would complement. Hence, if *9000* proved to be the titillating and exploitive fare that the General Film Corporation had a history of releasing, Motown could at least work to distance itself from the content.

## THE NARRATIVE

*Detroit 9000* was directed by Marks and written by Orville Hampton, who, prior to drafting the screenplay, had already enjoyed a lengthy career working in the television and film industries. His previous writing credits included episodes of *Sky King* (1956), *Perry Mason* (1957–66), *Bronco* (1958–62), *Flipper* (1964–67), and *Mission: Impossible* (1966–73). Additionally, Hampton had also penned films such as *Three Outlaws* (1956), *Hong Kong Confidential* (1958), *A Dog's Best Friend* (1959), *Operation Bottleneck* (1961), *Beauty and the Beast* (1962), and *One Potato, Two Potato* (1964). Importantly, *Potato*, with its focus on interracial marriage, was released in the 1960s among a small number of critically acclaimed black art-house films that provided intimate glimpses into African American experiences. Thus, Hampton's extensive industry experience, in conjunction with his previous foray into a film centering on black-white relationships, made him a viable choice to write *9000*.

*9000* stars Alex Rocco as Lieutenant Danny Bassett, Hari Rhodes as Detective Jesse Williams, and Vonetta McGee as Ruby Harris. The film opens at the Hail Our Heroes Ball, a posh event held in the African American community to celebrate the efforts of its most prominent leaders and activists. Always the consummate politician, black congressman Aubrey Hale Clayton (Rudy Challenger) attends the affair to announce his candidacy for governor and, more importantly, to begin raising funds for his campaign. After he has amassed $400,000 in contributions in the form of money and jewelry, armed masked robbers enter, stealing the donations as well as other valuables from the people in attendance. Because of the high-profile nature of the crime, the Detroit Police Department assigns its best cop to the case, white officer Danny Bassett. Meanwhile, black homicide cop Jesse Williams investigates a dismembered body pulled out of the Detroit River. After the two men develop a hunch that their cases are linked, Williams proposes that he and Bassett join forces to solve the mysterious crimes. Bassett initially rejects Williams's offer, until his precinct captain orders him to team up with Williams. The remainder of *9000* chronicles Bassett and Williams as they brave the rough Detroit streets to find the robbers and answer the burning question that is on everyone's mind: Are the criminals who dared rob the Hail Our Heroes Ball black or white?

With the film's focus on criminality and black-white relationships between Detroit citizens and the police, *9000* emerges as an examination of the very real and complicated racial politics that in the 1970s characterized the city. To fully understand the film, it is critical to discuss what is commonly referred to as the Detroit riot or rebellion, which on July 23, 1967, began when police raided a "blind pig," or an after-hours drinking establishment, on Twelfth and Clairmount Avenue, which was located in the middle of the city's poorest and most highly concentrated African American neighborhood.[7] As Harvard Sitkoff explains in *The Struggle for Black Equality*, "Recurring instances of police brutality had caused massive black resentment toward law enforcement officers and a constant, unrelenting low level of warfare between black citizens and white cops."[8] For many African Americans, the mass arrests of blacks frequenting the bar on July 23rd was the proverbial straw that broke the camel's back. For the ensuing six days and nights, enraged blacks filled the streets committing acts of vandalism, arson, and property damage. The aftermath was devastating, as the riot proved to be the bloodiest urban disorder and the costliest in property damage in U.S. history. According to Sidney Fine, "When it finally ended, forty-three people had been killed—thirty-three blacks and ten whites—over one thousand injured, and 3,800 arrested."[9] Further, Joe Darden and Richard Thomas explain, "Close to 5,000 people were left homeless, most of them black. More than 1,000 buildings had been burned to the ground. When the total damage was tallied, it soared to $50 million."[10]

Although July 23 will forever be remembered as the day that the Detroit uprising began, the impetus had been building for years. This is clearly outlined in the report filed by the National Advisory Committee on Civil Disorders, which came to be known as the Kerner Commission as a result of its chair, Illinois Governor Otter Kerner. On July 28, while the Detroit rebellion was ongoing and just a little over a week removed from the Newark riots, President Lyndon Johnson formed the eleven-man Kerner Commission, tasking it to answer three questions regarding the uprisings: (1) What happened? (2) Why did it happen? and (3) What can be done to prevent it from happening again?[11] After working for seven months to answer these questions, in February 1968, the Kerner Commission released its findings in a report that was a scathing indictment of U.S. racial practices. In particular, the commission cited white America's historical political, social, and economic oppression of African Americans as the true catalyst for the rebellion. Thus, as Darden and Thomas summarize, "white institutional racism in the form of urban renewal, expressways, and white suburban resistance were the major causes of the civil disorder, or rebellion, of 1967."[12]

The Kerner Commission was clear in its findings, yet as is common with such important work, its report did not transform Detroit into a racial utopia, as whites and blacks remained divided on the cause of the rebellion and, thus, on their views about American racism. For example, Fine notes in his study of the uprising, *Violence in the Model City*, "Whites and blacks just after the riot viewed what had happened and its consequences in very different ways. As two University of Michigan political scientists put it, 'for the most part it was as if two different events have taken place in the same city, one a calculated act of criminal anarchy, the other a spontaneous protest against mistreatment and injustice.'"[13] This black-white dichotomy was clear in surveys conducted just four months after the riot, which revealed that "31 percent of blacks believed the riot would 'help' black-white relations compared to only 4 percent of whites."[14] An additional survey taken eight months after the uprising revealed that "almost 70 percent of the white respondents now thought that blacks were pushing 'too fast' for what they wanted, and just over 67 percent believed that blacks in the central city had only themselves to blame for the fact that they had 'worse jobs, education, and housing than white people.'"[15] Thus, many whites held a "blame the victim" view, which Darden and Thomas cite as "a classic example of how white collective memory distorted history, and was often deliberately blank, or at least benignly ignorant, of the city's racist history prior to the 1967 riots, when blacks in Detroit routinely experienced discrimination in jobs, housing, public accommodation, and education."[16]

This brief discussion of the Detroit rebellion is in no way the definitive account of the years leading up to the uprising, the event itself, or the aftermath. That history is documented much more comprehensively in books such as Darden and Thomas's *Detroit: Race Riots, Racial Conflicts, and Efforts to Bridge the Racial Divide*, Susan Welch's *Race and Place: Race Relations in an American City*, Fine's *Violence in the Model City*, and Max Arthur Herman's *Summer of Rage: An Oral History of the 1967 Newark and Detroit Riots*. Instead, I recount the events surrounding the Detroit rebellion to contextualize *9000*'s predominant themes, which are critical for developing a richer understanding of the film. Because the film follows the relatively standard cops-and-robbers narrative, without at least a cursory understanding of the Detroit rebellion, *9000* might potentially be dismissed as just another police drama.

Further, I also focus on the rebellion to demonstrate that, like prior blaxploitation films such as *Sweet Sweetback's Baadasssss Song* and *Blacula* (1972), *9000* also features a plot that addresses the African American experience, a seminal characteristic of the movement. For example, *Sweetback* tells the story of a black renegade who goes on the run after killing two corrupt white police officers who brutalize a young African American, while in myriad ways, *Blacula* critiques the institution of slavery. Such stories made blaxploitation films wildly popular, as they functioned as allegories in which blacks overcame the racist white establishment. *9000* follows suit by centering the story on Detroit's history and racial politics; however, given that the film focuses primarily on a white protagonist, it differs greatly from other blaxploitation films.

In addressing Detroit's fragile racial politics six years removed from the rebellion, *9000* bears a striking resemblance to Hollywood's post–World War

II social problem films. Discussing these pictures in general, Charles Maland outlines several factors that are integral in defining the cycle.

> First, a social problem refers to an undesirable social condition affecting a significant number of people. Second, it must be perceived by a considerable segment of society to be a problem. Third, the definition of what constitutes a social problem presupposes power: an individual or a group must have enough power in society to get the matter into public debate, or the condition may never be considered a social problem. Finally, implicit in the very notion of the term "social problem" is the belief that something can be done about it—that the problem has a solution.[17]

Taking these factors into account, Maland contends,
> [The social problem film] is a feature film whose central narrative concern or conflict relates to or includes the presentation of a social problem. The social problem film also has a contemporary setting, though it may include scenes from the past that lead up to that contemporary setting and help to explain the roots of the problem. Finally, the social problem film is generally animated by a humane concern for the victim(s) or of crusader(s) against the social problem and, often, by an implicit assumption that the problem can be treated or even eliminated through well-intentioned liberal social reform.[18]

With that description in mind, Hollywood's post–World War II social problem films were conceived partly as a result of America's participation in the conflict. After fighting anti-Semitism during World War II, many soldiers returned home feeling that if racial inequality was unjust overseas, then the United States' treatment of African Americans was equally egregious. Recognizing this shift in the ideology surrounding America's skewed racial policies and, more importantly, declining ticket sales as a result of the proliferation of television, Hollywood turned to the production of social problem films in order to profit off U.S. citizens' newfound consciousness. In *From Sambo to Superspade*, Daniel Leab explains that Hollywood noticed that "movies with so-called 'adult' themes such as anti-Semitism, juvenile delinquency, and mental health did well at the box office, and the race problem seemed a topic ideal for raising profitable controversy."[19]

## A WHITE FILM FOR A BLAXPLOITATION AUDIENCE?

Working from that perspective, Hollywood studios produced several social problem films centering on black-white relationships, including United Artists' *Home of the Brave* (1949) and 20th Century Fox's *Pinky* (1949). The former tells the story of a black soldier, Peter Moss (James Edwards), who as a result of the racial discrimination that he experienced during combat suffers from amnesia and hysterical paralysis. Fortunately, a good-hearted white psychiatrist commits himself to curing Moss, a goal that he eventually accomplishes by engaging in a form of verbal shock treatment in which he calls Moss a "dirty nigger." *Pinky*, on the other hand, centers on the title character (played by white actress Jeanne Crain), a tragic mulatto who, after passing for white while attending nursing school in the North, returns home to the South, where she endures discrimination at the hands of racist whites. Pinky is faced with the decision of whether to return to the North, where she can live a good life passing with her white fiancé, or persevering as a black woman in the racist South. With the help of Miss Em (Ethel Barrymore), an old white woman whom she nurses until her death, Pinky accepts her ethnicity and opens a nursing school for African American women on the plantation that Miss Em leaves her in her will.

Though *Brave* and *Pinky* may seem contrived, in 1949 the studios' theory that race-themed pictures would lead to big returns at the box office proved valid. The films grossed $2 million and $4 million in domestic film rentals, respectively.[20] Nevertheless, it is important to keep in mind that *Brave* and *Pinky* were geared toward white audiences, as African Americans were not truly recognized as a viable demographic until the emergence of blaxploitation cinema.[21]

Much like *Brave* and *Pinky*, black-white racial politics in the aftermath of a terrible event is the social problem that *9000* works to overcome. Though the Detroit rebellion is not analogous to World War II, it was a major battle in the struggle for racial justice that further exposed the problems that existed in Detroit. *9000* seeks to mend the wounds through its superficial narrative, which depicts racism as a difficulty that can easily be conquered if blacks and whites could only learn to work together. As a result, both African American and white characters alike emphasize this integrationist message throughout the film, in essence presenting the solution that Maland explains is key to the social problem film. Given the complexity of Detroit's black-white relationships, *9000*'s overarching message is problematic. However, it perfectly aligns with the contrivances presented in *Home* and *Pinky*, while also demonstrating one of the main shortcomings of a white film that is trying to pass as black.

## THE PROTAGONISTS

In addition to featuring a narrative that is simply a re-presentation of those featured in post–World War II social problem films, *9000* also borrows heavily from another cycle that enjoyed success in the late 1960s and early 1970s—the white buddy film, which seemingly paved the way for a return to the examination of the relationship between black and white men in movies as well. To be clear, the interracial buddy movie had been a staple of Hollywood for years, as evidenced by films focusing on black-white racial politics such as *The Defiant Ones* (1957) and *In the Heat of the Night* (1967). However, as Ed Guerrero explains in *Framing Blackness*, the "1970s cycle of white male buddy movies was launched in 1969 with the release of *Easy Rider*, *Butch Cassidy and the Sundance Kid*, and *Midnight Cowboy*."[22] These films were different from their race-themed predecessors in that they valorized white masculinity through a number of tropes, including "the marginalization or absence of women . . . , an absence of home and the narrative articulation of a journey."[23] As a result of these recurring themes, many critics and scholars attributed the rise of the white buddy film to the emergence and subsequent success of the women's movement.[24]

Given the tremendous success of *Rider*, *Kid*, and *Cowboy*, among other white buddy films, it is unsurprising that the General Film Corporation sought to capitalize on the cycle. The company shifted the focus from a pair of white comrades to a set of interracial protagonists, ultimately producing an updated and violent retread of Norman Jewison's critically acclaimed social problem film *In the Heat of the Night*. *Night*, a study of southern racial politics, tells the story of African American Philadelphia homicide detective Virgil Tibbs (Sidney Poitier), who, while traveling through Sparta, Mississippi, after visiting his mother in the South, is arrested for the murder of a prominent white developer. After discovering that Tibbs is a homicide detective, the tough-talking, outspoken Chief Gillespie (Rod Steiger) hesitantly asks Tibbs to view the victim's body. During the examination, Gillespie realizes that Tibbs possesses expertise that will greatly improve the Sparta Police Department's attempts to solve the crime. Though Tibbs initially wants to leave Sparta, he agrees to stay on and work the case after Gillespie swallows his pride and admits that he needs Tibbs's assistance. The remainder of the film depicts the two men overcoming their preconceived notions about race as they work to achieve a common goal—catching the killer.

With the film's strong cast and its timely integrationist theme, *Night* won Academy Awards for Best Picture, Best Actor (Rod Steiger), Best Screenplay, Best Sound, and Best Editing. Further, the film performed well at the box office, grossing $10,910,000 in domestic film rentals.[25] Melvin Donalson explains in *Masculinity in the Interracial Buddy Film* that *Night*'s success clearly indicated that it "resonated with viewers and their integrationist mood, confirmed by the passing of the Civil Rights Act and the Voting Rights Act in 1964 and 1965, respectively."[26] This is not to suggest that *Night* is without its problems. For example, Poitier emerges as the token black character representative of the type of good Negro easily accepted by whites. Further, scholars Hernán Vera and Andrew M. Gordon contend, "*In the Heat of the Night* proposes another false dichotomy typical of Hollywood film: white racism is a disease confined to the South, and all Northerners are liberal. . . . Such portrayals allow white Northerners to congratulate themselves on their open mindedness in comparison to these benighted Southern rednecks."[27] Still, *Night* has its merits and warrants its sustained celebration in cinematic history.

With *9000*'s focus on race and the partnership between a white police officer and a black detective, the film more closely resembles *Night* rather than the blaxploitation films that it imitates. Like Tibbs and Gillespie, Bassett and Williams form a reluctant partnership in which each represents his respective race. This interracial partnership changes one of blaxploitation's most essential characteristics—the black hero or heroine who was significant for three distinct reasons: (1) they cut against the stereotypical images that had traditionally circumscribed the black cinematic image; (2) they were capable of navigating the oppressive system while maintaining their blackness; (3) they were connected to and thus fought on behalf of the black community.[28] These characteristics are evident in films such as *Sweetback*, *Coffy* (1973), and *Cleopatra Jones* (1973), in which the title heroes and heroines are proud African Americans who struggle to overcome problems such as police brutality and the drug trade that are plaguing African American municipalities. Since *9000* was not conceived as a black-themed film, it disrupts this essential convention, instead focusing more heavily on Bassett. As Marks explained, "We thought of it as a white film. . . . What happens in a Black city to a White police department, a white cop?"[29] Hence, in recounting the investigation of a case that occurred in a black community suffering from systemic racism in both the film's diegesis and the real world, *9000* privileges white masculinity, suggesting that Bassett's experiences dealing with African Americans are the most compelling.

Discussing 1980s biracial buddy films like *Lethal Weapon* (1987), Guerrero asserts, "in too many instances the buddy formula has pushed blacks into the background or reduced them to subordinate, updated 'loyal sidekick' roles that subtly reinscribe the cinematic racial hierarchies of old."[30] Here, I would like to use Guerrero's description retroactively to include *9000*, as it also functions

Lt. Danny Bassett (*left*) listens as his superior (*right*) informs him that he is being assigned to the Hail Our Heroes Ball case. (*Detroit 9000* DVD, Buena Vista Home Entertainment)

much like the 1980s interracial buddy films on which he focuses his analyses. Similar to the films that Guerrero describes, *9000*'s most pressing questions and complex issues surround Bassett. When audiences are initially introduced to the character, he is being informed by his captain that he has been assigned to the Hail to Our Heroes Ball case. Upon hearing this news, Bassett becomes defensive, claiming that the case is a lose-lose-lose whether he solves it or not. He explains that if he discovers that blacks pulled off the robbery, then African Americans will be upset, while if he finds that whites committed the crime, Detroit's Caucasian citizens will claim that the police department is placating the black community. Bassett concludes that in the event that he is unable to solve the case, then he will get into trouble with his superiors. This dialogue is significant because it immediately establishes Bassett as the victim instead of those who were robbed at the ball or Detroit's black citizens, who had historically endured racism at the hands of white police officers.

The Bassett character is further developed in an ensuing scene between him and his wife, who, as a result of an undisclosed illness, is in a state hospital. Unhappy with the facilities, in part because of all of its black attendants, she complains about her living conditions. Bassett responds, explaining that he does not have the funds to move her to a different location. At this point, audiences learn that he is an honest cop when his wife reprimands him for never taking bribes from the criminals who have offered him money in return for being allowed to run their illegal operations. This exchange is extremely significant in further establishing his character. First, audiences learn that while Bassett's wife is racist, he is not, a point that demonstrates that he is trustworthy and that he will work hard to solve the Hail Our Heroes Ball case. That Bassett does not take bribes further establishes that fact, and thus, he emerges as a good white cop who has been forced to work in a corrupt black space.

In addition to positioning Bassett as the victimized good cop, *9000* goes to great lengths, using subtle and overt cues in the diegesis, to establish him as an integrationist who has an affinity for black people. For example, one scene depicts Bassett slapping five with an African American officer, a soulful move that showcases his familiarity with the customs generally associated with black culture. In a more overt yet bizarre sequence, Bassett visits a brothel run by a madam friend of his who operates as an informant of sorts. After watching as her employees saunter around the mansion, Bassett expresses his satisfaction over the fact that her assortment of scantily clad workers is integrated. Later in the same sequence, he saves an African American call girl from being raped at the hands of a white man. In each of these instances, Bassett potentially endears himself to the black audiences that had grown accustomed to cheering on heroes and heroines who looked like them.

Perhaps the most glaring scene that positions Bassett as trustworthy occurs when he appears on a re-creation of *Buzz the Fuzz*, an actual thirty-minute radio program that in January 1971 began airing on Detroit's WJLB 1400. Billed as "your chance to call The Man," *Fuzz* was conceived as a result of the Detroit rebellion, with the distinct goal of creating dialogue between the public and the Detroit Police Department. Martha Jean "The Queen" Steinberg, a popular radio personality who had remained on air for forty-eight hours straight encouraging citizens to remain calm during the uprisings, hosted *Fuzz* alongside then–Detroit police commissioner Jerry Nichols.[31] Both Steinberg and Nichols make cameo appearances in *9000* on a fictional installment of *Buzz the Fuzz*, fielding calls from residents upset about the Hail Our Heroes Ball robbery. During the program, a black caller bluntly questions the panelists regarding the case, and he and Bassett engage in the following exchange.

> **Caller**: Was it whites ripping off blacks, or was it brothers ripping off brothers?
>
> **Bassett**: I don't really give a damn.
>
> **Caller**: You mean you're a honky racist like the rest of the pigs. You don't care what happens to black people as long as they keep their place, huh?

Martha Jean "The Queen" Steinberg and former Detroit police commissioner Jerry Nichols on *9000*'s staged episode of *Buzz the Fuzz*. (*Detroit 9000* DVD, Buena Vista Home Entertainment)

**Bassett**: No, what I mean is I don't care whether the bastards are black, brown, blue, or green. When an asshole commits a felony, I'm going to do my goddamndest to bust him! That's what I mean.

This exchange further positions Bassett as color-blind, hard-nosed, and ultimately down for justice. Moreover, it functions as a foreshadowing of Williams's final summation of the Hail Our Heroes Ball robbers, a point that I return to shortly.

Since *9000* primarily focuses on Bassett, his African American counterpart, Jesse Williams, is far less developed. While Bassett emerges as a complex three-dimensional character, audiences learn very little about Williams other than the fact that he is a former professional football star turned hard-nosed cop. Keeping intact blaxploitation characteristics from films like *Shaft* and *Super Fly*, which establish their protagonists as ladies' men, Williams is constructed similarly, providing audiences with the display of black sexuality that defined the African American–themed pictures. In particular, he appears in a scene with his steady girlfriend, who despite engaging in a serious dialogue is unable to keep her hands off him. What makes the scene odd is that in the early stages of his girlfriend's seduction, Williams engages her in a conversation about Bassett, further illustrating that the white detective is *9000*'s main focus. Hence, even when Bassett is not onscreen, the narrative centers on him, as Williams is preoccupied with his motives. Eventually, Williams succumbs to his girlfriend's advances,

Det. Jessie Williams and his girlfriend share an intimate moment. (*Detroit 9000* DVD, Buena Vista Home Entertainment)

providing audiences with a glimpse of the display of black sexuality that had become a staple of blaxploitation cinema.

Perhaps Williams's most important role in *9000* is to validate Bassett's notions about police work and criminality as they pertain to their case. As previously mentioned, Bassett is committed to bringing the Hail Our Heroes Ball robbers to justice, regardless of their ethnicities. After learning that the gang responsible for the crime is composed of whites, blacks, and a Native American and overcoming them in a bloody shootout, Williams delivers a brief but important integrationist diatribe: "Do you know everybody's screwed up? This whole city? Everybody but Danny. He's the only one that saw it the way it was, man. Just another rip-off. It's like he said, assholes are only—assholes." That Williams quotes Bassett to describe the villains validates the views that the liberal white detective had espoused to the caller on the *Buzz the Fuzz* radio program. Inherent in Williams's dialogue is the assumption that criminality is an equal-opportunity endeavor, and thus, his delivery of the line renders the social, economic, and political discrimination that blacks had historically endured in Detroit moot.

*9000* does not conclude after Williams and other officers gun down the Hail Our Heroes Ball robbers, because they have yet to recover the stolen loot. At this point, the focus shifts back to Bassett, again making apparent that he is the true subject of the film. Having found the money and jewels unbeknownst to Williams and the other police officers, he arranges a meeting with Oscar

(George Skaff), the buyer to whom the robbers intended on selling the jewelry. During Bassett's interactions with Oscar, it is unclear whether he is planning to arrest him after the sale or if he intends to take the money, which will allow him to acquire better care for his ailing wife. Meanwhile, upon realizing that Bassett has found the stolen goods, Williams recalls a conversation that they had, during which Bassett explained that if he were ever to go on the lam, he would do so on a cruise ship, because the police generally do not think to search them for fleeing criminals. Williams goes to the docks in search of Bassett, whose meeting goes awry when Oscar exposes his cover, informing him that the seller that he arranged to purchase the goods from was supposed to be a black man. Bassett attempts to escape, but Oscar's henchman shoots him. Williams then happens upon the meeting, killing the gunman and apprehending Oscar. Though paramedics arrive and attend to Bassett, he succumbs to his wounds, leaving Williams and the black audiences that expected to see another blaxploitation hero overcoming the system pondering the white protagonist's true intentions. Appropriately, then, in a final scene with Williams and his girlfriend in which they once again discuss Bassett, the black detective concludes, "You know what's gonna bother me the rest of my life? Just trying to figure it. If he was the worst cop I ever knew or the best?"

## THE AIP EFFECT: MARKETING *DETROIT 9000*

In making and marketing *9000*, Marks implemented AIP's formula, which involved campaigns that guaranteed audiences nudity, violence, or horror beyond belief, depending on the genre of the film that the company was advertising. In bringing its titillating fare to the public, AIP followed a fairly simple formula:

> observe trends in emerging taste.
>
> know as much as possible about your audience.
>
> anticipate how you will sell your chosen subject.
>
> produce with prudence, avoiding expense for what won't show on-screen.
>
> sell with showmanship and publicity.
>
> have good luck.[32]

Following these tenets, AIP enjoyed success releasing films on a low budget of approximately $500,000 each. As a result of the minuscule budgets and the relatively inexperienced casts and crews it employed in making its films, the company consistently turned a profit on its motion pictures regardless of whether they delivered on the promises made in the ad campaigns. This is evidenced by AIP's enduring presence on the cinematic exhibition landscape as it released films for decades, including the successful blaxploitation films *Slaughter* (1972), *Blacula*, *Coffy*, *Black Caesar* (1973), and *Foxy Brown* (1974), among others.

Similar to AIP, Marks implemented a "give the audience what it wants" approach to sell *9000*. This is readily apparent in the ads that he and his General Film Corporation colleagues devised for the film. Marks explains that while shooting the film in Detroit, there was a "whirlwind of excitement, predominantly from Black people."[33] Despite garnering interest from African Americans, Marks and the General Film Corporation executives wanted *9000* to play across the United States rather than being confined to theaters in predominantly black locales. "When we released *Detroit 9000* originally we weren't going to sell it as a Black film. We thought of it as a white film and the first campaign we made was a white campaign."[34] With that in mind, the initial poster for *9000* prominently features Bassett in the foreground with Williams behind him, emerging from the flashing light that sits atop a police car that reads "Detroit 9000" on the base. Here, the characters' positioning makes it readily apparent that Bassett is the star of the film. Further, the film's supporting cast members, who are presented on a smaller scale than Bassett and Williams, are visible in the light, which I can only speculate is meant to represent the city of Detroit and all of the corruption housed within it. *9000*'s tagline emphasizes the danger associated with Detroit as well as Bassett's precarious situation, as it boasts, "It's the Murder Capital of the World. The Black Rip-Off of the Decade and a White Cop Squeezed in the Middle." It is important to note that Bassett's positioning in the poster also implies that he will rise above the corruption and solve the case.

Although *9000*'s original marketing campaign was geared toward white audiences, the film's demographic changed after the film was released. According to Marks, "When *Detroit 9000* opened in the Madison Theater in Detroit, it was such a hit, it was taking $50,000 a week out of that house. We got a call from a chain that wanted the picture, but they wanted it as a Black picture. We knew that if we sold it to the Chicago Theater, which is the biggest house outside of New York, at 3,000 seats, that we had a Black picture on our hands because the momentum would carry it into a Black audience."[35] While momentum alone may have carried *9000* to a black audience, Marks and the General Film Corporation steered the picture in that direction by remarketing it as an African American–themed movie. The company redesigned the poster, emphasizing Williams over Bassett by simply switching the detectives' original positions. Hence, for the

*Detroit 9000* posters for the black-themed advertising campaign (*left*) and the marketing campaign geared toward white audiences (right). (Gerald Martinez, Diana Martinez, and Andres Chavez, *What It Is . . . What It Was! The Black Film Explosion of the 1970s in Words and Pictures* [New York: Hyperion, 1998].)

campaign geared toward blacks, Williams appears in the foreground with Bassett behind him, while the other, smaller images remain the same. The tagline, however, was changed to read, "It's the Murder Capital of the World. And the Biggest Black Rip-Off of the Decade. It's Gonna Get Solved . . . or the Town's Gonna Explode." This altered slogan plays on Detroit's tenuous racial politics and the rebellion that had occurred just six years earlier, as it either intentionally or inadvertently connotes that if the act of criminality against African Americans is not solved, blacks might once again erupt into violent protest.

In addition to referencing Detroit's racial divide to sell *9000* to black audiences, the redesigned poster and tagline also brought it in line with the promotional materials that by 1973 studios relied on to release blaxploitation pictures en masse. Not only is the black supporting character prominently featured to give African American filmgoers the impression that the picture centers on him, but the slogan is also imbued with the danger, attitude, and bravado that characterized other marketing campaigns for blaxploitation films. For example, the tagline for *Cleopatra Jones* proclaimed that its title character was "6 feet 2" and all of it Dynamite!" while the slogan for *Coffy* boasts, "She's the Godmother of them all.... The baddest One-Chick Hit-Squad that ever hit town!" The familiar imagery and the slogan further contribute to *9000*'s sustained categorization as a part of blaxploitation lore in the popular psyche.

Unlike the posters, I have been unable to validate the existence of two trailers—one white and the other black—for *Detroit 9000*, despite Marks's assertion that there were two separate marketing campaigns for the picture. However, from my perspective, the theatrical trailer that is readily available on various Internet sites features several characteristics of a film aimed at black audiences. Thus, my presumption is that either the trailer is the reedited version intended for African Americans or it is evidence that *9000* is such a convoluted film that it was difficult to market. The trailer begins with a voice-over in which the narrator exclaims, "Trouble? When you've got the biggest rip-off of the decade in the murder capital of the world, you've got more than trouble. You've got disaster!" This tagline omits key elements that defined the white and black marketing campaigns. In particular, it does not refer to the Hail Our Heroes Ball robbery as a black rip-off, mention Bassett as the white cop "squeezed in the middle," or allude to the danger that might ensue if the Detroit Police Department fails to investigate the caper properly. Yet, as the trailer progresses, it becomes apparent that *9000* centers on Bassett, as he receives top billing. His name appears on the screen first and is followed by Rhodes's and McGee's. Though the names all remain on the screen together for approximately five seconds, Rocco's remains on top for the duration, with the others beneath it. After setting up the film's premise by showing the robbers infiltrating the Hail Our Heroes Ball, the trailer further establishes Bassett as the central character by introducing him first in a scene in which a black man operating as a police informant is shown punching him, so that he can maintain his cover. As this action occurs, the narrator comments, "Dan Bassett is the man," a calculated choice of words given that in the 1970s African Americans routinely used the phrase "The Man" in reference to the unjust system that worked to keep them oppressed. It seems logical, then, that the events unfolding onscreen out of their appropriate context, in conjunction with the narration, potentially masked the fact that *9000* actually centered on Bassett. The remainder of the trailer serves as further evidence that Marks followed AIP's marketing strategy, as it introduces Williams and then focuses heavily on the violent content that characterizes *9000*. Moreover, the advertisement also includes scenes in which the film's supporting black characters complain about racial injustice, while the narrator uses 1970s slang commonly associated with African Americans to introduce various characters and onscreen actions.

Finally, the action presented in the trailer unfolds to songs that function as the perfect aural accompaniment to the pictorial images. The majority of the trailer features Luchi De Jesus's instrumental theme, which articulates the sound of the 1970s that Isaac Hayes popularized with his *Shaft* soundtrack. The advertisement also cleverly uses Holland, Dozier, and Holland's gospel-infused track "Touch Me Jesus" in the sequence depicting the Hail Our Heroes Ball robbery, a move that suggests that the criminals interrupted a sacred event. While these songs feature prominently in the *9000* trailer, it seems that Motown reneged on its deal to release the soundtrack, as I have been unable to find any substantial information detailing the company's association with the album. If that is indeed the case, the General Film Corporation primarily relied on posters and trailers to market *9000* at a time when other studios producing black-themed pictures were using the soundtracks to advertise the films as well.

*9000*'s marketing campaign proved effective, as the film performed well at the box office, largely due to black filmgoers—the very audience that the General Film Corporation had originally attempted to avoid gearing the picture toward exclusively. After selling the film to the Chicago Theater and expanding to other houses in African American communities in pursuit of the almighty dollar, Marks recounts the surge in *9000*'s performance: "It was taking $90,000 out of Chicago, and then jumped, not only in Chicago, but went to the State Lake and played both of them. The handwriting was on the wall. It just couldn't be avoided. Except for maybe a handful, *Detroit 9000* never played a white theater in the United States."[36] Thus, *9000*, like *Sweetback*, *Shaft*, *Super Fly*, *Blacula*, and other blaxploitation films released prior to it, performed well with African American audiences, grossing $1.2 million in domestic film rentals.[37] This box-office success illustrated that at the height of the blaxploitation movement, even a film with a semblance of "blackness" could perform beautifully at the box office.

## CONCLUSION

In *Teenagers and Teenpics*, Thomas Doherty writes that when used to describe motion pictures, "exploitation" has three different meanings that at times overlap. In its first sense, it refers to the advertising and promotion used to lure the audience into the theater.[38] The second definition refers to the manner in which a film endears itself to audiences, while in its third categorical sense, the term defines a particular kind of film.[39] Further, in 1946, *Variety* columnist Whitney

Williams spoke of exploitation pictures as "films with some timely or currently controversial subject which can be exploited, and capitalized on, in publicity and advertising."[40] Taking these definitions into account, *Detroit 9000* is pure exploitation, as its narrative played on Detroit's complicated racial politics to lure audiences to theaters. Moreover, although the film focuses primarily on a white protagonist, after gaining interest from theater owners in predominantly black communities, Marks and General Film Corporation executives developed a second ad campaign that played on the timeliness of the blaxploitation movement to endear *9000* to African American audiences.

I now return to my original, more specific questions regarding the term "blaxploitation": Who or what did the African American–themed films exploit? As this chapter illustrates, *9000* exploits the black audience, as well as the blaxploitation movement as a whole. Marks and the General Film Corporation were so effective in the implementation of the black film cycle's most prominent conventions that *9000* is commonly regarded as a blaxploitation film. As if that is not problematic enough, if one looks carefully at *9000*'s credits, she or he will find Junius Griffin listed as an executive producer. Thus, the person who inadvertently coined the term "blaxploitation" in protest of the African American film boom played a role in selling a white film to the very blaxploitation audiences that he discouraged from attending the motion pictures. Perhaps as a result of the film's integrationist themes, Griffin, who had once worked as a speech writer for Dr. Martin Luther King, Jr., and later served as a publicist for Motown, deemed *9000* superior to pictures like *Shaft* and *Super Fly*. Yet it is also possible that his motives for helping bring the picture to silver screens were purely financial. Given his very public denunciation of blaxploitation films, if the latter is indeed the case, then it adds even more truth to the assertion that at the end of the day, "assholes are only assholes."

## NOTES

1. "NAACP Blasts Super-Nigger Trend," *Variety*, August 16, 1972, 2.
2. The film's title plays on the police code that means "officer down."
3. Ed Lowry, "Dimension Pictures: Portrait of a 1970s Independent," in *Contemporary American Independent Film: From the Margins to the Mainstream*, ed. Chris Holmlund and Justin Wyatt (New York: Routledge, 2005), 46.
4. "Motown Picture Gets New Title in Settlement," *Jet*, August 2, 1973, 58.
5. "Gordy Suing over Use of 'Motown' in Film," *Jet*, July 5, 1973, 54.
6. Gerald Martinez, Diana Martinez, and Andres Chavez, *What It Is . . . What It Was! The Black Film Explosion of the '70s in Words and Pictures* (New York: Hyperion, 1998), 96.

7. Joe T. Darden and Richard W. Thomas, *Detroit: Race Riots, Racial Conflicts, and Efforts to Bridge the Racial Divide* (East Lansing: Michigan State University Press, 2013), 3.
8. Harvard Sitkoff, *The Struggle for Black Equality: 1954–1992*, rev. ed. (New York: Hill and Wang, 1993), 188–89.
9. Sidney Fine, *Violence in the Model City: The Cavanaugh Administration, Race Relations, and the Detroit Riot of 1967* (East Lansing: Michigan State University Press, 2007), 299.
10. Darden and Thomas, *Detroit*, 1.
11. Steven M. Gillon, "'Separate and Unequal': Revisiting the Kerner Commission," *Huffington Post*, May 13, 2015. www.huffingtonpost.com/steven-m-gillon/separate-and-unequal-revi_b_7268382.html.
12. Darden and Thomas, *Detroit*, 3.
13. Fine, *Violence in the Model City*, 369.
14. Ibid.
15. Ibid.
16. Darden and Thomas, *Detroit*, 3.
17. Charles Maland, "The Social Problem Film," in *Handbook of American Film Genres*, ed. Wes D. Gehring (Westport, CT: Greenwood, 1988), 306.
18. Ibid., 307.
19. Daniel Leab, *From Sambo to Superspade: The Black Experience in Motion Pictures* (Boston: Houghton Mifflin, 1975), 146.
20. Ibid., 156.
21. This is not to suggest that blacks did not attend screenings of *Brave* and *Pinky*. Rather, I am calling attention to the fact that aside from a small number of failed attempts to target the African American audience with all-black films such as *Hallelujah* (1929), *Green Pastures* (1936), *Cabin in the Sky* (1943), and *Thousands Cheer* (1943), Hollywood largely ignored black filmgoers until the 1970s, when their buying power resonated loudly at theaters screening blaxploitation cinema.
22. Ed Guerrero, *Framing Blackness: The African American Image in Film* (Philadelphia: Temple University Press, 1993), 127.
23. Ibid.
24. Ibid.
25. James Robert Parish and George H. Hill, *Black Action Films: Plots, Critiques, Casts, and Credits for 235 Theatrical and Made-for-Television Releases* (Jefferson, NC: McFarland, 1989), 178.
26. Melvin Donalson, *Masculinity in the Interracial Buddy Film* (Jefferson, NC: McFarland, 2006), 36.
27. Hernán Vera and Andrew M. Gordon, *Screen Saviors: Hollywood Fictions of Whiteness* (Lanham, MD: Rowman and Littlefield, 2003), 160.
28. Novotny Lawrence, *Blaxploitation Films of the 1970s: Blackness and Genre* (New York: Routledge, 2007), 18–19.
29. Quoted in Martinez, Martinez, and Chavez, *What It Is . . . What It Was!*, 99.
30. Guerrero, *Framing Blackness*, 128.

31. George Bulanda, "Martha Jean 'The Queen' Steinberg, 1969: The Way It Was," *Hour Detroit*, January 31, 2012, www.hourdetroit.com/Hour-Detroit/February-2012/The-Way-It-Was/.
32. "AIP Formula—Not Foolproof, but It Pays Off," *Variety*, October 27 1970, 54.
33. Quoted in Martinez, Martinez, and Chavez, *What It Is . . . What It Was!*, 99.
34. Ibid.
35. Ibid.
36. Ibid.
37. Parish and Hill, *Black Action Films*, 125.
38. Thomas Doherty, *Teenagers and Teenpics: The Juvenilization of American Movies in the 1950s* (Philadelphia: Temple University Press, 2002), 2.
39. Ibid., 5–6.
40. Quoted in ibid., 36.

## WORKS CITED

"AIP Formula—Not Foolproof, but It Pays Off." *Variety*, October 27, 1970.

Bulanda, George. "Martha Jean 'The Queen' Steinberg, 1969: The Way It Was." *Hour Detroit*, January 31, 2012. www.hourdetroit.com/Hour-Detroit/February-2012/The-Way-It-Was/.

Darden, Joe T., and Richard W. Thomas. *Detroit: Race Riots, Racial Conflicts, and Efforts to Bridge the Racial Divide*. East Lansing: Michigan State University Press, 2013.

Doherty, Thomas. *Teenagers and Teenpics: The Juvenilization of American Movies in the 1950s*. Philadelphia: Temple University Press, 2002.

Donalson, Melvin. *Masculinity in the Interracial Buddy Film*. Jefferson, NC: McFarland, 2006.

Fine, Sidney. *Violence in the Model City: The Cavanaugh Administration, Race Relations, and the Detroit Riot of 1967*. East Lansing: Michigan State University Press, 2007.

Gillon, Steven M. "'Separate and Unequal': Revisiting the Kerner Commission." *Huffington Post*, May 13, 2015. www.huffingtonpost.com/steven-m-gillon/separate-and-unequal-revi_b_7268382.html.

"Gordy Suing over Use of 'Motown' in Film." *Jet*, July 5, 1973.

Guerrero, Ed. *Framing Blackness: The African American Image in Film*. Philadelphia: Temple University Press, 1993.

Herman, Max Arthur. *Summer of Rage: An Oral History of the 1967 Newark and Detroit Riots*. New York: Peter Lang, 2013.

Lawrence, Novotny. *Blaxploitation Films of the 1970s: Blackness and Genre*. New York: Routledge, 2007.

Leab, Daniel. *From Sambo to Superspade: The Black Experience in Motion Pictures*. Boston: Houghton Mifflin, 1975.

Lowry, Ed. "Dimension Pictures: Portrait of a 1970s Independent." In *Contemporary American Independent Film: From the Margins to the Mainstream*, edited by Chris Holmlund and Justin Wyatt, 41–52. New York: Routledge, 2005.

Maland, Charles. "The Social Problem Film." In *Handbook of American Film Genres*, edited by Wes D. Gehring, 305–29. Westport, CT: Greenwood, 1988.

Martinez, Gerald, Diana Martinez, and Andres Chavez. *What It Is . . . What It Was! The Black Film Explosion of the '70s in Words and Pictures*. New York: Hyperion, 1998.

"Motown Picture Gets New Title in Settlement." *Jet*, August 2, 1973.

"NCAAP Blasts 'Super-Nigger' Trend." *Variety*, August 16, 1972.

Parish, James Robert, and George H. Hill. *Black Action Films: Plots, Critiques, Casts, and Credits for 235 Theatrical and Made-for-Television Releases*. Jefferson, NC: McFarland, 1989.

Sitkoff, Harvard. *The Struggle for Black Equality: 1954–1992*. Rev. ed. New York: Hill and Wang, 1993.

Vera, Hernán, and Andrew M. Gordon. *Screen Saviors: Hollywood Fictions of Whiteness*. Lanham, MD: Rowman and Littlefield, 2003.

Welch, Susan, Lee Sigelman, Timothy Bledsoe, and Michael Combs. *Race and Place: Race Relations in an American City*. Cambridge: Cambridge University Press, 2001.

# 7

# AS FOXY AS CAN BE

## THE MELODRAMATIC MODE IN BLAXPLOITATION CINEMA

### JOSEPH S. VALLE

WHY IS SUFFERING SO PREVALENT IN BLAXPLOITATION CINEMA YET rarely mentioned or remembered in the popular and critical discourse of the movement's legacy? With that question in mind, I hope to answer Linda Williams's call to "recognize melodrama when we see it, and analytically to recognize the power of its ability to make us feel the aggrieved virtue of racial sufferers whether black or white."[1] My aim is to evaluate blaxploitation cinema through the melodramatic mode, because melodrama illuminates the visual, sonic, thematic, and historical nuances within many blaxploitation films. Melodrama, above all other modes, fully reveals the blaxploitation hero/heroine's suffering and why it is important to recognize not only their pride and physical prowess but also the emotions that make them vulnerable and soulful.

The melodramatic mode is the primary address of blaxploitation cinema for three specific reasons. First, it is important to recognize how revolutionary thought and actions from the Black Power movement inspired and shaped blaxploitation films. This leads me to consider the connection between revolution and melodrama, beginning with the first melodramas inspired by the French Revolution. Second, the blaxploitation oeuvre of the iconic actress Pam Grier startlingly resembles the serial-queen melodramas from silent cinema. Serial-queen melodramas were the first action films to feature the adventures of virtuous, albeit tough (white) heroines who gallantly fought the villains and saved the day. Grier's heroine-centered blaxploitation films closely follow this popular narrative trope and feature her frequently agonized raced and gendered body in jeopardy, which adds a provocative twist to melodrama scholarship about heroine-centered action films. Grier's body maximizes the melodramatic mode similarly to, albeit more graphically than, serial queens, when their bodies are at risk from the villains in their respective films. Finally, I argue that the bases of all narrative films and genres have melodramatic roots and why melodrama is still a viable and pertinent mode when applied to blaxploitation cinema.

Before delving into the textual analysis of *Foxy Brown* (Jack Hill, 1974), it is important to foreground and historicize melodrama's definition and why, at least for the benefit of this chapter, it is better to understand melodrama as a mode instead of a genre. Film scholar Agustín Zarzosa explicates the difference between genres and modes in his monograph *Refiguring Melodrama in Film and Television: Captive Affects, Elastic Sufferings, Vicarious Objects*: "Critics have theorized the difference between mode and genre in four distinct ways: the first conceives of modes as a higher taxonomic group than genres; the second understands modes as a cultural imaginary or as a structure of feeling; the third envisions modes as representational strategies; the fourth proposes that modes and genres follow disparate principles in classification."[2] The definition of melodrama greatly expands when it is seen as a mode, and it transforms into a vital strategy that helps us understand blaxploitation cinema beyond its generic elements. Melodrama as a genre severely limits the potential discourse of how it exists outside a constricting set of stylistic and thematic conventions, while the melodramatic mode is flexible and fluid and stretches across film genres. Blaxploitation cinema is also not a genre but a film movement that produced action, gangster, and horror motion pictures.[3] Zarzosa defines "melodrama as an elastic system that redistributes the visibility of suffering to the community."[4] This metaphor of melodrama as an "elastic system" exists not only in a variety of genres but also in other media, histories, rhetoric, politics, and social movements, as long as the display of excessive emotions and suffering is dominant and duly noted by the audience, and it has been a primary mode in Western theatrical entertainment for over 225 years.

Melodrama's modern origins began during the French Revolution when the Third Estate overthrew the monarchy due to their interest in establishing a democratic government. Revolutionaries believed that the French monarchy bankrupted the country and exploited peasant labor. They came to the realization that royals were not revered figureheads anointed by God but corrupt and hedonistic humans. The concept of melodramatic vigilante justice arguably derives from the French Revolution, when people rebelled against their immoral rulers. Peter Brooks states, "The Revolution attempts to sacralize law itself, the Republic as the institution of morality."[5] Initially, French revolutionaries created a violent moral order during the twilight of the Enlightenment, which privileged humanism and sciences over sacred institutions such as the church and the monarchy. The cultural product from this time period was theatrical protomelodramas. These plays lampooned European monarchies by exaggerating their decadence in order to stir and agitate French audiences.[6]

According to Brooks, "the word melodrama means, originally, a drama accompanied by music. It appears to first have been used in this sense by Rousseau, to describe a play in which he sought a new emotional expressivity through a mixture of spoken word, pantomime, and orchestral accompaniment."[7] Melodrama's theatrical origins underscore the performative and sonic cues that currently define the melodramatic mode in cinema. Music is instrumental in defining melodrama by directly alerting the audience to an emotional moment when a character is seized with pathos. Performances rooted in pantomime emphasize virtuous or evil characteristics, which is especially apparent in both silent and sound cinema. This exaggerated and indiscreet emoting through facial and body gestures is the epitome of melodrama's performative style.

Thematically, melodramas contain simple narrative variations that uphold good/evil binaries. Brooks posits, "[Melodrama] is inherently a dramatic form, in which the humble of the earth stand up to overbearing tyrants and express home truths, about the value of the good heart, the sanctity of the domestic hearth, the essential moral equality of all and the fraternity of the virtuous, and win through to see villainy punished, and virtue rewarded, in spectacular fashion in the last act."[8] Melodrama specifically addresses ethical and moral concerns in a postsacred world and advocates for humanness and social justice. Melodrama elevates the domestic sphere to high esteem, despite relishing in its fragility and corruptibility. It is a democratic form of theatrical entertainment, and its purpose is to incite strong emotions in the widest possible audience. Brooks adds, "While its social implications may be variously revolutionary or conservative, it is in all cases radically democratic, striving to make its representations clear and legible to everyone."[9]

Brooks's supple description also complements blaxploitation cinema's thematic and narrative interests and illuminates the blaxploitation hero/heroine's role as protector of hearth, family, and community from societal forces such as racism, exploitation, and absolute evil. Brooks asserts, "The polarization of good and evil works toward revealing their presence and operation as real forces in the world. Their conflict suggests the need to recognize and confront evil, to combat and expel it, to purge the social order."¹⁰ The blaxploitation hero/heroine, like French revolutionaries, create their own codes of law and order as a response to a system that is designed to oppress them. The hero/heroine uses his or her superior intellect and physical prowess to fight villainy, because the white antagonists function as the personification of racism in blaxploitation cinema.¹¹

Williams contemplates the significance of melodrama in American popular culture and reminds us that "racial melodrama takes on an enormous importance as the engine for the generation of legitimacy for racially constituted groups whose very claim to citizenship lies in these spectacles of pathos and action."¹² If we first acknowledge that melodrama in fact exists in blaxploitation cinema and use the melodramatic mode to investigate the movement's popularity and legacy, we will then have a richer understanding of the movement's historical and commercial relevance.

According to Novotny Lawrence, "The black exploitation or blaxploitation movement (1970–75) began as a result of a combination of three main social, political and economic factors: the Civil Rights Movement, the historic misrepresentation of blacks in motion pictures and Hollywood's financial trouble."¹³ However, melodrama is rarely acknowledged for contributing to the success of blaxploitation cinema, yet as Williams argues, it is the most popular mode for addressing race in American popular culture, beginning with the publication of the controversial abolitionist melodrama *Uncle Tom's Cabin* by Harriet Beecher Stowe in the mid-nineteenth century.¹⁴ Williams believes that "melodrama has been for better or worse, the primary way in which mainstream American culture has dealt with the moral dilemma of having first enslaved and then withheld equal rights to African-Americans."¹⁵ Blaxploitation cinema, then, is the cinematic representation of this predicament, and melodrama cannot erase the groundbreaking, edgy, and at times radical aim of blaxploitation cinema. In fact, it historicizes the movement's most progressive qualities by pointedly countering and parodying long-held racist stereotypes about African Americans circulating within American popular culture. Arguably, melodrama, with its special emphasis on emotionality and the spectacular, is one of the reasons why blaxploitation cinema initially became popular with black and white audiences in the 1970s and for its nostalgic resurgence in American popular culture at the dawn of the twenty-first century.

Furthermore, melodrama's revolutionary roots solidify the relationship between melodrama and blaxploitation cinema, because the movement is a cultural and commercial product from the civil rights and Black Power movements, in which the struggle for black equality created a social revolution in the United

States. The civil rights movement effectively used civil-disobedience tactics and boycotts to fight for the basic legal rights of southern African Americans that were denied to them by local and state governments. This tireless and courageous activism led to remarkable social change and had a monumental and transformative impact on American society. However, blaxploitation cinema is more closely aligned with the Black Power movement due to its reliance on violence as a form of self-defense, especially in black working-class communities. Historian Harvard Sitkoff explicates, "Unlike the civil-rights movement, which had largely focused on the aspirations of the burgeoning black middle class, Black Power drew attention to the needs of the lower classes, and to the root of their plight: powerlessness."[16] Many civil rights activists did not fully acknowledge the struggles of urban African Americans from northern states, target the African American underclass, or address internalized racism. The civil rights activists fought valiantly for integration and social equality, but cultural pride was not as explicitly addressed as it was in the Black Power movement. They also did not arm themselves with weapons as a form of self-defense or engage in violent tactics to further their political causes.

Besides fighting for social equality against a hostile government, the Black Power movement psychologically uplifted its followers by acknowledging the importance of self-worth. "Accordingly, the major thrust of Black Power was to make blacks proud to be blacks, a psychological precondition for equality. It fostered a new sense of racial pride and self-confidence that helped revolutionize the black perspective."[17] Filmmakers appropriated this burgeoning racial pride into their work by creating heroes/heroines inspired by the social and cultural revolution of the late 1960s.

At first glance, blaxploitation characters might lack "complexity," but examining them through the melodramatic mode reveals nuances that have seemingly gone undetected by scholars and audiences alike, especially in Pam Grier vehicles. In particular, the pain and suffering that her characters experience make them three-dimensional and virtuous,—characteristics that scholars and critics have generally glossed over, instead focusing on their sassy attitudes, physical prowess, and comeliness. Though it is easy to celebrate Grier's characters' courage and heroics, their humanity and vulnerability also need to be duly noted, because they reveal the occasionally painful experience of living as an African American woman in a racist, patriarchal, white-dominated American society, which features so prominently in *Foxy Brown*.

*Foxy Brown*'s preproduction began when independent film studio American International Pictures (AIP) wanted to produce a sequel to its previous year's hit

Pam Grier vehicle *Coffy* (Jack Hill, 1973). *Coffy* is the first action film starring an African American actress, and it features the title heroine as a vengeful nurse who wants to murder the drug dealers who left her preteen sister in a catatonic state from an overdose. Prior to *Coffy*, Grier began her career as a supporting actress before costarring in low-budget women-in-prison films that were shot in the Philippines. These films, which include Jack Hill's *The Big Doll House* (1971) and *The Big Bird Cage* (1972), featured salacious narratives in which the female characters were frequently put into homosocial scenarios in which they excessively displayed their nude bodies. While in terms of plot the women-in-prison film left much to be desired, Grier stood out in the controversial subgenre, demonstrating that she had the charisma to attract audiences, because she had the grit, gumption, and athleticism to become a convincing action star.

Despite AIP's initial enthusiasm in working with Hill and Grier again, the direction of *Foxy Brown* changed when the company deemed a sequel to *Coffy* too financially risky. In an interview with Calum Waddell, Jack Hill reveals, "Just before we started shooting, the sales department at AIP decided that sequels weren't very good for business. They had released some sequels that had done horrible business but they were terrible movies and they didn't differentiate between rubbish and a good sequel—they just decided they didn't want anymore sequels."[18] As a result, AIP decided to keep the action-revenge formula that had made *Coffy* a hit in place but changed the title character's name and incorporated more spectacular action sequences, which was ambitious for a low-budget film.

*Foxy Brown* tells the story of a young, upstanding African American woman on the cusp of creating a new life with her boyfriend, Michael Anderson (Terry Carter), who works as a federal agent. After gathering enough evidence to bring a drug cartel to justice, Anderson fakes his death and undergoes plastic surgery in an effort to keep himself safe until he testifies against the drug ring. However, Foxy's drug-dealing, ne'er-do-well brother Link (Antonio Fargas) works for the drug cartel and recognizes Anderson from an old newspaper photograph in Foxy's house. Wanting Miss Katherine Waugh (Kathryn Loder), the leader of the drug ring, to forgive the outstanding debts that he owes her, Link betrays his sister, telling his employer that Anderson is alive. He then gives Miss Katherine Foxy's home address so her goons will murder Anderson. Foxy discovers Link's betrayal, and just as she is about to warn her boyfriend, Miss Katherine's hit men shoot and murder him. After his death, Foxy decides to exact revenge on Anderson's murderers.

*Foxy Brown*'s plot is pure melodrama and positions the audience to root for Foxy because she loses her lover. She is forced into action after her personal life is shattered. The diabolically evil and racist villains inflict so much pain and anguish on her that the audience feels complete sympathy for her and hopes that she will execute vigilante justice. *Foxy Brown* evokes silent cinema's serial-queen melodramas, which were the first action films that featured heroines in roles in which they were the central driving force of the spectacular action sequences. Ben Singer, in his groundbreaking research on serial-queen melodramas, explains why these series were quite progressive and share some of the same narrative and sensational characteristics of *Foxy Brown*: "The most intriguing element in the serial-queen melodramas of the Teens is their extraordinary emphasis on female heroism. Within a sensational action-adventure framework of the sort most associated with male heroics, serials gave narrative preeminence to an intrepid young heroine who exhibited a variety of 'masculine' qualities: physical strength and endurance, self-reliance, courage, social authority, and freedom to explore novel experiences outside the domestic sphere."[19] Once Foxy is forced into action, she exhibits all of the aforementioned qualities. However, before proclaiming that *Foxy Brown* is at least a descendant of the serial-queen melodrama, it is vital to understand their differences. In order to do so, I will share a summary of one of the first and most famous serial-queen melodramas still in circulation, *The Perils of Pauline* (The Electric Company, 1914).

*The Perils of Pauline* follows the episodic adventures of a rich, brash young heiress, Pauline (Pearl White), as she travels the world, races cars and horses, rides submarines, and flies in hot-air balloons. She is engaged to her cousin Harry Marvin (Crane Wilbur), who encourages her to stay at home to avoid unnecessary danger. Despites his protests, Pauline decides to prolong her engagement because she yearns for a year of adventure before marriage. After Harry's father dies, Pauline's inheritance is left in the hands of her evil guardian, Koerner (Paul Panzer), who in a string of episodes attempts to murder Pauline, because he will inherit her fortune after her demise.

*The Perils of Pauline* centers on a woman who demands agency and reaps the benefits of modernity. Pauline is the cinematic representation of the New Woman, a fashionable, single, independent female who lived her life outside the domestic sphere. While this New Woman was the product of modernity and first-wave feminism, in society there was much hesitation about her relative freedom. Singer contends, "The New Woman epitomized the profound cultural discontinuity of modern society; traditional ideologies of gender, essentially stagnant for centuries, became objects of cultural reflexivity, open to doubt and revision."[20] Pauline is celebrated for her adventurous spirit, but she is also reprimanded for defying widely accepted stereotypical constructions of femininity. In many of the episodes, if Harry is not also

Miss Katherine's gang torments Foxy Brown and threatens her with physical violence. (*Foxy Brown* DVD, MGM Home Entertainment)

captured beside her, he rescues her from peril. Occasionally, after the rescue, Harry treats Pauline like a child, while Koerner constantly takes advantage of her naïveté by constructing scenarios in which he or his henchmen attempt to murder her. Harry views Pauline's adventurous streak as an immature phase that she will grow out of before she settles into womanhood, while Koerner exacerbates it. Nevertheless, Pauline is an extremely privileged woman, who has the economic and racial agency to be a New Woman. Such freedom and independence were rarely afforded to African American women in the early 1900s; therefore, race and class privilege separate the formidable, womanly Foxy Brown from the adventurous, albeit girlish Pauline. Despite these differences, Foxy Brown is conceivably the New Black Woman, who emerged from the Black Power movement and second-wave feminism.

Undeniably, though, the blaxploitation heroine is a cinematic construction that did not fit into any previous African American female cinematic archetypes. Charlene Regester, in her definitive account of the careers of prominent African Americans actresses from the birth of cinema to the beginning of the civil rights movement, describes how the physical presence of black performers such as Hattie McDaniel and Louise Beavers primarily functioned as a contrast to the whiteness of the female stars. She describes McDaniel and Beavers as operating as shadows in their films and argues, "a shadow self is a reflection of another subject, darker and less distinct in form and substance than the subject the shadow reflects."[21] Regester uses this beautiful yet tragic shadow metaphor to describe the careers of

African American actresses who were never granted the chance to play a role that was not a mere reflection of their white counterpart. Throughout early film history, the purpose of African American actresses was to illuminate the effervescence of white actresses whom they appeared alongside. Pam Grier certainly did not fit into this category during the blaxploitation movement, which represents the peak of her career. Foxy Brown's vibrancy and character traits, which Grier ably performs, come from the serial queens, while her radicalism and power ironically come from the historical constrictions that previous African American actresses endured in their careers, because there are many moments when their dignity and grace shone through their often one-dimensional roles.[22]

Both *Foxy Brown* and serial-queen melodramas feature heroines under constant threat of misogynistic violence, which underscores their marginal status as women in the public sphere. Mia Mask, in a political analysis of Pam Grier's early filmography, argues, "misogynist imagery emerges in reaction to the instability of patriarchy at moments of feminist achievement."[23] The heroines' suffering and defenselessness against seedy male villains is amplified throughout *both* serial-queen and blaxploitation melodramas, and it is no coincidence that these films were produced during feminist movements as a way to deal with the anxiety of women's liberation and to control its representation in popular culture. Despite the heroines' courage, physical prowess, and tenaciousness, serial-queen melodramas and Pam Grier blaxploitation vehicles create titillating spectacles that exploit the heroines' victimization. Singer explains, "the genre as a whole is thus animated by an oscillation between contradictory extremes of female prowess and distress, empowerment and imperilment."[24] He elaborates on the theme of female distress and pathos further: "The heroine systematically would be assaulted, bound, and gagged, terrorized by instruments of torture and dismemberment, hurled out windows or off bridges, and threatened with innumerable means of assassination. The genre thus coupled an ideology of female power with an equally vivid exposition of female defenselessness and weakness."[25]

*Foxy Brown*, which follows a similar narrative trope, demonstrates how Grier's body transforms into a vessel loaded with pathos and suffering because of her race and gender. The violence she endures at the hands of the villains is greatly emphasized throughout the film's narrative and propels the plot forward. She is punished for exhibiting agency and defending herself against violence.

The misogyny in the film becomes apparent when Foxy Brown infiltrates Miss Katherine's prostitution ring by posing as Misty Cotton, a sex worker who will do anything to make fast money. Miss Katherine immediately realizes Foxy's sexual appeal and hires her to seduce a judge who will preside over a case involving Miss Katherine's drug dealers. Foxy and a high-strung prostitute, Claudia (Juanita Brown), purposely humiliate the judge by teasing him about his inadequate manhood and then lock him out of his hotel room while he is in his underwear. Foxy and Claudia escape from the hotel to hide from Miss Katherine's thugs but are soon discovered. After a physical struggle, Claudia escapes from the henchmen, but Foxy is captured. Foxy is taken to Miss Katherine and her boyfriend, Steve (Peter Brown), who decide to send Foxy to a place where she will be injected with heroin, raped, and subsequently trafficked to the "islands," where she will work in a bordello as a drug-addicted prostitute. This synopsis sets up the most melodramatic scene in *Foxy Brown* and warrants a detailed analysis.

The establishing shot is the exterior of a decrepit cabin that the villains call "the ranch." There is nondiegetic banjo music accompanying the scene, which is quite different from the funky score that provides sultry rhythms that complement the urban setting in the rest of the film. The jarring banjo music juxtaposed against a smooth R&B soundtrack foreshadows the physical threat Foxy is under and constructs the rural landscape as sinister. There is a cut to a medium close-up of a sweaty, disheveled Foxy asleep on a bed. She has a black eye, and her shirt is fully unbuttoned, displaying her bra and cleavage. Foxy wakes up disoriented, stands, and stumbles barefoot around the cabin. She ties her shirt into a knot, opens a door, and finds Miss Katherine's henchman Slauson (Boyd Red Morgan) sleeping on a couch. Unlike Miss Katherine's other employees, who wear suits, Slauson is dressed in dirty, ill-fitting clothing. In an analysis of how a rural setting and its inhabitants function as a threat to the heroine in the horror genre, Carol Clover argues, "More to the point, country people live beyond the reaches of social law. They do not observe the civilized rules of hygiene or personal habit. If city men are either clean-shaven or wear stylish beards or moustaches, country men sport stubble. Likewise teeth; the country is a world beyond dentistry. The typical country rapist is a toothless or rotten-toothed single man with four-day growth."[26] Slauson represents a slave warden at a plantation, because the mise-en-scène constructs him as a lower-class hillbilly and more importantly as a southerner. Further, his grimy costume foreshadows the upcoming horror that Foxy faces in her attempt to escape from the ranch.

Soon after Foxy silently walks past Slauson, she hears someone singing outside the cabin. She looks out the window and sees a large bald man in blue coveralls, named Brandi (H. B. Haggerty), putting gasoline in a tank. He sings, "I know a girl who lives on a hill. She won't put out, but her sister will." Slauson

## AS FOXY AS CAN BE

Foxy Brown's agonized state just before her off-screen rape. (*Foxy Brown* DVD, MGM Home Entertainment)

follows Foxy outside, cracks a whip, which wraps around her neck, and drags her to him. Once they are inside, Slauson ties Foxy to the bed. He insults her by calling her a "big-jugged jigaboo" and "a lucky nigger." Brandi enters the cabin and prepares an injection of heroin. There is a cut to a close-up of Foxy saying, "I don't need anymore. I'm doing fine." Brandi ignores her pleas and injects her with the needle. She swears at him, while Slauson ties her feet to the bed frame. Brandi leers at her and says, "Me, oh my. I'm beginning to get that old feeling." He then fondles her breasts, tears off her bra, and smells it, which functions as a clear indication that he plans to rape her. Slauson encourages Brandi while he removes his coveralls. There is a close-up of Foxy as her eyes widen in terror and a cut to a low-angle shot of Brandi as he moves closer to her. There is a cut back to Foxy's terrified face in an extreme close-up. The camera cuts back to Brandi, as he gets closer to the camera. His face becomes blurry, distorted, and then fades out to the next scene.

The rape scene clearly evokes rape between white men and black women in the antebellum South. The whip and ropes are the tools used for human bondage and sadistic punishment. Brandi and Slauson work as representatives of the sex traffickers Miss Katherine and Steve, who metaphorically represent the mistress and master of the plantation because they treat their African American drug dealers and prostitutes, like Link and Claudia, as if they were slaves. Link and

Claudia are threatened with bodily harm if they make any mistakes or try to escape. Thus, Link and Claudia's attempts at escaping "their masters" strongly connote a slave's escape from a plantation in the nineteenth century.

Foxy's rape is an attempt to strip her of power, victimize her, and control her sexuality. She survives a debased, heinous crime, which not only makes her revenge an act of vigilante justice but also gives her virtue, which is one of the most important characteristics of a heroine in melodrama. Williams posits, "The key function of victimization is to orchestrate the moral legibility crucial to the mode, for if virtue is not obvious, suffering—often depicted as the literal suffering of an agonized body—is."[27] The only way Foxy can regain her innocence is through revenge, because it will return her to a time before unwarranted tragedy, when her world was not destroyed by moral disorder. Unfortunately, time plays cruel tricks on the virtuous in melodrama, and it is one of the most villainous elements in the melodramatic mode. Williams notes, "The teasing delay of the forward-moving march of time has not been sufficiently appreciated as basic to the cinematic application of theatrical melodrama. . . . It needs to be linked with melodrama's larger impulse to reverse time, to return to the time of origins and the space of innocence."[28] Foxy wishes she could return to a time when she could have saved Michael and Link from Miss Katherine and Steve, when her domestic sphere was safe, and when she was just about to settle down with Michael. However, "do overs" are impossible in life, but such wish fulfillment is quite prevalent in melodrama. The villains took everything Foxy accomplished and loved away from her. Her only objective is to make them suffer the same way they made her suffer. After her rape, she has nothing else to lose and is hell-bent on escaping and murdering her rapists.

The camera fades into a close-up of Foxy waking up and breathing a sigh of relief that the rape is over. Slauson returns from town and laughs as a long shot reveals that Foxy is still tied to the bed. He walks out of the room. Foxy looks around and notices a razor blade that was left on the bed stand beside her. She moves to it, which reveals her breasts in a close-up. Foxy's partially nude body is on ample display for the audience to "admire" while she is in the midst of an agonized state. This graphic nudity differs from other nude scenes in the film, in which shots of Grier's breasts are fleeting and obscured by careful blocking, dark lighting, and camera trickery. These filmic tactics were quite unusual for an AIP film, because the studio was notorious for its lewd content, thereby emphasizing the scene's sensationalism and lasciviousness.

On the other hand, Waddell notes, "Hill not only shows us the aftermath of his character's violation—and, while it is not an appealing sight, it is arguably all the more powerful for being left to the imagination."[29] Thankfully the audience is not subjected to viewing the actual rape. The melodramatic mode creates enough pathos in this and the previous scene through the film's score, mise-en-scène, dialogue, performances, and especially its symbolism of slavery. The filmic elements overpower pornographic undertones and diligently reveal the rapists' brutality. However, Foxy never sheds tears after being raped. She is always put into situations that make her vulnerable, but the viewer barely sees her express anguish. The only moment she cries in the film is when Anderson dies in her arms. Arguably, she does not have any time for an emotional breakdown, because her life is in mortal danger. She also has no one to rescue her, so she only depends on herself to display resilience and perpetual determination no matter how traumatic the conflict is.

Next, Foxy picks up the razor with her mouth to cut the rope. The camera cuts to Slauson in the other room and then cuts back to Foxy removing the rope that binds her feet. There is also a fast cut to Brandi outside the cabin, underneath a car. Foxy silently walks to the closet and creates a weapon out of wire hangers. Then she sneaks into the kitchen and retrieves a gasoline hose that is hanging on the windowsill. She sucks on the hose until gas flows, and she begins to fill a bucket. Slauson enters the room as she continues to fill the bucket. Mercilessly, she slashes him with her weapon, and his eye pops out of its socket. Brandi hears him screaming and sees Slauson writhing on the floor. Foxy yells, "Hey, skinhead," and splashes Brandi with gasoline. She then throws lit matches at him, which set him on fire. He stumbles around the room and crashes through the wall. Foxy runs outside and ducks behind a car, and then the cabin explodes.

The viewer feels gratified with Foxy's revenge in the immediate aftermath of her rape. Her resourcefulness is admirable, and her spectacular assault on the rapists mildly diffuses the tragedy from the previous scene. According to theater studies historian David Grimstead, "In melodramatic politics, of which vigilante chronicle is a sub-genre, the stress was always on the self-righteous pleasure of blood atonement needed for communal cleansing, where heroes proved their virtue by their enthusiasm for killing vice."[30] Earlier, I argued that Foxy's rape solidifies her virtue. However, what if it is vigilantism that constructs it? It is important to note that Foxy is seeking revenge not only for herself but also for her community that lives in fear of the drug cartel. Foxy realizes that she cannot destroy the drug ring on her own, so she enlists the help of her friends in the Anti-Slavery Committee, which is modeled after the Black Panther Party, to aid her in her efforts. Initially, they are skeptical of her plans, but they eventually realize that the law will not help them in their efforts to rid their neighborhood of Miss Katherine, Steve, and their gang.

Earlier in the film, Michael expresses his hesitancy about vigilante justice, and Foxy cleverly replies, "It's American as apple pie." If we continue to examine the film in the melodramatic mode, we will gain more insight into her simple answer and understand that the concept of vigilantism is part of the American vernacular. "The vocabulary of American life is absolutist; people talk about democracy, justice, law, Constitution, freedom, order, right, rights, individualism, community, as if they were self-evident and perfect, translucently clear."[31] Frequently, these concepts, when stripped of ethical complications, create conflicts between the heroes and villains in melodramas, because the villain interferes with the hero's pursuit of attaining and reveling in American privilege. Blaxploitation cinema complicates this formula, because its heroes/heroines fight against white supremacy, in order to gain the same autonomy as white American citizens. This battle is prominently featured in the climaxes of blaxploitation films. Brooks explains how villainy functions in the formulaic climaxes of revolutionary theatrical melodramas, which *Foxy Brown* also conventionally follows: "the body of the villain is publicly branded with its identity, exposed in a formal judgment scene, then, if not put to death in hand-to-hand combat, driven from the stage and banished from human society."[32]

The final scene begins with an establishing shot of a framed black-and-white headshot of Steve cleverly juxtaposed with the previous scene's final shot of him screaming as he is "branded" by the Anti-Slavery Committee. The camera cuts to a medium-long shallow-focus shot of Miss Katherine walking over to the photograph. She picks up the picture from the marble table and passionately kisses and strokes it. The house alarm rings, which startles her. There is a cut to a long shot of Foxy dressed in a black leather jacket and pants and sporting a large afro, which is a clear reference to the Black Panther's uniform. She carries a large, red leather bag. Once inside, she gazes down at a smug Miss Katherine sitting on her couch with an alcoholic beverage in hand. Two of Miss Katherine's armed henchmen come into the frame behind her. One of them approaches Foxy from the right and says, "Hold it right there, spook." Foxy follows his command and raises her hands. Miss Katherine says, "I want to know what she is doing here." The henchman grabs Foxy's bag and says, "I'll take that, big mouth." Foxy says, "Sure. I brought it for you, Ms. Pimp. Like I said, it's a present from your faggot boyfriend." The henchman brings Miss Katherine the bag. She opens it and recognizes the object in the jar as Steve's penis. She screams, "Steve!" and drops it on the floor. Foxy takes a pistol out of her afro and shoots the henchmen dead.

The camera cuts to a long shot of Miss Katherine as she takes a gigantic knife out of its holster, a hilarious metaphor for the castrated Steve. She raises it as she slowly moves toward Foxy, who shoots her in the arm. She moans, falls to the floor, and asks, "Why don't you kill me too? Go on, shoot. I don't want to live anymore." The camera cuts to Foxy in a low-angle point-of-view shot as she says, "I know. That's the idea," and then back to Miss Katherine as she cries. Foxy says in voice-over, "The rest of your boyfriend is still around, and I hope you two live a long time, so you get to feel what I feel. Death is too easy for you, bitch. I want you to suffer." The camera cuts to Miss Katherine shaking and then returns to Foxy as she makes her grand exit from the scene. The final shot is of Miss Katherine sitting on the floor dramatically screaming and moaning in despair for all that she has lost. Her suffering, Steve's castration, and her ultimate defeat at the hands of Foxy deplete her of all her phallic power. Finally, as the New Black Woman, Foxy regains her lost innocence after making the villains who ruined her life suffer in grand theatrical style. Such gleefully twisted punishment exists only in films that intentionally address the audience through the melodramatic mode by adroitly examining the iconic, pathos-laden moving images in the films.

The melodramatic mode is greatly apparent in *Foxy Brown* due to the agonizing emotional and physical suffering that the heroine and villains endure throughout the film. The film's thematic connection to serial-queen melodramas also provides a strong historical connection to silent cinema and further historicizes the relationship between the blaxploitation film movement and global political and social movements that happened before the 1960s and 1970s.

Gender also plays a significant role in understanding how melodrama works in blaxploitation films, because it is more difficult to find overt scenes of agonized suffering in the hero-centered films. Besides Grier's characters, blaxploitation heroines like Diana "Sugar" Hill in *Sugar Hill* (Paul Maslansky, 1974) and Serena in *The Muthers* (Cirio Santiago, 1976) are routinely exposed to racist *and* misogynistic violence throughout the film narratives, in which their bodies are under constant peril. However, much work needs to be done for the melodramatic mode in blaxploitation cinema to gain traction in academic scholarship. Hopefully this analysis is a useful blueprint to examine the melodramatic mode in blaxploitation cinema as we continue to find innovative ways to engage with such a fascinating, iconic, and complex film movement.

# NOTES

1. Linda Williams, *Playing the Race Card: Melodramas of Black and White from Uncle Tom to O. J. Simpson* (Princeton, NJ: Princeton University Press, 2001), 309.
2. Agustín Zarzosa, *Refiguring Melodrama and Television: Captive Effects, Elastic Sufferings, Vicarious Objects* (Lanham, MD: Lexington Books, 2012), 9.
3. Novotny Lawrence, *Blaxploitation Films of the 1970s: Blackness and Genre* (New York: Routledge, 2007), 34.
4. Zarzosa, *Refiguring Melodrama and Television*, 9.
5. Peter Brooks, "The Melodramatic Imagination," in *Imitations of Life: A Reader on Film and Television Melodrama*, ed. Marcia Landry (Detroit: Wayne State University Press, 1991), 60.
6. Peter Brooks, "Melodrama, Body, Revolution," in *Melodrama: Stage, Picture, Screen*, ed. Jacky Bratton, Jim Cook, and Christine Gledhill (London: British Film Institute, 1994), 16.
7. Brooks, "Melodramatic Imagination," 59.
8. Brooks, "Melodrama, Body, Revolution," 16.
9. Brooks, "Melodramatic Imagination," 60.
10. Ibid., 59.
11. Lawrence, *Blaxploitation Films of the 1970s*, 26.
12. Williams, *Playing the Race Card*, 44.
13. Novotny Lawrence, "Fear of a Blaxploitation Monster: Blackness as Generic Revision in AIP's *Blacula*." *Film International* 39 (2009): 14.
14. Williams, *Playing the Race Card*, 6.
15. Ibid., 44.
16. Harvard Sitkoff, *The Struggle for Black Equality: 25th Anniversary Edition* (New York: Hill and Wang, 2008), 201.
17. Ibid., 202.
18. Calum Waddell, *Jack Hill: The Exploitation and Blaxploitation Master, Film by Film* (Jefferson, NC: McFarland, 2009), 127.
19. Ben Singer, *Melodrama and Modernity: Early Sensational Cinema and Its Contents* (New York: Columbia University Press, 2001), 220.
20. Ibid., 14.
21. Charlene Regester, *African American Actresses: The Struggle for Visibility, 1900–1960* (Bloomington: Indiana University Press, 2010), 2.
22. Some fine examples include Juanita Moore's Annie in *Imitation of Life* (Douglas Sirk, 1959) telling her spoiled friend Lora (Lana Turner) with pride that she has a rich life outside their friendship, and Maidie Norman's Elvira in *What Ever Happened to Baby Jane?* (Robert Aldrich, 1962) defiantly standing up against the monstrous Baby Jane's (Bette Davis) treatment of her sister, Blanche (Joan Crawford), which ultimately leads to Elvira's tragic murder.
23. Mia Mask, *Divas on Screen: Black Women in American Film* (Urbana: University of Illinois Press, 2009), 75.
24. Singer, *Melodrama and Modernity*, 222.
25. Ibid., 255.

26. Carol Clover, *Men, Women, and Chainsaws: Gender in the Modern Horror Film* (Princeton, NJ: Princeton University Press, 1992), 125.
27. Williams, *Playing the Race Card*, 29.
28. Ibid., 3.
29. Waddell, *Jack Hill*, 139.
30. David Grimstead, "Vigilante Chronicle," in *Melodrama: Stage Picture Screen*, ed. Jacky Bratton, Jim Cook, and Christine Gledhill (London: British Film Institute, 1994), 211.
31. Ibid., 210.
32. Brooks, "Melodramatic Imagination," 22.

## WORKS CITED

Brooks, Peter. "Melodrama, Body, Revolution." In *Melodrama: Stage, Picture, Screen*, edited by Jacky Bratton, Jim Cook, and Christine Gledhill, 11–24. London: British Film Institute, 1994.

———. "The Melodramatic Imagination." In *Imitations of Life: A Reader on Film and Television Melodrama*, edited by Marcia Landry, 50–67. Detroit: Wayne State University Press, 1991.

Clover Carol. *Men, Women, and Chainsaws: Gender in the Modern Horror Film*. Princeton, NJ: Princeton University Press, 1992.

Grimstead, David. "Vigilante Chronicle." In *Melodrama: Stage Picture Screen*, edited by Jacky Bratton, Jim Cook, and Christine Gledhill, 199–213. London: British Film Institute, 1994.

Lawrence, Novotny. *Blaxploitation Films of the 1970s: Blackness and Genre*. New York: Routledge, 2007.

———. "Fear of the Blaxploitation Monster: Blackness as Generic Revision in AIP's *Blacula*." *Film International* 39 (2009): 14–26.

Mask, Mia. *Divas on Screen: Black Women in American Film*. Urbana: University of Illinois Press, 2009.

Regester, Charlene. *African American Actresses: The Struggle for Visibility, 1900–1960*. Bloomington: Indiana University Press, 2010.

Singer, Ben. *Melodrama and Modernity: Early Sensational Cinema and Its Contents*. New York: Columbia University Press, 2001.

Sitkoff, Harvard. *The Struggle for Black Equality: 25th Anniversary Edition*. New York: Hill and Wang, 2008.

Waddell, Calum. *Jack Hill: The Exploitation and Blaxploitation Master, Film by Film*. Jefferson, NC: McFarland, 2009.

Williams, Linda. *Playing the Race Card: Melodramas of Black and White from Uncle Tom to O. J. Simpson*. Princeton, NJ: Princeton University Press, 2001.

Zarzosa, Agustín. *Refiguring Melodrama and Television: Captive Effects, Elastic Sufferings, Vicarious Objects*. Lanham, MD: Lexington Books, 2012.

PART III

# WAS, IS, OR ISN'T BLAXPLOITATION

# 8

## STOMPING ON STEPIN FETCHIT

### HISTORICIZING "BLACKNESS" IN AFRICAN AMERICAN FILM CULTURE OF THE 1970S

#### ALLYSON NADIA FIELD

THE TERM "BLAXPLOITATION" CONNOTES THE NUMEROUS FILMIC ITERAtions of black urban life, politics, and style visible in the proliferation of hip, eroticized, and often-violent urban-themed films that burst onto American screens in the early 1970s. In the popular imagination as well as in scholarship and criticism, the sexploitative and stereotypical imagery of the more sensational examples of these films has suggested a greater homogeneity to black-themed films than is evinced by the wide range of genres, styles, narratives, structures, and production circumstances. Blaxploitation, to be sure, could not be avoided. Whether embracing or rejecting the term, African American writers, directors, and producers repeatedly grappled with the pervasiveness of the movement's presumption of a categorical and symbolic definition of "blackness."

In this essay, I focus on one form of an enactment of "blackness" in 1970s black filmmaking, paying particular attention to the intertextual assertions of notions of "blackness" that put contemporary black film in dialogue with film history. Specifically, I look at how black film history is mobilized in three films directed by African American directors that bracket the peak years of the black film boom of the early 1970s: *Watermelon Man* (dir. Melvin Van Peebles, 1970), *Amazing Grace* (dir. Stan Lathan, 1974), and *Car Wash* (dir. Michael Schultz, 1976). Each film has a narrative that pivots on notions of "blackness," yet they enact their inquiries through the legacy of black film history. Although this happens in different ways, the films share a strategy that revolves around the casting of an older generation of black actors in cameo roles. These actors were prominent character actors in Hollywood's golden age—a time when most roles for African Americans conformed to white stereotypes and caricatures of blackness. By taking up the reappearance of Mantan Moreland, Stepin Fetchit, and Clarence Muse, this essay aims to reveal the complex negotiation with a significant part of film history as it is presented at a time when the legacy of black representation was a pressing question. Making such an argument will require a composite methodology: close analyses of the films in which the actors appear in cameos, studies of representation (both the actors and the characters they portray), an understanding of the production histories of the films, and broader accounts of extrafilmic discourse. It is only by looking at these aspects in relation to one another that the full complexity with which black films of the 1970s engage the history of race and cinema can emerge.

## BLAXPLOITATION AND BLACK FILM HISTORY

The proliferation of black-themed films in the 1970s is generally taken to have been catalyzed by Van Peebles's *Sweet Sweetback's Baadasssss Song* (1971), the film he released immediately following *Watermelon Man*. Though the impact of *Sweetback* is undeniable, a more accurate periodization of blaxploitation would account for the significance of the popularity of earlier releases leading to the production of a greater number of black-themed films in the early 1970s such as United Artists' *Cotton Comes to Harlem* (dir. Ossie Davis, 1970), starring Godfrey Cambridge (who made *Watermelon Man* immediately following the completion of principal photography on *Cotton*).[1] After the success of these films, black-themed movies were generally marketed through the iconography of blaxploitation regardless of the narrative content of the film. This meant that films with predominantly black casts and/or themes surrounding race were seen at the time as occupying the same discursive space.

Conceptions of blaxploitation thus dominated all black-themed films released in this period, regardless of narrative or style or if they were capitalizing on—or offering a counterimage to—the dominant iconography of the black film boom. In this context, it is important to remember that blaxploitation is *not* a retronym, though the term has been consistently misunderstood and arguably more contentious than the films it supposedly categorizes. As Ed Guerrero writes, "More than a bit of irony figures in the term *Blaxploitation*."[2] The most striking irony concerns the origin of the term, coined by Junius Griffin, the then-president of the Hollywood branch of the NAACP, as a critique of what he saw as a "cancer . . . gnawing away at the moral fiber of our community."³ Griffin, who in 1972 founded the Coalition Against Blaxploitation (CAB), vehemently denounced the films: "We will not tolerate the continued warping of our black children's minds with the filth, violence and cultural lies that are all-pervasive in current productions of so-called black movies. The transformation from the stereotyped Stepin Fetchit to Super Nigger on the screen is just another form of cultural genocide. The black community should deal with this problem by whatever means necessary."⁴ Similarly, Roy Innis, the national director of the Congress of Racial Equality (CORE), wrote in the *New York Times*, "I view the present Black movie phenomenon with a strong suspicion that the Black youth of America are being programed in a subliminal, subtle way that, in its ultimate destruction of the minds of Black youth, is potentially far more dangerous than "step-n-fetch-it" and his lot."⁵

Though blaxploitation is often seen as oriented by tropes of "presentness," a strong sense of black film history, as well as cultural history more broadly, runs through the more expansive group of films made by black filmmakers in the 1970s.⁶ Films such as *Soul Soldier* (dir. John Cardos, 1970), *Man and Boy* (dir. E. W. Swackhamer, 1971), *Buck and the Preacher* (dir. Sidney Poitier, 1972), *The Legend of Nigger Charley* (dir. Martin Goldman, 1972), *Charley-One-Eye* (dir. Don Chaffey, 1972), *Thomasine and Bushrod* (dir. Gordon Parks, Jr., 1974), *Take a Hard Ride* (dir. Antonio Margheriti as Anthony M. Dawson, 1975), and *Boss Nigger* (dir. Jack Arnold, 1975) all reference the history of Race Westerns prolific in the late 1930s (like *Harlem Rides the Range* and *The Bronze Buckaroo*).⁷ While slavery and its media representations were used as a subject of titillation by exploitation producers in films such as *The Arena* (dir. Steve Carver, 1973) and *Passion Plantation* (dir. Mario Pinzauti, 1976), slavery was also a site of social critique (even if of questionable efficacy) in films such as *Skin Game* (dir. Paul Bogart, 1971), *Blacula* (dir. William Crain, 1972), *Mandingo* (dir. Richard Fleischer, 1975), and *Mandingo*'s sequel, *Drum* (dir. Steve Carver, 1976).

This logic structures the cameos given to older black actors. As Donald Bogle has noted, Stepin Fetchit (born Lincoln Perry) had a talent for gauging popular tastes.⁸ Fetchit's characters were designed to appeal to white audiences.⁹ Bogle notes that he perfected and emblematized the popular "coon" type: "lazy, no-account, good-for-nothing, forever-in-hot-water, natural-born comedians."¹⁰ Fetchit became known for a "whining nearly indecipherable speech pattern" in his portrayal of slow-speaking, "slothful" characters.¹¹ While controversial, this was a highly lucrative shtick; throughout the 1930s, Fetchit was the highest earning black actor in Hollywood. The popularity of these comedic roles led to the proliferation of "Stepin's step-chillun," in Bogle's terms, as Willie Best and Mantan Moreland "picked up Fetchit's mantle" in their studio roles.[12] Best (also known as Sleep n' Eat), played slow-witted servants, porters, and janitors. Moreland was known for wide-eyed expressions of fear, which were on prominent display during his appearances in the Charlie Chan series (though he also had a substantive career making race films). Clarence Muse, on the other hand, portrayed "the dignified, humanized tom" at a time, as Bogle notes, "when being black and human in the movies was neither easy nor expected."[13] In the 1930s and 1940s, these figures were relegated to the margins of the screen as servants or other supporting roles to white principals.

Fetchit became perhaps *the* symbol of such pernicious screen roles, invoked as a cautionary tale during the Black film boom. In the wake of the civil rights movement and the rise of Black Power, Fetchit seemed positively outmoded. Indeed, the Coalition Against Blaxploitation was explicitly concerned about a trajectory from the Willie Best, Mantan Moreland, Stepin Fetchit characters to Sweetback, Shaft, and *Super Fly*'s Youngblood Priest. Yet Fetchit was not universally reviled, and some scholars offered subversive readings of his art, noting the great skill his performances evince. One counterargument was that the true object of Fetchit's mockery was black stereotype itself, specifically the "white man's vision of the black," in the terms of Joseph McBride in his fascinating profile of the actor in *Film Quarterly* in 1971. McBride suggests that Stepin Fetchit's art "can now be seen as a secret weapon in the long racial struggle."[14] Fetchit himself endorsed such a reading, and his 1971 assertion that he "was the first Negro militant" coincided with the release of Melvin Van Peebles's *Sweet Sweetback's Baadasssss Song*, whose image of black militancy inspired Huey P. Newton to proclaim it "the first truly revolutionary Black film made."[15]

On the surface, it might appear that Fetchit, Moreland, and Muse fit Bogle's schema of stereotypes—Fetchit as "arch-coon," Moreland as "a round-faced, wide-eyed, cherubic coon," and Muse as an "archetypal tom"—yet they are each more complexly figured in their 1970s cameos.[16] Fragments within a film—that is, the cameos of these veteran actors—are indicators of a serious and deep engagement with film history. They are not merely homages, inside jokes, or subtle critiques (though they are also these things), but they are at the heart of how these films work and how the films engage with black film history. The films show that these directors were attuned to and interested in the complexity of the caricatures they employed. Rather than being relegated to the past, Mantan Moreland, Stepin Fetchit, and Clarence Muse functioned as reminders of the persistence of stereotype, the dangers of asserting a monolithic notion of "blackness," and cinema's uneasy relationship with its own history. They reemerged, not coincidentally, at a time when the stakes of black film, African American representation, and the popular cinema were most acute.

## *WATERMELON MAN*: CRITIQUE THROUGH INDIRECTION

At a basic level, the question these cameos raise involves the work they are doing in these films. What narrative and extrafilmic functions do they perform? Clearly, these appearances carry baggage of signification, but what does their presence evoke—and to whom? In the case of *Watermelon Man,* Mantan Moreland's cameo is a reference to a type as well as an ironic commentary on that type.

A farce, *Watermelon Man* chronicles the experiences of a white bigot named Jeff Gerber who turns Black overnight (loosely ascribed to a sunlamp accident). Gerber, played by Godfrey Cambridge initially in whiteface, learns to negotiate life with black skin. Through subsequent encounters with his family, colleagues, and neighbors, he gains insight into racism and discrimination and ends up accepting his situation and thriving as a black man. The film concludes with Gerber rejecting his now-estranged wife and joining a black self-defense group, implicitly becoming politicized.

Moreland spent one day on set and was paid $300 for the role of Joe the "Negro Counterman," who works at the diner frequented by Gerber.[17] He was the only cast member that Van Peebles insisted on hiring for the film, presumably because the director wanted to "give the brother a chance."[18] However, Moreland's casting in this role does significant work. In this film about the multiple meanings of "blackness" in American society, it is especially striking that Mantan Moreland represents an idea of "authentic blackness" in contrast to Gerber's refusal to accept how others see him. It is Joe who essentially calls him out on his fakeness. While Joe was obsequious to Gerber when white (calling him "Mr. Gerber" and laughing at his racist jokes), he switches to slang and treats Gerber as a peer when Gerber shows up with black skin. When the now-black Gerber gets upset, Joe tells him, "Cool it, Jeff, that's why they don't want us in these places now," and Gerber, still a bigot, balks at his use of "us." Enraged, Gerber threatens to sue the NAACP and angrily points to his hand and exclaims, "Here! Look at my skin!" Joe retorts, "I don't have to look at your skin! I can look at my own!" In the film, Moreland delivers the line with increasing annoyance, though the script indicates the line is to be given with "growing anger," permitting Moreland

Mantan Moreland in *Watermelon Man*. (*Watermelon Man* DVD, Columbia Tristar Home Entertainment)

a range of emotion not allowed by his circumscribed studio roles; anger in particular was an emotion rarely permitted for a sympathetic black character.[19] The manager intervenes to appease the customer, nervous about "trouble," telling him, "I've always gotten along well with members of your race. Ask Joe here!" to which Moreland nods and smiles in agreement.

Moreland's rapid code switching provides much of the comedy in this sequence, but it also serves as an homage to the actor's talent, a kind of recuperation of his legacy that lays bare the constructedness of such a stereotype. The casting of Moreland as the "authentic" foil to Cambridge's masquerade functions ironically for a spectator familiar with Moreland's legacy (or at least those who would recognize the "type" that his portrayal of an obsequious counterman would evoke). In a film about literally becoming comfortable in one's skin, the confrontation between Moreland and Cambridge works both narratively and extrafilmically to underscore the myth of an authentic blackness. This was not without its difficulties. The studio's advertising strategy reveals anxiety about the film and how it envisioned the comedy. Through this lens, we can better understand how Moreland's cameo works; it functions, in the language of Columbia's advertising approach for the film, through "indirection."

Columbia emphasized the comedic aspects of *Watermelon Man* as a way to mitigate the possible perceptions of a "message." By this time, the question of whether movies should or should not contain a message of social significance, or be made with a particular didactic purpose, was long-standing. Concerning Van Peebles, the box-office analysis stated that he "is one of the few black directors to make a major film at a major studio. It is he who gives the picture its authentically black viewpoint and the fresh, young, unhandcuffed-by-tradition approach that has 'today' stamped on it in black print." Internal memos reveal that the studio was concerned with marketing the film as a comedy, not a message film: "The advertising approach should appeal to the amusement-seeking audience, and should strongly indicate that this is a picture they will enjoy. Any message and/or social commentary inherent in the film will make its point as it was intended to—by *indirection*.... No attempt should be made to hide the basic plot—and we should get our main mileage out of the fact that this idea is treated with humor."[20] Elsewhere, "It is a sharply comedic look at the black-white racial situation. It has serious undertones, but is made strictly for entertainment. As everyone knows by now, it is the story of a middle-class, middle-income white man who wakes up one morning to find himself black. This, of course, is pure fantasy—but played against a realistic background, it has some valid comments to make about the contemporary racial scene."[21]

These anxieties are apparent in the taglines for the film (then titled *The Night the Sun Came Out on Happy Hollow Lane*, the title of Herman Raucher's original novel and adapted screenplay):

Suggested Ad Lines:
There's something funny
about Jeff Gerber . . .


Last night he was white.


But when he looked
In his mirror this morning . . .
Everything went Black!


There's something *very* funny
About Jeff Gerber.
In fact, hilarious.

For Godfrey Cambridge
A Change of Pace
Face
And
Race

The blackest night
Of Jeff Gerber's life—
"The Night The Sun Came Out"

There are all kinds
Of black comedy—
This is the funny kind

Jeff Gerber looks
In his mirror
And turns white . . .

But it doesn't show . . .

Because he's just
Turned black![22]

The advertising strategy indicates that the studio was imagining the comedy to be at the expense of Black people, hence addressed to white audiences—blackness as nightmare providing the humor to white anxieties about race. (According to Van Peebles, the studio had wanted him to shoot a version of the ending in which Gerber wakes up and it was all a nightmare, an ending untenable to the director.)

In this context, Moreland's cameo is a clear example of indirection—though not in the way the studio envisioned the term. The cameo functions as a critique targeted at the studio and American film industry itself, creating irony by way of an embrace of history. Moreland plays a man playing a role; we are shown both the masquerade and the fact of the masquerade. In this sense, he draws from not only his career in Hollywood productions as the stereotyped "coon" of Bogle's critique (such as the bulging eyes that he was known for) but also his long history in race films made for African American audiences. There, he was able to bring greater nuance to his characters than in his studio roles. Further, in his race-film performances, Moreland's "coon" comedy was contextualized within a range of other black characters, permitting audiences, as Julia Leyda argues, to "feel freer to enjoy the slapstick humor of the character without feeling betrayed, angry, or ashamed."[23]

The complex dynamics involved in black spectatorship prevent simple categorization of Moreland's performances or how black audiences perceived them. Jacqueline Stewart has traced these dynamics focusing on the late teens and twenties: "During this period, Black viewing practices can be read as a reconstructive process, whereby Black viewers could reconstitute themselves as viewing subjects in the face of a racially exclusionary cinematic institution and social order."[24] She writes, "In relation to a variety of film stars, Black moviegoers could read alternatively with and against the disparate racial identities being performed on screen."[25] Stewart's concept of "reconstructive spectatorship" permits us to see Moreland's cameo in *Watermelon Man* as critique-by-indirection. In this sense, Van Peebles's choice of Moreland as foil to Gerber's boorish racism (both when white and when newly Black) harnesses the history of Hollywood representation of African Americans in a sharp satire of racialized anxieties. According to Van Peebles, he told Moreland, "Don't make it too clear that we're saying 'fuck you.'"[26]

## *AMAZING GRACE*: CRITIQUE THROUGH AMBIVALENCE

Without a doubt, the black film boom enabled films to be made that might not have been green-lit without the box-office success of so-called blaxploitation titles. As a result, films that had nothing to do with blaxploitation but featured predominantly black casts were marketed in those terms or with blaxploitation as a reference point. Films such as *Black Girl* (dir. Ossie Davis, 1972), about an aspiring dancer, and *Emma Mae* (dir. Jamaa Fanaka, 1976), centering on a country cousin's move to the city, were advertised with posters that played up violence and/or sex, obfuscating their actual subject; *Black Girl* was advertised with the slogan, "She's got to cut it . . . or cut out" over the image of a woman brandishing a knife, and *Emma Mae* was released by Xenon as *Black Sister's Revenge*. Other films more actively worked with that legacy. In the promotional materials for

*Amazing Grace*, the film both draws from blaxploitation's iconography and ironically comments on it.

The trailer for *Amazing Grace* begins with a voice-over and scrolling text announcing "the motion picture debut of America's most talented, most beautiful, most exciting, most glamorous female superstar." This is followed by clips of Moms Mabley accompanied by a voice-over description of her character: "She's sweet, she's sexy, she's tough, she's tender, she's courageous, she's contagious, she's outrageous, she's Moms Mabley and she's Amazing in *Amazing Grace*." The trailer features the actors and cameo appearances including those of Butterfly McQueen and Stepin Fetchit. With a drawing of Mabley standing in the backseat of a Rolls Royce, arms outstretched, parading through a crowd of celebrating Black folks, the poster posited the film in the visual discourse of blaxploitation (and referenced posters for films such as *Sweet Jesus, Preacher Man*, *Cleopatra Jones*, *Black Caesar*, and *Come Back, Charleston Blue*), but the trailer based its rhetoric on ironic humor, where the "joke" is Mabley's age and feistiness.

At the time of the film's release, the press by and large announced it as the first starring role for Mabley. They were off by nearly thirty years: she had starred in the 1948 race film *Boarding House Blues*, directed by Josh Binney for All-American. (All-American also produced *Killer Diller* the same year, featuring Mabley and McQueen.) *Boarding House Blues* showcased Mabley's vaudeville-circuit comedy and captured her signature stances and expressions. Mabley runs a boardinghouse for entertainers and refers to the boarders as her children. In the concluding scene, in which the rent has been secured and the show can go on, she tells her lodgers, "When my children are happy, believe it make me feel good inside." Her invocation of an expansive adoptive view of maternal protection was a recurring comedy routine for Mabley, one that serves as the foundation for her role in *Amazing Grace*.

In contrast to the broad advertising aimed at a white/crossover audience, the studio took a different tack in marketing to black audiences. Mabley recorded a two-and-a-half-minute "sermon" distributed by United Artists' field agents across the country to churches and community and educational groups.[27] As reported by the *New Pittsburgh Courier*, an African American newspaper, this publicity tool emphasized "her new status as a motion picture star" and served as an invitation to audiences "of all ages and all groups."[28] Despite having suffered a heart attack on set, Mabley also traveled in the film's promotional tour and participated in a number of interviews to promote the film. For WGBH's black public-affairs program *Say Brother*, Mabley responded to the reporter's question about the difference between *Amazing Grace* and the "so-called black films that are out these days," stating that the difference is "day and night" and that her film is a family movie that audiences can take their children to see. As she says, "I wouldn't do anything [on the screen] that would hurt my children."[29] In the interview, she also emphasizes that she is "color blind": "I don't know the difference. I only know you're a human being, and you're my children."[30]

The critical reception of the film positioned it in the context of blaxploitation but also made its relation to black film history explicit. In reporting on the completion of the film's shooting, the *Chicago Defender* went so far as to suggest that *Amazing Grace* was a powerful corrective to the damage perpetrated by the proliferation of black action films. Reporting on the release of the film, the *Defender* described it as "an original screen super production that will lead to a possible solution of the black exploitation films."[31] Without critiquing the actor or mentioning his legacy, the paper reported, "'Step' was pleased to return to the screen in this kind of motion picture that places its emphasis on comedy rather than violence and the gross evil in the black community." The *Defender* lauded the film's "universal appeal" and its "mix [of] past and present cultural expressions."[32] Two things are particularly striking in the *Defender*'s article: how it squarely contextualizes the film against black exploitation films and how the attack on blaxploitation comes from black film history. The "mix" that the *Defender* refers to is a pithy way of referring to older and younger stars in a film together. Stepin Fetchit, referred to as "the legendary black film star," is particularly singled out as part of this project of recuperating black representation from the distortions of blaxploitation.[33] Upon the film's release, the *Defender*'s entertainment reporter Earl Calloway wrote, "Its emphasis differs from the novel presentation of overt sex and violence and centers its appeal in a beautiful, heartwarming story of affection for the opposite sex and a down-to-earth story of everyday people."[34] Calloway lauds the portrayal of the friendship between Slappy White's and Moms Mabley's characters, implying that the "affection" between these senior citizens serves as a corrective to the hypersexualized roles prevalent in blaxploitation.

Reporting on the film's premiere in Pittsburgh, Greg Mims wrote in the *New Pittsburgh Courier* that the film is "spotty" but is "one of the newer type Black oriented movies that are increasingly revealing our positive aspects as opposed to the exploitative rash of 'street dramas.'"[35] In the same article, Mims parenthetically reflects on meeting Stepin Fetchit at the premiere and Jim Brown at an event a week prior: "[Lincoln] Perry's visit gave this writer an opportunity to meet both the beginning (Perry) and new beginning (Brown) in Black film history."[36]

Fetchit appears twice in the film. In the first instance, he has a brief cameo at the start of the film as himself yet fictionalized as a cousin of Moms Mabley's character, Grace Teasdale Grimes. Grace is returning to Baltimore from a family reunion. Standing on the train platform, she is saying a lengthy goodbye to her relatives, much to the consternation of the conductor. Fetchit intervenes in a half-coherent ramble: "I think the lady, Grace, the VIP, said don't move that train. And also, until she finishes farewells to her family reunion relatives, I—her cousin Lincoln from the artistic archives of Hollywood as its first universal unique movie star—do hereby himself in person as Stepin Fetchit agrees with her that you don't move this train."[37]

Stepin Fetchit's reference to the "artistic archives of Hollywood" is an odd one and almost certainly ad libbed, but it makes sense for a film that mobilizes figures from African American film history as a means of dialoguing with contemporary black film culture. Fetchit himself was reportedly given this cameo by Matt Robinson, the film's writer and producer, when he was on set coaching Slappy White.[38] A loyal friend of the older actor, White facilitated Fetchit's entrée on the set, and once there, he lobbied for a role with "pestering determination," as Robinson recalls.[39] For the young writer and producer, Fetchit's cameo was motivated by the actor's venerable Hollywood legacy: "it would be a piece of history if I put him in this film."[40] The film's director, Stan Lathan, expressed more ambivalence:

> I was a product of the '60s. So "Stepin Fetchit" was synonymous in my mind with an Uncle Tom. And that's how I felt about Step when I first met him. But with Moms Mabley, Slappy White and Step, there was a lot of time spent on the set just reminiscing about the old days. And I began to realize the kind of career that Step had had and I gained a great respect for him. I considered him a wise old man. My whole feeling about him changed. The 1960's created symbols, many of them negative. And those of us who bought into them really were missing the big picture. Lincoln Perry became one of those people who I developed an admiration for. *Because* of his accomplishments.[41]

United Artists spun his appearance as a recuperative one. In its publicity material, it stated, "Fetchit agreed to appear in 'Amazing Grace' on one condition—that he be able to do something that he'd never been able to do in a film before.... 'I want to tell off a white man,' declared Stepin Fetchit with a wide grin."[42] While relatively mild, Cousin Lincoln's exchange with the train conductor might be the closest thing to a confrontation with a white man in Fetchit's career.

Fetchit also accompanied Mabley and the cast members on the promotional tour for the film. During the tour, he waged a campaign of self-recuperation in what one newspaper called a "bitter truth-telling session which stemmed from Fetchit's memories of a career he never had, and a place in black history, he's never been offered.... He is regarded by the current generation as an irrelevant, an Uncle Tom, a Coon buffoon."[43] Yet while celebrating Fetchit through this featured—albeit weird—cameo, *Amazing Grace* exhibits its own ambivalences about his representation of caricatures of blackness.

In Fetchit's second appearance in the film, he is represented through a crumpled and discarded flyer with his name in bold block letters and multiple images of what appear to be caricatures of him. The earlier cameo appearance presented Fetchit as both fictional and real: as Grace's cousin and as Lincoln Perry. These conflicting identities are reduced to a discarded flyer that Grace and Forthwith literally tromp on. The scene is a musically accompanied montage sequence in which Grace and Forthwith leave an unsuccessful rally for Welton J. Waters, their candidate for mayor of Baltimore.[44] (The film has a very loose narrative surrounding Grace's efforts to elect Waters mayor of Baltimore, all to showcase Moms Mabley's comedy). The flyer is on-screen for only a few seconds, hardly perceptible to a theatrical audience. Yet it is there, and the rather aggressive treatment it receives at the hands (or feet) of Slappy White and Moms Mabley is in a distinctly different tone than that of the opening cameo (and the cameo of Butterfly McQueen, who plays a friend of Grace). Moreover, the scene of Grace and Forthwith stepping on Stepin Fetchit's flyer is immediately followed by an altercation between Grace and Waters's wife, the not-so-subtly-named Creola (Rosalind Cash). In a self-loathing drunken rant, Creola taunts Grace for being poor. Grace threatens Creola, who balks, "Don't you dare put your hands on me," to which Grace replies, "I don't need no hands. I'm going to use my feet. Baby, I'm going to *stomp* you!" She then attacks Creola (and the camera/audience) and manages to pull off her wig, shaming Creola in front of a crowd of onlooking neighbors. In this sequence, Grace threatens Creola with stomping—but has already stomped on Stepin Fetchit.

If Mabley's character is the "authentic" foil to Creola's self-loathing social climber, similar to the way Moreland's counterman puts Gerber's bigotry into relief, then how is it to be understood in relation to Stepin Fetchit's cameo? As "cousin Lincoln," Fetchit plays Grace's kin just as the elderly actors shared a long

Stepin Fetchit's name and previous cinematic image are literally stepped on. (*"Moms" Mabley "Amazing Grace"* DVD, MGM Home Entertainment)

history in American entertainment. As Stepin Fetchit, however, he is the object of Grace's dismissive stomp. Unlike Moreland's position within *Watermelon Man*, *Amazing Grace* is deeply ambivalent about Stepin Fetchit, at once celebrating him as a performance legend and rejecting the kind of performance for which he was most famous. Through this ambivalence, the film mobilizes black film history as a way of navigating filmmaking in the wake of blaxploitation.

*Amazing Grace* is deeply imbued with a consciousness about its position as both a product of the 1970s black film boom and a work that draws from and showcases black performative talent from an earlier era. The mother-children relationship epitomized by "Moms" as an actor and performer is thematized in *Amazing Grace*, where the generational divide is bridged through the shared purpose of electing a black mayor of Baltimore. After a stern talking to from Grace, Welton J. Waters renounces his plan to be a stooge candidate for the white power interests and decides to run a sincere campaign, with Forthwith as his campaign manager and Grace as a kind of rally leader. Launching the campaign at Morgan State, Waters tells the students, "I was cured not by a radical movement, but by a lady who lives next door. *She* is what we all must be if we are to be anything." Grace then takes the podium and tells the students that they have the power to elect Waters. Yet the emphasis of her speech is on her relationship to the youth. In a break from the comedic tone of the film, she tearfully tells the students, "I ain't nothing but an old church sister, . . . but

Moms Mabley telling it like it is. (*"Moms" Mabley "Amazing Grace"* DVD, MGM Home Entertainment)

you Children are something else.... Y'all don't know me, but I'm your mother, honey.... You're *all* my children." And Grace tells the kids what to do. When one student resists becoming involved in the campaign, telling Grace, "I've got a revolution to deal with," she responds with a classic Moms jibe: "I'm going to revolution you if you don't do as I tell you to do." Forthwith follows up, "I know what you've got to do if you're going to call yourself Black, Negro, Colored or us." In a film so highly self-conscious about its references, the allusions to Mabley's legacy as a popular comedian function cross-textually with the contemporary climate of black filmmaking and its youth-oriented market. The generational rhetoric within the film is matched by the film's own generational ambivalences as a product of the black film boom whose leads and cameos are stars of a previous generation.

## *CAR WASH*: CRITIQUING THE "CLOWN SHOW"

Like *Watermelon Man* and *Amazing Grace*, *Car Wash* makes use of self-conscious cameos and casting choices that carry extrafilmic significance. In this film, chronicling a loose narrative structured around a day in the life of a Los Angeles car wash, much of the comedy works through the audience's recognition of figures such as George Carlin, Irwin Corey, the Pointer Sisters, and Richard Pryor. Universal pressured the producers to secure cameos, wanting marquee names for the film, and used Pryor's and Carlin's names and photos in subsequent advertising.[45] While these figures were contemporary stars, the appearance of Clarence Muse as Snapper, the car wash's shoeshine man, works differently. Regarding the casting of Muse, the film's director, Michael Schultz, emphasized his lengthy filmography, remarking, "that's incredible film history!"[46]

In the film's opening, Muse appears in four discrete vignettes made from single shots in the exposition.[47] He first appears when the boss, Mr. B. (Sully Boyar), arrives at the car wash in the morning with his would-be-leftist son Irwin (Richard Brestoff). Irwin greets Snapper (Muse) with a complicated handshake routine, described in the script as "a really jive, elaborate, cool, 'inside' handshake," which Snapper cannot follow, and Snapper responds, "I don't think I know that one."[48] The next shot that features Muse has him with Carlin asking about the prostitute that skipped out on Carlin's cab without paying the fare: "a big, tall, blond black chick," he says, emphasizing "blond black." The third shot shows Snapper kissing a framed portrait of Pryor before hanging it next to portraits of John F. Kennedy and Martin Luther King, Jr., positioned above his shoeshine stand. This shot is prior to the introduction of Pryor's character—Daddy Rich—so it is as if Muse were paying homage to the young comedian. The fourth vignette is a brief shot that shows him talking with Earl (Leonard Jackson), the car shiner, who tosses a coin in self-satisfaction.[49] This last shot prefigures Snapper's run-in with Earl shortly after the exposition. Snapper tells Earl he is on his way to see Slide (Garrett Morris), the numbers player, and wants Earl to play as well. Earl responds by calling him a fool for gambling. When Snapper retorts, "Who you calling fool? What makes you think you're so special?" Earl replies, "I'm the nigger who doesn't get wet around here. I'm the star." Snapper replies, "Just like me, shining, shining, only you stoop a lot lower, a lot lower."

In the scene featuring Pryor's cameo, Snapper is portrayed as a devoted disciple of Daddy Rich, a flamboyant televangelist modeled after Reverend Ike, a prominent prosperity preacher. Reverend Ike was slated to appear as himself but pulled out of the project at the last minute out of concern for his image.[50] Pryor was convinced (and generously paid) to do one day on set (and was talked into a second day).[51]

As Daddy Rich exits the car proclaiming, "Praise the Lord," Snapper is shown in close-up, with Daddy Rich's portrait over his shoulder, making a fist and saying, "Praise the Lord." The gesture of Black Power seems to contradict the verbal affirmation of allegiance to the preacher. This conflict embodied in the shot of Snapper is played out in the altercation between the Black radical

Abdullah (Bill Duke) and Daddy Rich. Snapper offers to shine Daddy Rich's shoes, and the preacher shares his goblet of wine with Snapper. Snapper tells Daddy Rich that ever since he has followed him, he got a new house and a color TV. Abdullah interjects, challenging the preacher and accusing him of making money off the poor and talking "just like a pimp." Snapper looks up at Daddy Rich and implores, "Answer him! Answer him, Lord!" The Pointer Sisters, as the Wilson Sisters, then challenge Abdullah in song while the chauffeur takes up a collection. As they sing, Daddy Rich comes down from the shoeshine pedestal as Snapper raises his fist again, looking to the heavens, repeating this contradictory gesture. As Daddy Rich and his entourage make their way back to their car, Abdullah retreats. As Daddy Rich drives off, he turns to Abdullah and tells him, "You've got it in you too, brother," and a reverse shot reveals Abdullah watching him drive off in scorn while Snapper looks on behind him. This connection between Abdullah and Snapper is reinforced in a subsequent scene in the locker room.

After Lonnie (Ivan Dixon) is visited by his parole officer and tells him not to bother him at work anymore, what seems to be extradiegetic music turns out to be a sound bridge to Abdullah playing the saxophone in the locker room, alone in the dark. As Abdullah plays, Snapper walks into the locker room in the background, hangs his jacket up in his locker, and listens. In addition to further linking Lonnie and Abdullah, and Abdullah and Snapper, this brief scene could be seen as a subtle homage to Larry Clark's *Passing Through*, in which Muse played Poppa Harris, a legendary jazz saxophonist.[52] In the script, there is extended dialogue between Snapper and Abdullah in which the older man tells the young would-be revolutionary that he is wasting his time in the car wash and that he should cultivate his talent. Abdullah responds bitterly, "I gave up my music for the 'Movement.' . . . No, the 'Movement' gave up." The script notes that "he is sad for a moment, then becomes bitter again." Abdullah tells Snapper, "An' don' you worry, ole man. . . . I wouldn' be here if my welfare hadn' run out." Snapper replies, "I used to know 'Bird,' . . . you know, Charlie Parker, . . . but all his friends used to called him 'Bird.' . . . So one day I says, 'Bird,' why don't you . . ." Abdullah tells him, "Cut the shit. . . . I'm sick of your mouth, . . . all the time shootin' off how you know this one and that one." Snapper insists that he did know the musician, but Abdullah retorts, "Yeah . . . then how come you shinin' shoes in a chicken shit car wash," and then storms out of the locker room.[53] The script indicates that "Snapper is hurt and confused." And he is then comforted by Lonnie, who tells him that Abdullah "didn' mean nothin'."[54] Muse's presence in the role of Snapper changes the scene. Instead of an extended dialogue about an elderly man's past as a jazz insider, we get a quiet portrait of the senior actor as a solitary saxophonist.

The studio executives hated the ending of *Car Wash*, insisting that comedy and drama could not mix.[55] But Schultz wanted the film to explore "the reality of the characters; they weren't just clowns."[56] At the end of the day, Abdullah confronts Lonnie with a gun, holding him up for the cash in the office safe. Lonnie talks him out of robbing the car wash, and the scene ends with a monologue Abdullah delivers to Lonnie: "It's all falling apart. I don't know, man, I don't know. I know I'm not crazy, but every day I have to come here and watch this clown show. Sometimes I just can't take it." The scene works doubly. Just as Abdullah complains to Lonnie about the "clown show" of the car wash, we can read this scene as Ivan Dixon serving as confidant to Bill Duke's criticism of the film itself. In this sense, the conclusion of *Car Wash* is a self-conscious critique of a "clown show" that reads as a critique of Hollywood's proliferation of blaxploitation titles. As Lonnie tells Abdullah that he will be with him and he is not alone, Ivan Dixon is also telling Bill Duke that he is with him. It is a discussion between an established director (Dixon directed the subversive *The Spook Who Sat by the Door*, 1973) and an aspiring one (Duke went on to become an accomplished director of films such as *The Killing Floor*, 1985; *A Rage in Harlem*, 1991; and the documentary *Dark Girls*, 2011). Schultz films Dixon and Duke as two men working in Hollywood (both in film and television) who share a moment of mutual distain for the "clown show" that surrounds them.

## CONCLUSION: BLAXPLOITATION AND HISTORIOGRAPHY

Along with the surge in black-themed films, the 1970s saw a proliferation in the publication of Black film histories: Jim Pines's *Blacks in the Cinema: The Changing Image* (1971), followed up with Pines's *Blacks in Films: A Survey of Racial Themes and Images in the American Film* (1975), Edward Mapp's *Blacks in American Films: Today and Yesterday* (1972), Donald Bogle's *Toms, Coons, Mulattoes, Mammies, and Bucks: An Interpretive History of Blacks in American Films* (1973), Daniel Leab's *From Sambo to Superspade: The Black Experience in Motion Pictures* (1975), Henry Sampson's *Blacks in Black and White: A Source Book on Black Films* (1977), Thomas Cripps's *Slow Fade to Black: The Negro in American Film, 1900–1942* (1977), and Cripps's follow-up *Black Film as Genre* (1978). While these texts are very different projects, they all address issues related to Hollywood's vexed history of representing blackness and the myriad ways in which performers worked within and against Hollywood's hegemonic parameters of signification. It is certainly not surprising that these studies came out during the black film boom of the 1970s. The academic interest in black film history and historiography found a parallel in black-themed films themselves and their interest in black film history, in particular from films directed by African Americans. Van Peebles, Lathan, and Schultz tap into the living legacies of black film history as a means of confronting the contemporary climate of African American cinema. Yet instead of a nostalgic or recuperative gesture, their casting of older actors in cameo roles is a critical assertion of a break from the past (represented by the figures and the legacies they bring to their cameos). It is also a critique of the contemporary popular film culture surrounding blaxploitation (demonstrated in how the figures are mobilized in the films).

This chapter argues that black film culture of the 1970s, as much as it engaged with the contemporary urban environment and the social and political issues that define the films of this period, was highly aware of its precedents. With these films' enactment of the confrontation of the past and present, youth and elders, they function as palimpsests of multiple narratives of the past. They are self-consciously in dialogue with these references, mobilizing them as part of a self-situating critique within the broader scope of 1970s black cinema. While much of the grounding rhetoric of 1970s black film culture points to cultural nationalism of the time, there was a concurrent interest in black film history at the same moment of the boom in black action-film production and the studios' discovery of the power of black box office. Black film culture of the 1970s mobilized its history as a way of negotiating blaxploitation and its attendant representational problematics. In this sense, blaxploitation—in the very broadest sense of the term—is a discourse and a mode that becomes the locus of black film historiography.

## NOTES

1. Columbia interoffice communication from Seymour Steinberg to Peter Guber, April 23, 1969, *Watermelon Man*, Billy Gordon Papers, Margaret Herrick Library, Academy of Motion Pictures Arts and Sciences, Beverly Hills, CA.
2. Ed Guerrero, *Framing Blackness: The African American Image in Film* (Philadelphia: Temple University Press, 1993), 69.
3. Junius Griffin, "Black Movie Boom: Good or Bad?," *New York Times*, December 17, 1972, D3.
4. Junius Griffin, quoted in "Blacks vs. Shaft," *Newsweek*, August 28, 1972, 88.
5. Roy Innis, "A Joke on Blacks?," *New York Times*, December 17, 1972, D19.

6. Paula Massood identifies a "presentness" in blaxploitation films and the way in which Black urban spaces are presented as "an entirely *contemporary* phenomenon." See Massood, *Black City Cinema: African American Urban Experiences in Film* (Philadelphia: Temple University Press, 2003), 88.
7. The star of these Race Westerns, Herb Jeffries, also enjoyed a resurgence in the 1970s with *Chrome and Hot Leather* (1971) and *Portrait of a Hitman* (1979) in addition to fairly regular work in television.
8. Donald Bogle, *Toms, Coons, Mulattoes, Mammies, and Bucks: An Interpretive History of Blacks in American Films*, 4th ed. (New York: Continuum, 2003), 41.
9. Charlene Regester, "Stepin Fetchit: The Man, the Image, and the African American Press," *Film History* 6, no. 4 (1994): 502.
10. Bogle, *Toms, Coons, Mulattoes, Mammies, and Bucks*, 41.
11. Mel Watkins, *Stepin Fetchit: The Life and Times of Lincoln Perry* (New York: Vintage Books, 2005), 86–87.
12. Bogle, *Toms, Coons, Mulattoes, Mammies, and Bucks*, 71.
13. Ibid., 55–56.
14. Joseph McBride and Stepin Fetchit, "Stepin Fetchit Talks Back," *Film Quarterly* 24, no. 4 (1971): 20.
15. Huey P. Newton, "He Won't Bleed Me: A Revolutionary Analysis of *Sweet Sweetback's Baadasssss Song*," *Black Panther Intercommunal News Service*, June 19, 1971.
16. Bogle, *Toms, Coons, Mulattoes, Mammies, and Bucks*, 41, 72, 53.
17. Day out of Days ledger for *Watermelon Man*, Billy Gordon Papers.
18. Racquel Gates, "The Subversive Politics and Production of Melvin Van Peebles' *Watermelon Man*," *Film Quarterly* 68, no. 1 (2014): 18.
19. *Watermelon Man* (handwritten over: "Mirror, Mirror"), screenplay by Herman Raucher, Final draft August 6, 1969, 73, Margaret Herrick Library.
20. Jack Atlas to Joe Ansen, December 17, 1969, *Watermelon Man*, Jack Atlas Papers, Margaret Herrick Library. Emphasis added.
21. Ibid.
22. Ibid.
23. Julia Leyda, "Black-Audience Westerns and the Politics of Cultural Identification in the 1930s," *Cinema Journal* 42, no. 1 (2002): 59.
24. Jacqueline Najuma Stewart, *Migrating to the Movies: Cinema and Black Urban Modernity* (Berkeley: University of California Press, 2005), 101.
25. Ibid., 113.
26. Gates, "Subversive Politics," 21n42.
27. "New Moms Mabley Disc Produced for 'Grace,'" *New Pittsburgh Courier*, August 17, 1974, 18.
28. Ibid.
29. *Say Brother*, episode 428, WGBH, June 12, 1975.
30. Ibid.
31. "'Moms' Mabley Finishes Film," *Chicago Defender*, October 6, 1973, 25.
32. Ibid.

33. Ibid.; and Earl Calloway, "'Moms' Mabley, Stepin' Fetchit Star in 'Amazing Grace,'" *Chicago Defender*, December 15, 1973, 20.
34. Earl Calloway, "Moms Mabley Makes Mirth in New Movie," *Chicago Defender*, June 1, 1974, A3.
35. Greg Mims, "Steel City Turns Out for 'Amazing Grace,'" *New Pittsburgh Courier*, June 29, 1974, 18.
36. Ibid.
37. In the July 1973 revised script by Matt Robinson, there is no reference to Cousin Lincoln. Margaret Herrick Library.
38. "'Moms' Mabley Finishes Film," 25.
39. Matt Robinson, unpublished interview with Mel Watkins, quoted in Watkins, *Stepin Fetchit*, 274–75. Robinson later wrote a play, *The Confessions of Stepin Fetchit*, which premiered at the American Place Theater in New York in 1993, directed by Bill Lathan and featuring Roscoe Orman.
40. Quoted in Watkins, *Stepin Fetchit*, 274.
41. Champ Clark, *Shuffling to Ignominy: The Tragedy of Stepin Fetchit* (Lincoln, NE: iUniverse, 2005), 126–27.
42. Ibid., 131.
43. Greg Mims, "Stepin Fetchit Voices Anger over Rip-Offs," *New Pittsburgh Courier*, August 24, 1974, 1, 3.
44. In the July 1973 revised script by Matt Robinson, there is no mention of the walk home.
45. Michael Schultz Q&A, UCLA Film & Television Archive, July 15, 2011.
46. Ibid.
47. I delineate the exposition as the opening through the theme song, *Car Wash*, as the car wash opens and the workday begins. Muse can also be seen in the background setting up his shoeshine stand as the employees come from the locker room and head to work. He looks up from the stand to watch Floyd and Lloyd practice their dance routine as they proceed to the wash.
48. Third draft screenplay by Joel Schumacher, 10, Margaret Herrick Library.
49. In the script, Snapper has dialogue in which he tells Earl that he has been in that spot for fifteen years—"I seen 'em all.... All come an' go"—and Earl ignores Snapper's musings. Ibid., 16.
50. Michael Schultz Q&A.
51. Larry Clark recalls that Muse, a perfectionist, told Michael Schultz, "Tell that son of a bitch, Pryor, if he don't get it on the first take I'm a leave. You know, I'm not going to be doing take 25 like he does." Clark recalls, "So on the day that they're going to shoot, Pryor's sweating bullets. And they get it on the first take. Pryor's happy, Clarence is happy, everybody's happy." Larry Clark, oral history interview with Michael Schultz by Jan-Christopher Horak and Jacqueline Stewart, June 2, 2010, L.A. Rebellion Oral History Project, UCLA Film & Television Archive.
52. Though the film was not completed and released until 1977, Larry Clark's *Passing Through* began filming prior to Clarence Muse's appearance in *Car Wash* and

following his role in *Buck and the Preacher* (1972), in which Muse appeared with Pamela Jones, who also starred in *Passing Through*. Jones suggested Muse to Clark for the role of Poppa Harris. Ibid.
53. Third draft screenplay by Joel Schumacher, 65.
54. Ibid., 64–65.
55. Michael Schultz Q&A.
56. Ibid.

## WORKS CITED

"Blacks vs. Shaft." *Newsweek*, August 28, 1972.
Bogle, Donald. *Toms, Coons, Mulattoes, Mammies, and Bucks: An Interpretive History of Blacks in American Film*. 4th ed. New York: Continuum, 2003.
Calloway, Earl. "Moms Mabley Makes Mirth in New Movie." *Chicago Defender*, June 1, 1974.
———. "'Moms' Mabley, Stepin Fetchit Star in 'Amazing Grace.'" *Chicago Defender*, December 15, 1973.
Clark, Camp. *Shuffling to Ignominy: The Tragedy of Stepin Fetchit*. Lincoln, NE: iUniverse, 2005.
Gates, Racquel. "The Subversive Politics and Production of Melvin Van Peebles' *Watermelon Man*." *Film Quarterly* 68, no. 1 (2014): 9–21.
Griffin, Junius. "Black Movie Boom: Good or Bad?" *New York Times*, December 17, 1972.
Guerrero, Ed. *Framing Blackness: The African American Image in Film*. Philadelphia: Temple University Press, 1993.
Innis, Roy. "A Joke on Blacks?" *New York Times*, December 17, 1972.
Leyda, Julia. "Black-Audience Westerns and the Politics of Cultural Identification in the 1930's." *Cinema Journal* 42, no. 1 (2002): 46–70.
Massood, Paula. *Black City Cinema: African American Urban Experiences in Film*. Philadelphia: Temple University Press, 2003.
McBride, Joseph, and Stepin Fetchit. "Stepin Fetchit Talks Back." *Film Quarterly* 24, no. 4 (1971): 20–26.
Mims, Greg. "Steel City Turns Out for 'Amazing Grace.'" *New Pittsburgh Courier*, June 29, 1974.
———. "Stepin Fetchit Voices Anger over Rip-Offs." *New Pittsburgh Courier*, August 24, 1974.
"'Moms' Mabley Finishes Film." *Chicago Defender*, October 6, 1973.
"New Moms Mabley Disc Produced for 'Grace.'" *New Pittsburgh Courier*, August 17, 1974.
Newton, Huey P. "He Won't Bleed Me: A Revolutionary Analysis of *Sweet Sweetback's Baadasssss Song*." *Black Panther Intercommunal News Service*, June 19, 1971.

Regester, Charlene. "Stepin Fetchit: The Man, the Image, and the African American Press." *Film History* 6, no. 4 (1994): 502–21.

Stewart, Jacqueline Najuma. *Migrating to the Movies: Cinema and Black Urban Modernity*. Berkeley: University of California Press, 2005.

Watkins, Mel, *Stepin Fetchit: The Life and Times of Lincoln Perry*. New York: Vintage Books, 2005.

# 9

# NORMAN . . . IT'S NOT ABOUT YOU

## DECENTERING BLACK GAYNESS IN *NORMAN . . . IS THAT YOU?*

### ALFRED L. MARTIN, JR.

HISTORICALLY AND CULTURALLY, BLACK-CAST FILM OF THE 1970S IS most often tightly connected to the blaxploitation cycle. While Ed Guerrero suggests that the cycle we collectively call blaxploitation existed between 1969 and 1974, smaller/independent filmmakers and production companies were producing black-cast films that *could* be subsumed into the categorization throughout the 1970s.[1] However, between 1969 and 1974, black-cast films were produced that were decidedly *not* blaxploitation films, including *Lady Sings the Blues* (1972), *Sounder* (1972), *Mahogany* (1975), and *The Bingo Long Traveling All-Stars and Motor Kings* (1976). In the interest of moving "beyond blaxploitation," as the title of this volume suggests, I am more interested in a film that is not often considered within the movement, the 1976 film *Norman . . . Is That You?* The media attention given to blaxploitation films meant that every black-cast film of the era was impacted by the movement.

Released September 29, 1976, *Norman* is based on a play with the same title written by Ron Clark and Sam Bobrick. The play and film deal with a couple coming to terms with the fact that their son is gay. More specifically, the comedic stage play is concerned with a Jewish couple who travel to New York and upon arrival discover that their son is gay. Attempting to capitalize on the popularity of the blaxploitation movement, the film version, like several other black-cast films in the 1970s, "blackened" "white" source material, as had *Dracula/Blacula* and *Little Caesar/Black Caesar*. In addition to utilizing a black cast, the location was shifted from New York to Hollywood.

Unlike many of the aforementioned films, *Norman* was more industrially scrutinized because it dealt with homosexuality—a topic that was still taboo in 1976 and arguably still is today. Upon initial review, the Motion Picture Association of America (MPAA) gave the film an R rating. However, MGM execs and the film's producer successfully appealed the rating, with the board ultimately agreeing that "the plot's primary premise of youthful homosexuality did not require parental presence when being watched, which was the reason the Code and rating Administration had put an initial R tag on the film."[2] Despite the film's more lenient PG rating, it was nonetheless condemned by several religious organizations, including the U.S. Catholic Conference, which lambasted *Norman* for its "treatment of homosexuality and its 'contempt' for parental authority."[3]

I am interested in *Norman* for three reasons. First, unlike the films historically categorized within the blaxploitation cycle, *Norman* was a star vehicle for Redd Foxx, who at the time was a hot commodity in Hollywood because of his hit NBC series, *Sanford and Son* (1972–77), and Pearl Bailey, the celebrated stage and screen star (and UN ambassador). The inclusion of two high-profile black celebrities gestured toward the increasing import of celebrity-driven fare in the 1970s as the film industry was clawing its way out of financial catastrophe. Second, like films within the blaxploitation movement, *Norman* was made quickly on a meager (by Hollywood standards) budget of $1 million. In order to accommodate such a budget, the director, George Schlatter, "scheduled only three days of rehearsals before the twelve-day shoot commenced on Stage 22" of the MGM lot.[4] Ultimately, the film went on to gross more than $3.2 million.[5] Third, the film is the first mainstream black-cast film to deal explicitly with black gayness. While blaxploitation films including *Sweet Sweetback's Baadasssss Song* (1971), *Blacula* (1972), and *Friday Foster* (1975) include black gay characters, often as tertiary to the central narrative, *Norman* attempts to narratively center black gayness. *Norman* does not simply feature a few scenes in which black gayness is an "issue"; rather, the black gay character serves a central narrative function. Certainly, black gayness had appeared outside the blaxploitation movement before *Norman*, most notably in *The Boys in the Band* (1970). However, *The Boys in the Band* was largely billed as a "gay film," whereas *Norman*, because of its stars, was simply released and marketed as a black-cast film.

This chapter focuses on *Norman* and its duplicitous approach to black gayness in the 1970s. On one hand, the film's narrative hinges on homosexuality— a first for a black-cast film. On the other hand, the film decenters gayness, ultimately making *Norman* a tale of parents coming to terms with the fact that their son is gay. I examine the film as a sitcom, arguing that the structure of the film resembles the way sitcoms of the 1970s engaged with homosexuality via the "Coming-Out Episode." Additionally, I use the black press to examine the ways in which magazine articles sought to distance Michael Warren, who portrays Norman, from his character in order to reify the notion that Warren is only donning gayface to play the character. Lastly, I examine the ways that the film, while decentering gayness, also seeks to position black homosexuality as inherently antiblack.

## BLACKNESS AND GAYNESS IN 1970S HOLLYWOOD

At the end of the 1960s, as Hollywood entered a period categorized as "New American Cinema," many films, like *The Graduate* (1967) and *Bonnie and Clyde* (1967), began to engage with the American sexual revolution by including sexuality, profanity, and nudity, partially in a bid to attract younger audiences to the movies. Included in this "wave" of more sexualized films were a small number of gay-themed movies including *Reflections in a Golden Eye* (1967) and *The Detective* (1968). Unsurprisingly given the social climate in which these films were released, many of them did not generate stellar box-office returns and were largely unsellable (initially) in television syndication, because their content was deemed too taboo for TV. The continued poor box-office performance of many of these films only added to Hollywood's financial struggles. For a short time in the early 1970s, following the box-office success of *Sweet Sweetback's Baadasssss Song* and *Shaft*, Hollywood became interested in a movement of film that ultimately came to be called blaxploitation.

Several black-cast films that centered on so-called positive images of black men and women were produced and distributed by major studios. Chief among these films were many of the motion pictures produced by Motown Productions, including *Lady Sings the Blues* (1972), *Mahogany* (1975), and *The Bingo Long Traveling All-Stars and Motor Kings*. While two of these Motown Productions starred Diana Ross, the then–Queen of Motown and arbiter of crossover appeal, the films, excepting *Lady Sings the Blues*, were largely understood as being for black audiences. These films and others, like *Sounder*, underscore the utility of the star system within Hollywood broadly and black Hollywood specifically. Diana Ross was the "draw" for the films in which she starred, while Billy Dee Williams (having been made a black leading man and heartthrob via *Lady Sings the Blues* and *Mahogany*) starred in *The Bingo Long Traveling All-Stars and Motor Kings*.

In addition, Cicely Tyson, known for her work on the groundbreaking series *Eastside/Westside* (1963–64), was the star of *Sounder*.

While it is a mistake to suggest that gay characters suddenly appeared in the 1970s, the decade certainly marked a turn in gay media visibility. Part of the increase in gay visibility in film can be credited to the Production Code Administration's 1961 decision to lift the prohibition on "sexual perversion," which was interpreted to broadly signify homosexuality.[6] One of the benefactors of this alteration was the 1969 film *Midnight Cowboy*. Centered on the relationship between a hustler and his roommate, *Midnight Cowboy* ultimately won three Academy Awards including Best Picture, Best Screenplay, and Best Director. Underscoring Hollywood's "star" strategy, the film starred Dustin Hoffman, who was a hot Hollywood commodity following his work in *The Graduate*, and Jon Voigt. While the film is not necessarily a "gay" film, Harry Benshoff and Sean Griffin suggest that because the relationship between the two men is the only "genuine expression of love" within *Midnight Cowboy*, it can and should be read as a gay film.[7]

However, the film that has been most enduring in histories of gay visibility in cinema, *The Boys in the Band*, was released at the beginning of the decade and included one black gay character within its ensemble cast. The film, which focuses on a group of gay men in New York dealing with love and life, seems a strange movie given that no films that could *really* be considered queer cinema emerged until the 1990s. However, as Benshoff and Griffin note, given Hollywood's financial doldrums, the industry was willing to try anything as it was looking for its "missing audience"—much of which was lost as television rose in stature as a source of home entertainment.[8]

While *The Boys in the Band* included a token black gay character, such characters were not wholly excluded from black film of the 1970s either. Several blaxploitation films included black gay characters in relatively tertiary roles, including *Sweetback*, *Blacula*, and *Friday Foster*. While Joe Wlodarz asserts that "blaxploitation films are notable for the ways they frequently situate 'normative' black male identity amongst a variety of ideological 'others' (women, homosexuals, other ethnicities) whose presence cannot simply be seen to solidify black manhood," I see the presence of these black gay men serving exactly that purpose.[9] These stereotyped effeminate characters in blaxploitation films serve to prop up and reify "proper" black masculinity. However, because I would not classify *Norman . . . Is That You?* as a blaxploitation film, what does the film do with its black gay body? I argue that the film's use of black gayness is to underscore the narrative growth of its heterosexual axial character, Ben Chambers.

## NEXT TO *NORMAN*: SITCOM STRUCTURE AND DECENTERING HOMOSEXUALITY

> It's easier to approach otherwise serious subject matter through the use of comedy.
> —Michael Warren in an interview with *Ebony* magazine[10]

Hollywood generally, and black Hollywood specifically, traffics in narratives that center heterosexuality. This is what makes the appearance of *Norman* so queer. I use "queer" here in the sense that it is odd that in the late 1970s, Hollywood would produce and broadly distribute a film that appears to center gayness in its main narrative story line. The title of the film, *Norman . . . Is That You?*, very clearly articulates that the question is being posed from an outside source (in this case, Norman's father, Ben), thus foreclosing on the notion that the film might focus on gayness within its narrative. In contrast to *The Boys in the Band*, which narratively centers the gay "boys" referenced in the title, *Norman*'s title suggests that to the "speaker," Norman is illegible. Put another way, as the speaker (ostensibly Ben Chambers) asks, "Norman . . . is that you?" Norman is understood as so far out of step with how this "old-fashioned man" understands the cultural and social scripts laid out for black men that he is unrecognizable.

Importantly, I argue that *Norman* uses the sitcom's narrative structure, importing it into the cinematic form. Certainly, the sitcom is one of the first places where the "other" appears. As the Michael Warren quote that opens this section underscores, when serious subject matter is placed within the comedic form, it is more palatable for the viewer. Therefore, it is not surprising that *Norman* employs the "Coming-Out Episode" model of 1970s televisual gayness to make the film into a kind of parable about homosexuality. The "Coming-Out Episode," as defined by Stephen Tropiano, typically concerns "a series regular who learns someone in his or her life . . . is gay, lesbian, bisexual or transgender."[11] As an illumination of this kind of episode, I turn to the short-lived 1977 series *Sanford Arms*, a spin-off of the long-running *Sanford and Son* and the first black-cast sitcom to feature a black gay character. In the series's third episode, "Phil's Assertion School," the secondary story line concerns a series regular, Angie, who is dating an attorney named Travis. While Angie is aware that Travis is gay, what makes this a coming-out episode is that Travis must ultimately reveal his homosexuality to the other lead (black male) characters so that they can "come to terms with his gayness." Ultimately, the episode, like all coming-out episodes, has little to do with Travis's gayness per se but how others will react to or accept the episodic gayness.

Extending this concept to *Norman*, the film is concerned with the detection and discovery of homosexuality, rather than the inner workings of homosexuality and homosexual relationships. I extend Lynne Joyrich's scholarship on gayness in television to film. In her work, she suggests that televisual gay representation is often concerned with the ways heterosexuals can detect/discover gay narrative interlopers.[12] Typically, the first act presents the players that audiences are supposed to care about, laying out the situation or, put more simply, the first act or the exposition. Much like the opening credits of a sitcom with its theme music and cast introductions, the opening credits serve as the exposition for *Norman*. Particularly, as the opening credits roll, a montage of shots featuring Ben Chambers as he takes a bus trip to Hollywood to visit his son, Norman (although the viewer is not privy to this information as the credits unfold), helps situate viewers within the narrative. The visual imagery and soundtrack are important here. Images of Ben Chambers are most prominent. As he is on the bus en route to Hollywood, Chambers is the only black man. In this way, the soundtrack can be read in three ways. As Smokey Robinson sings/narrates that Redd Foxx is an "old-fashioned man" in a "brand-new world," this world Ben inhabits *could* be read as placing Ben in a post-civil-rights era when segregation of black people from white people is no longer legally institutionalized. As the fraternization between the races on a bus to Hollywood occurs, we *might* be tempted to read this "brand-new world" as one concerned with race. In addition, we *might* interpret this new world as Hollywood, as Ben is supposed to be from Tucson, Arizona. Spaces like Tucson are mediated as wholly out of step with cosmopolitanism. However, I posit a third potential reading: this new world refers to his son's homosexuality as well as the "brand-new world" that has taken hold since the turbulent 1960s. Chief among these changes is the emergence of the gay-rights movement and the Stonewall riots. This reading is further underscored by the song lyrics, as they suggest that Ben is an "old-fashioned man" who is "trying to understand things he's not about" and that he is "lost in time in a place we left behind." Most important, the song's lyrics suggests that whatever viewpoints Ben holds are wholly old-fashioned. However, Ben is positioned as the axial character of the film, the one whose perspective viewers are instructed to privilege. Even as he is "old-fashioned," his viewpoint is the one to which black viewers are supposed to identify, because, presumably, black viewers also hold "old-fashioned" viewpoints with respect to homosexuality. As the song is meant to set the tone for the film (as opening credits/music do) and ease the viewer into the narrative world they

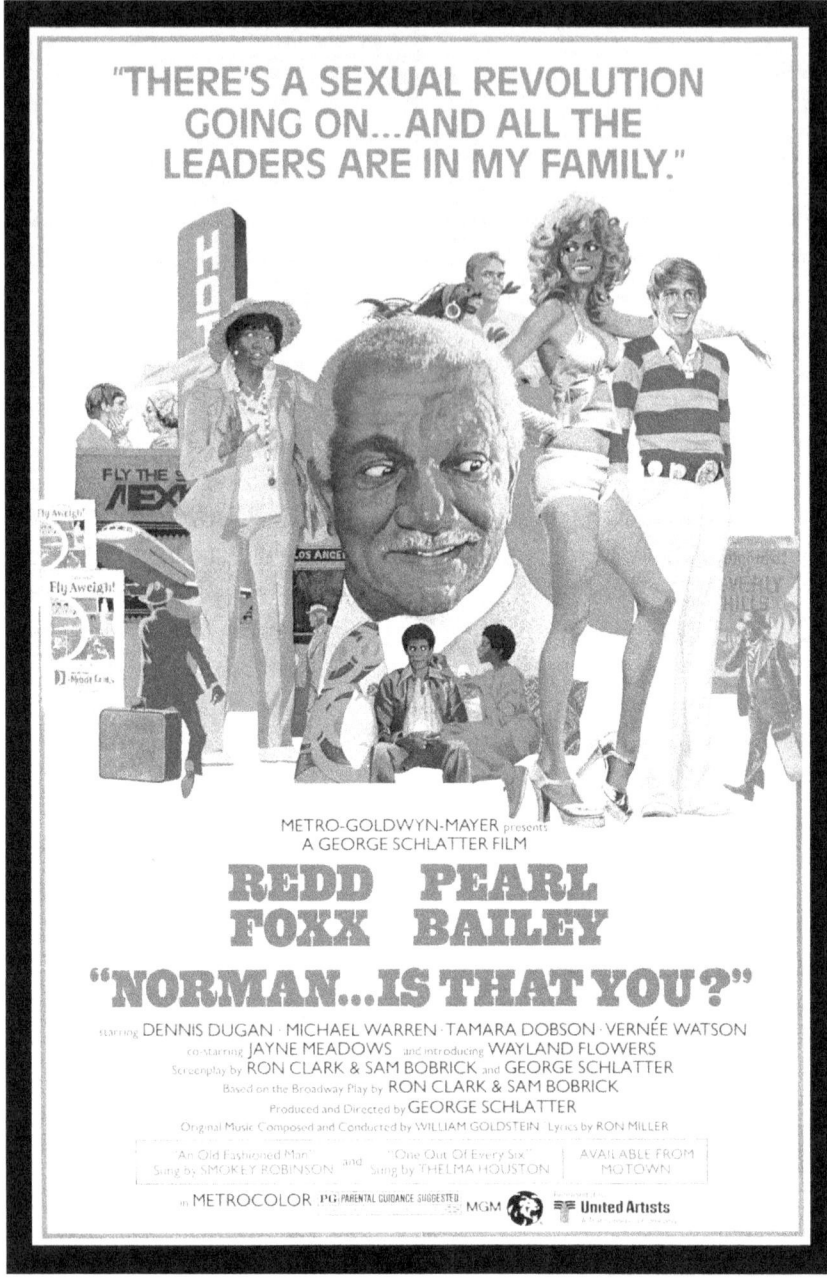

The promotional material for Norman both literally and figuratively centers the Ben Chambers character (Redd Foxx), rendering the gay character that the film allegedly focuses on to the margins. (Gerald Martinez, Diana Martinez, and Andres Chavez, *What It Is . . . What It Was! The Black Film Explosion of the 1970s in Words and Pictures* [New York: Hyperion, 1998])

will inhabit for approximately the next ninety minutes, the song immediately provides aural cues that something will undoubtedly be queer about the space to which Ben is traveling. The promotional material for *Norman* also centers the Ben Chambers character (Redd Foxx) both literally and figuratively.

*Norman*'s narrative arc, like that of the thirty-minute sitcom "Coming-Out Episode," is concerned with a series star (in this case, Foxx's Ben Chambers) discovering that someone he knows (his son, Norman) is gay. This is the nexus of the second act, or "complication." Within *Norman*'s narrative universe, we should understand the "complication" of the narrative as being unconcerned with gayness per se but rather with the detection and discovery of homosexuality. Importantly, the first scene within the second act hinges on a kind of hiding. Once Ben rings the doorbell at Norman's apartment, the camera cuts to the interior, where Norman is sleeping with an unknown person who is covered from head to toe with a blanket. As Norman attempts to stall his father's entry into his apartment, he runs back and forth between the bedroom and the front door, attempting to wake his still-unidentified lover. When Norman returns to his bedroom, his first line of dialogue, which is gender neutral and does not mention his lover's name, is, "We finally got caught. Get up! Come on, please! My dad is downstairs." This dialogue suggests a detection and discovery of Norman's heretofore-undisclosed gayness. While the first central conflict in the film is rooted in the detection and discovery of gayness, it is mostly concerned with how Ben will react to the "news" versus Norman's comfort within his own skin as a black gay man, who, according to his father, went to Hollywood to "find himself." Importantly, Norman is not in Los Angeles, or California generally, but in Hollywood, which is historically positioned as a liberal space where "anything goes." Next, the camera pans to a tight close-up to reveal that Norman's partner is a white man. The dialogue, in concert with the cinematic language, presents a "reveal" meant to surprise the audience. This is particularly true because Norman (and Michael Warren, the actor portraying him) does not display the markers audiences have been trained to use to read gayness. Unlike the "militant queen" in *Sweet Sweetback* or Ford Malotte from *Friday Foster*, Norman does not "look" and/or "sound" gay. Although it is later revealed that Norman works as a window dresser, the lisping speech pattern and otherwise "incorrectly feminine" behaviors that are often associated with gay men are absent from Norman.[13] Therefore, his gayness is illegible to a populace that has been instructed to read gayness in particular ways.

Furthermore, *Norman* employs none of the "gay pride" rhetoric that became popular in a post-Stonewall era; rather, Norman's homosexuality is shrouded in shame. He has been in a relationship with Garson for at least a year, yet while they have been "playing house," Norman is not ready to disclose his relationship to his parents. He even goes so far as to order Garson to temporarily move out of the apartment they share in order to keep his sexuality secret. This positioning of a "secret sexuality" sets the stage for the discovery that is imperative in the "Coming-Out Episode." Importantly, the discovery is not about Norman "discovering" that he is gay; rather, the heterosexual axial character must discover the character's "deviant" sexuality.

Although Ben has been using innuendo-laden words like "closet" and "lavender" to provide humor to the knowing audience, he does not discover Norman's homosexuality until roughly a third of the way through the movie. The "discovery" occurs when Garson returns to the apartment that he shares with Norman to pack his belongings while Ben attempts to track down his wife and brother in Mexico. As Garson attempts to leave the apartment with his clothes in a suitcase, including a silk robe thought to be a woman's robe, Ben asks why Garson is taking Norman's girlfriend's clothes. Garson answers, "I am she." Aside from the obvious gender inversion, which reifies heteronormative understandings of same-sex relationships, the "discovery" of Norman's homosexuality leads Ben on an introspective quest to understand and process the information he has received. In this way, like the sitcom, *Norman* employs a heterosexist gaze—a gaze preoccupied with recentering heterosexuality to explore how straight men come to "accept" this new information. Ben spends the next several minutes in the film going to a bookstore to look for books on "fairies" to help him understand homosexuality broadly and his son's homosexuality specifically. The use of derogatory words for homosexuality like "fairy" helps to underscore the ways the film is wholly unconcerned with exploring the contours of 1970s gayness; rather, *Norman* cares about centering heterosexuality. In this way, *Norman* utilizes its title character's homosexuality as a narrative hook to explore heterosexuality. In addition, to underscore the "horrors" of homosexuality, Ben suggests that he would rather have Norman be a drug addict than gay.

Many of the prerelease reviews provide synopses of the film that immediately decenter homosexuality. In a *Variety* review, the film is described as starring "Redd Foxx and Pearl Bailey as the perplexed and estranged parents of a gay son and his white lover."[14] Aside from syntactically making little sense (how can Foxx and Bailey be estranged parents of a gay son and his white lover?), the opening of this *Variety* review accomplishes two things. Aside from centering heterosexuality and the "effect" gayness has on heteronormativity, it immediately attempts to tether whiteness and gayness, which then positions gayness among black men as antiblack. Homosexuality is abjected from an "authentic" blackness because it is constructed as "the white man's disease."[15] In other words, homosexuality is antiblack. Black gayness is positioned as a threat to the legitimacy and respectability of blackness generally and black masculinity specifically. As Marlon Riggs succinctly puts it, "A strong, proud, 'Afrocentric' black man is resolutely heterosexual, not *even* bisexual."[16]

Additionally, one of the film's promotional posters declares, "There's a sexual revolution going on . . . and all the leaders are in my family," which, while also a line of dialogue from the film, as a piece of advertising, underscores and centers Ben's voice and (hetero)normativity. While this declaration also refers to his "deviant" wife, Beatrice, who has embarked on an affair with Ben's brother, because the film is titled *Norman . . . Is That You?*, this provides a semiotic linkage between the sexual revolution (understood here as gay rights) and Norman. This is particularly true because most synopses of the film do not mention Beatrice's sexual indiscretions, only Norman's homosexuality. *Ebony* magazine's Louie Robinson begins his five-page feature on the film thusly: "Take one distraught ex-marine father, one unfaithful wife, one homosexual son, and one—charming and gay—in every sense of the word—meddler in family affairs and you have the near perfect ingredients for Redd Foxx's first starring movie."[17] The sentence begins with Ben Chambers's feelings of distress and ends with Redd Foxx as the "star" of the film. As such, as a film that is ostensibly understood as broaching the topic of homosexuality within black culture, it is read as a film that is about homosexuality as an interloper into the sanctity of the heteronormative, hegemonic understanding of the idealized black family. This treatment of homosexuality is similar to the way black gayness was treated in a 1977 episode of *Sanford Arms* titled "Phil's Assertion School." This continues to be the case on the rare occasions that black-cast sitcoms deal with the "problem" of black homosexuality. In addition, the gay "meddler in family affairs" is actually Norman's partner, who by definition *should* be involved in the inner workings of family affairs. However, because gayness is positioned as antithetical to hegemonic notions of family generally, and the black family specifically, the meddlesomeness of Norman's partner, Garson, can remain uninterrogated.

The third act of *Norman . . . Is That You?*, the "resolution," is principally concerned with Ben "coming to terms" with his son's gayness. Importantly, this narrative closure is less concerned with homosexuality. The central question in *Norman* is, Will Ben come to accept his son's homosexuality?; therefore, without an answer to this question, the narrative would remain open, and viewers would likely feel unfulfilled. However, as the central question illuminates, the narrative closure has little to do with Norman. Norman, while explicitly mentioned in the title, is rendered a passive actor in the film's action. There is little Norman can do to move the narrative toward solving/answering the central problem/question, relieving the tension, or demonstrating that all can return to narrative stasis. The resolution of the film, then, is designed, like the sitcom narrative structure, to ensure an understanding that Ben no longer holds antigay viewpoints and will accept his son (and his son's partner) into his life.

Additionally, like the sitcom, *Norman* attempts to teach its characters and viewers of the film an important lesson about tolerance and unconditional love. While *Norman* depicts Ben learning that homosexuality (and homosexuals) should be accepted within our "brand-new world," it does so in problematic ways. First, while there are other gay characters within the narrative space (including a flamboyant Wayland Flowers in his film debut), those who are accepted (Norman and, by extension, his boyfriend, Garson) are welcomed because they attempt to mirror heteronormativity, or as Lisa Duggan calls it, homonormativity. Duggan deploys homonormativity to interrogate the ways gay men and lesbians adopt "a politics that does not contest dominant heteronormative assumptions and institutions, but upholds and sustains them," which ultimately creates a "depoliticized gay culture anchored in domesticity and consumption."[18] Because *Norman* can be read as a domesticom, a sitcom form rooted solely (or mostly) within the confines of the home, Norman and Garson are anchored in their apartment and thus are domesticated as depoliticized subjects who are largely segregated from a gay community and a 1970s gay politic. This domestication of Norman and Garson positions them as the "right" kind of gay subjects in a film wherein their gayness can be "accepted" and narratively resolved because it conforms to a reductive male/female binary in which heterosexual/ist viewers problematically map heterosexual gender roles onto gay and lesbian relationships.

Importantly, the film's narrative "happily ever after" is not necessarily by the acceptance of Norman's gayness; rather, it is provided by Ben and Beatrice's decision to reconcile, which provides the bookend for *Norman*'s heterosexist gaze. In fact, at the end of the film, there is no assurance that Norman and Garson will remain in their relationship, as Norman has decided to enlist in the army to "find himself (again)." Although Garson has been invited to move to Tucson with the Chamberses while Norman is in the army, Beatrice has already developed a plan to break the couple up by introducing Garson to another (presumably) gay man in Tucson. The physical separation of the gay couple by Norman's parents leads one to question the film's resolution.

In addition, *Norman*'s closing credits work to drive the "lesson" of the film home for viewers. While the last shot of the film features Ben, Beatrice, Norman, and Garson arm in arm, leaving Norman and Garson's apartment to have dinner together (with Norman and Garson on either side of the heterosexual couple), the shot freezes on the group. This, perhaps inadvertently, gestures toward the ways Ben and Beatrice have interfered in Norman and Garson's relationship. As the image dims and the closing credits begin to roll, the song "One Out of Every Six" begins to play. Sung by disco diva Thelma Houston, the song alludes to the estimation that roughly 16 percent of the American population is gay. With just a few notes of introduction, the song immediately starts with the lyric, "One out of every six is just like Norman"; thus, I argue, it attempts to explain to audiences that homosexuality is not a rarity and that queers are here, so heterosexual people should start getting used to it. The song goes on, "The other five get off their cookies by conforming." As the song ultimately closes out the film and drives the narrative lesson home, songwriter William Goldstein and lyricist Ron Miller turn a lens on heterosexuality and the failings of the institution as it attempts to uphold heteronormativity. Goldstein and Miller (and Houston in her delivery of the song) suggest that there is a voluntary conforming, in some ways underscoring what cultural theorist Antonio Gramsci asserts about hegemony; it "is characterized by the combination of force and consent, which balance each other reciprocally, without force predominating excessively over consent."[19] This set of lyrics is rhetorically rooted in holding a mirror up to the presumed heterosexual audience as if to say, those in glass houses should not throw stones. Driving this notion home, the first verse ends with, "Before we judge the one who rebels, let's take a good look at ourselves." As the song that provides the film's final narrative closure, it explicitly recognizes that this film does not seek to center gayness; rather, heterosexuality and the ways that the "brave new world" to which Smokey Robinson alludes in the film's opening-credits song, "Old Fashioned Man," should adapt to the presence of homosexuality.

While the "actual" film can be read as propping up particular ideologies with respect to homosexuality, examining what Jonathan Gray calls "critical paratexts" can provide an equally illuminating view of the ways *Norman* works to decenter gayness by ensuring that much of the viewing audience is clearly aware that Michael Warren is not gay in "real" life. As Gray notes, critical paratexts "form much of this realm of the 'between,' a realm through which we must travel in order to consume and make sense of a text."[20] I now turn to critical paratexts to underscore the ways the black press contributed to a narrative that ensured a discursive break between Michael Warren and Norman Chambers.

## MICHAEL WARREN IS *NOT* NORMAN CHAMBERS: THE BLACK PRESS AND DISCURSIVE GAYFACE

From a cultural studies perspective, paratexts are as important as the text itself. Gray rightly suggests that paratexts, which can include media discourse about a text, can work to structure, encourage, and/or discourage the ways audiences engage with a film.[21] In this section, I examine the ways that the black press contributed to forwarding a narrative that underscored the film's deployment of gayface, which conversely worked to decenter gayness.

In post-civil-rights America, the black press, particularly *Ebony* and *Jet* magazines, proved incredibly important for many black Americans. The magazines, as weekly and monthly providers of national news and entertainment centered on/in blackness, reported information that the mainstream press often chose not to cover. These two historically and culturally important magazines provide a rich site to examine the paratextual creation of what I am calling "discursive gayface" within black media.

"Gayface" is a relatively contemporary term, often rooted in popular culture. While the *Us vs. Them* blog defines the term as "that little something about a dude's face, expression, I don't know, . . . something that let's [sic] you know that he may be driving off from the ladies [sic] tees, swanging [sic] from the other side of the plate or helping his boys over the fence," I am seeking a more academic and historical rooting of the term.[22] This chapter operationalizes gayface as a performative strategy that is an outgrowth of the blackface and minstrelsy traditions—whereby heterosexually identified black actors embody black gay characters in media. Additionally, "discursive gayface" refers to not only the ways that gayface is entrenched within the culture industries but also the ways a possessive investment in its heterosexual performative properties in media is reinforced. Discursive gayface is concerned with the mass-mediated moves made to distance the actor from his gayface performance and place him firmly within the realm of the heterosexual.

Gayface has its roots in blackface traditions. Largely based on a series of stereotypes, these performances often featured white actors "blacking up" their faces, exaggerating their features (particularly the lips), and speaking "Negro dialect" in order to depict black people in early stage performances. Blackface was not just integral in the formation of American popular culture, demonstrating its adaptability to media forms including film and radio; it has proved to be *enduring* in American popular culture.

What is both important and problematic about blackface is that white actors helped to popularize the tradition. According to Donald Bogle, the blackface tradition began in slavery when black people were not permitted to appear and perform onstage. "Troupes of white minstrels blackened themselves with burnt cork to better mock and caricature the plantation slaves they imitated."[23] Because blacks were not initially allowed to perform their own versions of an "authentic" blackness, the caricatures created by white actors served as the cultural script from which the foundations of mass-mediated blackness were written. By the time slavery was abolished and blacks were allowed to perform on the stage, they too had to use burnt cork to darken their skin and perform exaggerated notions of blackness if they wanted to obtain gainful employment on the stage.

Having white, often racist, actors creating the cultural scripts of blackness illuminates the problematic nature of blackface as a performative practice. Those who hold social, political, and cultural power are allowed to create the scripts from which U.S. and global citizens came to understand blackness. This thin and one-dimensional construction of blackface can be transferred onto gayface, a practice whereby heterosexual actors, writers, and producers are the purveyors of mass-mediated representations of black gay men.

I am more interested here in the ways that gayface is rooted in a possessive investment in heterosexuality. This investment undergirds Michael Warren's mass-mediated star text as he dons gayface to portray Norman Chambers. It is this set of discursive moves that works to distance "the real" Warren from the character Norman Chambers. Because at the time of *Norman*'s release, Michael Warren was not the "star" that either Redd Foxx or Pearl Bailey were, *Ebony* magazine's feature story on the film begins discussing the actor and his role as Norman by providing biographical details and his decision to take the part. The paragraph begins, "It was for 30-year-old actor Michael Warren, whose first child was born on the last day of filming, that Norman perhaps posed the greatest dilemma."[24] Having a child in 1976, at the time of *Norman*'s release, would have been viewed as a possibility only within heterosexual coupling. After mentioning the birth of Warren's child, further biographical details are provided including that Warren played basketball for UCLA and refused an offer to join a professional team. In this way, the article hinges on an assumption that proficiency in sports is incongruous with homosexuality, which the author implicitly links with more hegemonically feminine behaviors. In 1976, sports, particularly played at a level that one could be considered to play professionally, was meant to exclude homosexuality from the realm of possibility. Rather, gay men are understood within a mainstream public's stereotypical imagination to be proficient in interior design, hair styling, and other professions commonly regarded as "women's work." Thus, the mention of Warren's firstborn child and his basketball prowess work to semiotically construct his heterosexuality and, at the same time, link him to gayface performance. If Warren is only "playing gay," as is highlighted in the *Ebony* piece, then it provides a level of comfort for readers (and viewers by extension), liberating them from grappling with complex internal struggles regarding the acceptance or even tolerance, for that matter, of "real" homosexuality.

In Warren's interview with *Ebony*, he further seeks to distance himself from the role (and, by extension, homosexuality) by embodying a heterosexist anxiety with relation to homosexuality. He explains, " Once I had actually gotten the part, I began wondering what my friends would think. If I did a good job, I wondered if they might start saying that perhaps some latent traits were emerging. I honestly began questioning my own masculinity, which was kind of crazy, but that's what happened."[25] The anxiety about homosexuality is palpable in Warren's response, which underscores that he very clearly understands the boundaries of "authentic" black masculine scripts. It is also important to note that not only could playing a role that could be perceived as a sympathetic gay character be detrimental to one's career, but it was also far less socially acceptable to play such a character. In the 1970s, the dominant scripts of the "proper" black masculine subject largely derived from images from blaxploitation film. These cinematic black men, including the *Shaft* series's (both film and TV) title character and *Super Fly*'s Youngblood Priest, became the ways that black men (and American culture more broadly) came to understand a 1970s black man who refused to be a submissive subject in the face of white hegemony. Ronald L. Jackson and Celnisha L. Dangerfield assert, "the public narratives pertaining to Black men's lives comply with several racialized social projections about the Black masculine body as (1) violent, (2) sexual, and (3) incompetent."[26] While certainly reductive, the words "violent" and "incompetent" rarely, if ever, are ascribed "positive" connotations. And while being deemed sexual can be read as having far more "positive" connotations, when applied to black men, sexuality is often construed as dangerous. Historically, these scripts have been a permanent part of the mass-mediated representational landscape and have helped (over)determine the ways we culturally come to understand black masculinity. The virile and violent black man initially appeared as a result of the necessity for whites in late eighteenth- and early nineteenth-century America to justify slavery. The overarching presumption was that if black men were set free, they would rape and defile white women (and, perhaps more horrifically in these minds, reproduce mixed-race children). As Stuart Hall details, although 1970s blaxploitation films attempted to reclaim this imagery and refashion it as a source of pride among black people generally, and black men specifically, the result of its attempt at transcoding was mixed at best.[27] However, this transcoding was successful in its solidification of a hegemonic and ontological understanding of black masculinity for black men. Within this imagining of the hegemonic black masculine, "negro faggotry" serves as a controlling image to police its boundaries.[28] Marlon Riggs, who theorizes "negro faggotry," asserts,

> What lies at the heart . . . of black America's pervasive cultural homophobia is the desperate need for a convenient Other *within* the community, yet not truly *of* the community, an Other onto which blame for the chronic identity crises afflicting the black male psyche can be readily displaced, an indispensible Other that functions as the lowest common denominator of the abject, the base line of transgression beyond which a black man is no longer a man, no longer black, an essential Other against which black men and boys maturing, struggling with self-doubt, anxiety, feelings of political, economic, social, and sexual inadequacy—even impotence—can always measure themselves and by comparison seem strong, adept, empowered, superior.[29]

In other words, heterosexual black masculinity is preserved because to not conform is to be constructed as "gay." Linguistically, words like "punk," "soft," and "fruity" are associated with homosexuality, whereas "strength" and "sexual prowess" become generally conflated with heterosexual masculinity, specifically heterosexual black masculinity.

Not only does *Ebony* participate in the distancing of Michael Warren from his Norman character, but *Jet* magazine includes an article titled "Gay Film Role Gets Straight Actor All Kinds of Propositions" that functions similarly. The article opens by suggesting that Warren played his role too well in the film. Implicit in the article title and opening is that Warren engaged in gayface for a film role. Additionally, the article explain what Warren's role in *Norman* "has wrought: An interview from a newspaper for gays; calls in the middle of night from men making offers and from women who vow to 'convert' him; . . . and cat calls and whistles from friends who teasingly refer to Warren as 'Normie.'"[30] The list of "issues" that Warren dealt with in the aftermath of playing the Norman character begins with the assumption that audiences are unable (or refuse) to separate the actor from the role. This, then, provides the impetus for the "need" to write such an article—to assist in separating Warren the actual man from his turn as Norman, the fictitious gay character. As Chris Rojek suggests about celebrity broadly, this article suggests an inability for fans to make a "split between the private self and a public self" of Michael Warren.³¹

Like the author of the *Ebony* article, *Jet*'s Ronald E. Kisner provides details about Warren's career on UCLA's basketball team before ultimately closing the piece with, "For the record, Warren is married and has a six-month-old."³² *Jet* engages in "discursive gayface" to very clearly articulate the split between Michael Warren and Norman Chambers. I am in no way suggesting that *Jet* or Kisner hold antigay sentiments; however, I am arguing that their articles seethe of the sentiment that while there may be nothing "wrong" with being gay, a "real" black man does not want to be accused of being gay. To that end, Michael Warren and black media outlets conspire to clearly articulate a differentiation between Warren's veridical self and the character he plays in *Norman . . . Is That You?* Ultimately, "discursive gayface" works as a strategy to decenter "real" gayness, by distancing the actor from his role as a gay person.

## CONCLUSION: FIVE OUT OF EVERY SIX ARE JUST LIKE BEN CHAMBERS

While Ben Chambers utters the line, "There's a sexual revolution going on," this sensual insurgency is not apparent in *Norman . . . Is That You?* Rather, while viewers understand via the dialogue that one in every six men has had a homosexual experience, the film centers on the five men, who are assumed to be heterosexual, who have not. *Norman* purports, then, to be about tolerance of gay men and women, particularly when they are part of one's family. However, as Suzanna Danuta Walters argues, the acceptance trope that dominates neoliberal understandings of gayness makes no space for gay men and lesbians who "don't fit the poster-boy image of nonstraight people and who can't be—or don't want to be—assimilated."³³ Particularly problematic with respect to Norman and Garson is that Norman's parents accept his homosexuality under the (comedic) guise of hatching a scheme to dissolve their relationship.

The discursive framework within which *Norman* operates makes apparent the cooperation of the script and related publicity. As I have demonstrated, the black press participated in the discursive distancing of Michael Warren from Norman Chambers. Through the use of sports as the ultimate arbiter of masculinity and the exercise of reproductive abilities, Warren is positioned as a heterosexual actor donning gayface for a role in a film. Ultimately, this helps to reify the film's heterosexist gaze.

While a long legacy of historical misrepresentations of gayness existed long before the blaxploitation cycle, the ways black queer bodies were presented in blaxploitation film became the racialized template from which other film and television representations of black queer bodies sprang, including those that traded on a fey representation of queerness. Among these characters are television's Dion (portrayed by Eddie Murphy) on *Saturday Night Live* (1975–present) and Blaine Edwards and Antoine Meriwether from *In Living Color*'s (1990–94) "Men On . . ." sketches (portrayed by Damon Wayans and David Alan Greer, respectively) and cinematic representations like Banana Man (portrayed by Damon Wayans) in *Beverly Hills Cop* (1984) and Lamar Latrell (Larry B. Scott) in *Revenge of the Nerds* (1984). In this way, *Norman* was a departure from the ways black gayness has historically been represented in media.

However, unlike these texts, which seem to be designed to prop up ideals about black masculinity, *Norman* remained broadly disinterested in homosexuality as a kind of sexuality that should be explored. Rather, like a thirty-minute sitcom, heterosexuality remained the normative narrative center. Ultimately, the question in the film's title, *Norman . . . Is That You?*, is rearticulated through the film's narrative positionality to suggest the declarative statement, "Norman . . . it's not about you." And indeed, *Norman* is not really about the title character.

## NOTES

1. Ed Guerrero, *Framing Blackness: The African American Image in Film* (Philadelphia: Temple University Press, 1993), 69.
2. "MGM Upgrades 'Norman' to PG; Ok Gay Theme," *Variety*, September 15, 1976, 284.
3. "Catholics Condemn 'Norman': Call Slant on Homosexuality Regrettable and Hits Scorn on Parental Authority," *Variety*, November 3, 1976.
4. Michael Seth Star, *Black and Blue: The Redd Foxx Story* (Milwaukee: Applause Books, 2011), 199.
5. "Movie Reviews," *Jet*, December 23, 1976, 54.
6. John E. Semonche, *Censoring Sex: A Historical Journey through American Media* (New York: Rowman and Littlefield, 2007), 123.
7. Harry Benshoff and Sean Griffin, *America on Film: Representing Race, Class, Gender, and Sexuality at the Movies*, 2nd ed. (New York: Wiley-Blackwell, 2009), 135.
8. Ibid., 332–33.
9. Joe Wlodarz, "Beyond the Black Macho: Queer Blaxploitation," *Velvet Light Trap* 53 (Spring 2004): 11.
10. Louie Robinson, "Norman . . . Is That You?," *Ebony*, November 1976, 60.
11. Stephen Tropiano, *The Prime Time Closet: A History of Gays and Lesbians on TV* (New York: Applause Books, 2002), 191–92.

12. Lynne Joyrich, "Epistemology of the Console," in *Queer TV: Theories, Histories, Politics*, ed. Glynn Davis and Gary Needham (New York: Routledge, 2009), 15–47.
13. For a fuller discussion, see Mary E. Kite and Kay Deaux, "Gender Belief Systems: Homosexuality and Implicit Inversion Theory," *Psychology of Women Quarterly* 11 (1987): 83–96.
14. Murph, "Film Reviews: *Norman . . . Is That You?*," *Variety*, September 29, 1976, 30.
15. See Eldridge Cleaver, *Soul on Ice* (New York: Delta Books, 1991).
16. Marlon Riggs, "Black Macho Revisited: Reflections of a Snap! Queen," in *Out in Culture: Gay, Lesbian, and Queer Essays on Popular Culture*, ed. Corey K. Creekmur and Alexander Doty (Durham, NC: Duke University Press, 1995), 471.
17. Robinson, "Norman," 54.
18. Lisa Duggan, *The Twilight of Equality? Neoliberalism, Cultural Politics, and the Attack on Democracy* (Boston: Beacon, 2003), 50.
19. Antonio Gramsci, "Hegemony, Intellectuals and the State," in *Cultural Theory and Popular Culture: A Reader*, ed. John Storey (Harlow, UK: Longman, 2009), 75.
20. Jonathan Gray, *Show Sold Separately: Promos, Spoilers, and Other Media Paratexts* (New York: NYU Press, 2010), 36.
21. Ibid.
22. Lake Arlington, "Is It Just Me or Does Tyler Perry Have Gay Face?," *Us vs. Them* (blog), May 14, 2008, http://uvtblog.com/2008/05/is-it-just-me-or-does-tyler-perry-have-gay-face/.
23. Donald Bogle, *Toms, Coons, Mulattoes, Mammies, and Bucks: An Interpretive History of Blacks in American Films* (New York: Viking, 1973), 25.
24. Robinson, "Norman," 51.
25. Ibid., 60.
26. Ronald L. Jackson and Celnisha L. Dangerfield, "Defining Black Masculinity as a Cultural Property: An Identity Negotiation Paradigm," in *Intercultural Communication: A Reader*, ed. Larry A. Samovar and Richard E. Porter (Florence, KY: Wadsworth, 2002), 123.
27. Stuart Hall, "The Spectacle of the Other," in *Representation: Cultural Representation and Signifying Practices*, ed. Stuart Hall (London: Sage, 2011), 270.
28. Riggs, "Black Macho Revisited," 470.
29. Ibid., 471, emphasis in original.
30. Ronald E. Kisner, "Gay Film Role Gets Straight Actor All Kinds of Propositions," *Jet*, February 17, 1977, 54.
31. Chris Rojek, *Celebrity* (London: Reaktion Books, 2001), 11.
32. Kisner, "Gay Film Role," 54.
33. Suzanna Danuta Walters, *The Tolerance Trap: How God, Genes, and Good Intentions Are Sabotaging Gay Equality* (New York: NYU Press, 2014), 3.

# WORKS CITED

Arlington, Lake. "Is It Just Me or Does Tyler Perry Have Gay Face?" *Us vs. Them* (blog), May 14, 2008. http://uvtblog.com/2008/05/is-it-just-me-or-does-tyler-perry-have-gay-face/.

Benshoff, Harry, and Sean Griffin, *America on Film: Representing Race, Class, Gender, and Sexuality at the Movies*. 2nd ed. New York: Wiley-Blackwell, 2009.

Bogle, Donald. *Toms, Coons, Mulattoes, Mammies, and Bucks: An Interpretive History of Blacks in American Films*. New York: Viking, 1973.

"Catholics Condemn 'Norman': Call Slant on Homosexuality Regrettable and Hits Scorn on Parental Authority." *Variety*, November 3, 1976.

Cleaver, Eldridge. *Soul on Ice*. New York: Delta Books, 1991.

Duggan, Lisa. *The Twilight of Equality? Neoliberalism, Cultural Politics, and the Attack on Democracy*. Boston: Beacon, 2003.

Gramsci, Antonio. "Hegemony, Intellectuals and the State." In *Cultural Theory and Popular Culture: A Reader*, edited by John Storey, 75–80. Harlow, UK: Longman, 2009.

Gray, Jonathan. *Show Sold Separately: Promos, Spoilers, and Other Media Paratexts*. New York: NYU Press, 2010.

Guerrero, Ed. *Framing Blackness: The African American Image in Film*. Philadelphia: Temple University Press, 1993.

Hall, Stuart. "The Spectacle of the Other." In *Representation: Cultural Representation and Signifying Practices*, edited by Stuart Hall, 223–85. London: Sage, 2011.

Jackson Ronald L., and Celnisha L. Dangerfield. "Defining Black Masculinity as a Cultural Property: An Identity Negotiation Paradigm." In *Intercultural Communication: A Reader*, edited by Larry A. Samovar and Richard E. Porter, 120–31. Florence, KY: Wadsworth, 2002.

Joyrich, Lynne. "Epistemology of the Console." In *Queer TV: Theories, Histories, Politics*, edited by Glynn Davis and Gary Needham, 15–47. New York: Routledge, 2009.

Kisner, Ronald E. "Gay Film Role Gets Straight Actor All Kinds of Propositions." *Jet*, February 17, 1977.

Kite, Mary E., and Kay Deaux. "Gender Belief Systems: Homosexuality and Implicit Inversion Theory." *Psychology of Women Quarterly* 11 (1987): 83–96.

"MGM Upgrades 'Norman' to PG; Ok Gay Theme." *Variety*, September 15, 1976.

"Movie Reviews." *Jet*, December 23, 1976.

Murph. "Film Reviews: *Norman . . . Is That You?*" *Variety*, September 29, 1976.

Riggs, Marlon. "Black Macho Revisited: Reflections of a Snap! Queen." In *Out in Culture: Gay, Lesbian, and Queer Essays on Popular Culture*, edited by Corey K. Creekmur and Alexander Doty, 470–75. Durham, NC: Duke University Press, 1995.

Robinson, Louie. "Norman . . . Is That You?" *Ebony*, November 1976.

Rojek, Chris. *Celebrity*. London: Reaktion Books, 2001.

Semonche, John E. *Censoring Sex: A Historical Journey through American Media*. New York: Rowman and Littlefield, 2007.

Star, Michael Seth. *Black and Blue: The Redd Foxx Story*. Milwaukee: Applause Books, 2011.

Tropiano, Stephen. *The Prime Time Closet: A History of Gays and Lesbians on TV*. New York: Applause Books, 2002.

Walters, Suzanna Danuta. *The Tolerance Trap: How God, Genes, and Good Intentions Are Sabotaging Gay Equality*. New York: NYU Press, 2014.

Wlodarz, Joe. "Beyond the Black Macho: Queer Blaxploitation." *Velvet Light Trap* 53 (Spring 2004): 10–25.

# 10

## MAKING EXPLOITATION BLACK

### HOW 1970S "BLAXPLOITATION" DISCOURSE MARGINALIZED INDUSTRY HISTORY AND CONSTRUCTED BLACK VIEWERS' TASTES

#### LAURA COOK KENNA

> The denial of lower, coarse, vulgar, venal, servile—in a word, natural—enjoyment, which constitutes the sacred sphere of culture, implies an affirmation of the superiority of those who can be satisfied with the sublimated, refined, disinterested, gratuitous, distinguished pleasures forever closed to the profane. That is why art and cultural consumption are predisposed, consciously and deliberately or not, to fulfil a social function of legitimating social differences.
> —Pierre Bourdieu, *Distinction*

THE TERM "BLAXPLOITATION" CAME INTO BEING IN AUGUST 1972, ABOUT two years into a flurry of black-oriented moviemaking that opened the 1970s. In the wake of *Super Fly* (1972) and its cocaine-dealer antihero, Youngblood Priest (Ron O'Neal), a number of civil rights organizations banded together, creating the Coalition Against Blaxploitation (CAB) and coined "blaxploitation" as a critique of these films. The term was intended to emphasize that the film industry was exploiting black audiences or blackness itself in the new cycle of black action films. "Blaxploitation" acted as a kind of accusation but also as a refusal of alternative terms like "black film" or "black cinema." That is, the CAB and other objectors seemed to declare that if a "black cinema" were possible or even imminent on the cultural horizon, the set of films making box-office cash registers sing by relying on sex, drugs, and criminality was not yet it. In the pages of the mainstream and especially the black press, African American leaders fought over the political ramifications of the black film cycle and its popularity. The once entirely pejorative term "blaxploitation" persisted long after films and protests had ceased, however, becoming the quasi-neutral, usual means for critics, scholars, and fans alike to refer to the films of the black movie boom.

The robust protests and debates over black-themed films during the 1970s has become the dominant historical context through which these films are positioned, and rightly so. In light of the variety of civil rights and other black-liberation projects competing for influence and fighting inequality, the story of the 1970s film cycle sheds light on the cultural front of those battles and the important disagreements between black culture makers about what would count as progressive racial representation and political ideology. Blaxploitation histories add vivid detail to the histories of Hollywood stereotyping of black characters and raise questions about the limits of "uplift," reappropriation, and "independent" cinema as strategies.[1] The stories of these films recount the responsiveness—however compromised—of mass culture to the seismic shifts in American racial politics in the late 1960s and early 1970s. Blaxploitation history also has stories to tell us about black artists, tradespeople, and marketing professionals overcoming the odds and making inroads into the film industry.[2]

The dominant focus on the immediate 1970s historical context of blaxploitation and its very specific racial politics, however, functionally disconnects these films and the debates they inspired from a longer pattern of film-related criticism in the African American press. As illuminated by Anna Everett's painstaking work on black film criticism from before *The Birth of a Nation* through the era of Hollywood's "social problem films," African American artists and critics had a rich history of using other black media to "talk back" to Hollywood images.[3] Jacqueline Stewart's work on black Chicagoans at the movies during the Great Migration also suggests historical continuity between the blaxploitation controversy and earlier discourses about the role of black movie viewers—not just movie images—in defining black city space and the political stakes that suffused black leisure.[4] Black newspapers and critics had a complex relationship to the movie industry as purveyors of stereotypical content and to black movie viewers as the patrons of representations that were sometimes less than "progressive" or "respectable."

The primary concern with these films as participants in 1970s black politics, however appropriate, nevertheless threatens to cordon them off from consideration as 1970s films per se, inadvertently reproducing their marginalization from related industry and aesthetic histories. As significant contributors to the recovery of Hollywood's tenuous economic footing, the spate of race-oriented pictures from the early seventies are also artifacts of the particular industrial practices that prescribed their production, their style, and their approach to representing race. As Novotny Lawrence has argued, the catchall classification "blaxploitation" applied as a generic category often precludes analysis of how these films and the role of race in them also made changes within established Hollywood genres like the detective or horror film.[5] I want to press his argument a bit further, making certain to think about these often-generic blaxploitation films in relationship to the history of that division of the American film industry known as exploitation cinema.

The independently produced and distributed films of exploitation operated in parallel to the studio system that submitted its films to the gerrymandered morality of the Production Code Administration and adhered to the aesthetic and narrative conceits now identified as the "classical Hollywood cinema."[6] This circuit of films that were not produced and distributed by studios carved out a profitable niche by quickly making and exhibiting low-cost films that filled out (especially independent, non-first-run) exhibitors' needs. While low-budget, "B" movies were made by some studios, exploitation fare distinguished itself by featuring those subjects forbidden by the mainstream industry's code. Thomas Doherty's *Teenagers and Teenpics* defines exploitation cinema around not only its low cost but its emphasis on sensational, publicity-ready content. But Doherty's narrowly focused topic threatens to confine scholars' application of the exploitation category to the quickly made, teen-focused 1950s and 1960s genre films of his study.[7] Eric Schaefer's impressive historical work attests that production and circulation of exploitation films were more diverse and extended as far back as the late nineteen-teens. Exploitation films involved frank nudity, explicit violence and gore, and an undisguised, objectifying gaze on its subjects.[8] In the wake of the studio system's collapse and as young directors, actors, and writers trained in exploitation houses landed mainstream Hollywood work, the influence of exploitation cinema—its racier content, heavier emphasis on marketing, and lower budgets—wended its way to the mainstream during the late 1960s and early 1970s, a trend that included but was certainly not limited to black films.[9]

This chapter begins to reconnect the history of black film criticism and the history of the exploitation film to the history of 1970s black cinema. Doing so reveals how much of the aesthetic practices and marketing strategies of the black movie boom were connected to a half-century-old mode of production that was characteristic of neither "mainstream" Hollywood nor "race films." Ed Guerrero's influential analysis credits three factors in the emergence of blaxploitation: the "rising political and social consciousness of black people," black leaders' "dissatisfaction with Hollywood's persistent degradation of African Americans in film," and the "near economic collapse" of the Hollywood studios.[10] This chapter, then, focuses on the third industrial factor to better imagine how the ideological shifts he and so many others describe actually ended up on the screen and took the form that they did. It also insists that the 1970s controversy over black-oriented movies be made sense of in light of a longer tradition of how the black press critiqued movies as a site in the struggle over black artists' representational burdens and the role of culture in racial progress.

In some ways, these historical maneuvers make blaxploitation films and their controversies less exceptional by situating them as an important and historically peculiar but not entirely novel development in either black cultural history or American cinema. This different perspective, nonetheless, points out how black exploitation operated very differently than other exploitation fare despite common production tactics, how the politics of race exceeded the frame and made these films something far more than cheap genre pictures. Linking the blaxploitation debates to earlier critiques of Hollywood representations also helps establish that these controversies about black representations on the screen have also consistently been about black moviegoers' role as black representatives in front of the screens. That is, this chapter begins to unravel some of the ideas about black viewers' pleasures and politics and about the sufficiency or deficiency of their tastes, which reappear as common threads woven through many questions about blackness in cultural production.

This chapter argues that, in light of these connections to both exploitation cinema practices and the history of black film criticism, it took cultural work to make exploitation black. Understanding blaxploitation as a market response to black viewers' tastes or as the black moviegoers' problematic box-office preference involved the work of film producers, marketers, reviewers, and reporters. It also required the work of black audiences and those who would defend them— either their right to be entertained by or to be free from black exploitation imagery. While my investigation addresses the systems of representation and cultural production that governed the making of black film images, its argument rests less on the idea of a powerful few working in concert than on the occurrence of an uncoordinated conjuncture of discourses, resources, and actors that together rested the explanation for blaxploitation's existence and excesses at the feet of black viewers' taste. The process of making exploitation black happened through structures while also requiring immaterial, yet no less substantial, work like historical forgetting, racial marginalizing, and marking out class distinctions. Once that work was completed, "blaxploitation" became more than just a categorical shorthand for the early 1970s black film cycle or a buzzword signaling one's disapproval of the movement. "Blaxploitation" was no longer just a neologism but a morpheme, an irreducible unit of meaning wherein black film and exploitation film became a single concept that fused ideas about race, class, viewership, and taste.

## THE TURN TOWARD EXPLOITATION

Histories of early 1970s American film have dubbed the era "a 'golden age' of exploitation cinema" that included black-oriented movies along with kung-fu pictures, hard-core porn flicks, and gory horror films.[11] As noted earlier, exploitation outfits had a history of providing cinematic treatments of sensational topics forbidden by the Production Code Administration, such as drug use and sex hygiene, among others. With the rise of new independent production companies like American International Pictures (AIP) in the 1950s, exploitation also came to include cheaply filmed pictures aimed at teens that rehabilitated B-movie staples like the "creature feature" genre.[12] Exploitation features, however, were defined by more than their relatively over-the-top content and reliably undersized budgets. These pictures were produced independently of Hollywood studios and developed alternative aesthetic and storytelling practices. Specifically, they addressed their viewers outside the conventions of the classic Hollywood cinema's "straight corridor" narratives and did not rigorously affect the naturalism cultivated by the continuity system.[13]

The promise of screen spectacle affected both the topics of exploitation cinema and ways the films address the spectator. More in line with preclassical Hollywood, exploitation pictures operate by what Tom Gunning named "the cinema of attractions," which emphasizes film as an act of spectacle and display. As Gunning describes, the viewing pleasures of the attractions model are less about absorption and more about "the excitement of curiosity and its fulfillment."[14] While (especially later) exploitation films may not have addressed the audience as directly as preclassical magician films, they nonetheless centered their appeals to the audience (in marketing as well as in the mode of address) on spectacle. Eric Schaefer, discussing the centrality of spectacle to the exploitation aesthetic in his book *"Bold! Daring! Shocking! True!,"* defines spectacle as anything "presented to fascinate the eye of the spectator. . . . Spectacle invariably exerts an immediate, affective response in the spectator."[15] Many tactics of exploitation—such as prefatory warnings about what audiences were about to see, recycled and recut footage from other films, or shocking close-ups—aligned with the visibly lower-budget quality of the films and "consistently reminded the viewer that he or she was watching a film, either through the display of spectacle or because of the crumbling continuity."[16] These pictures addressed their audience as people who wanted a good look at something or someone.

That exploitation fare eventually became a major influence within—rather than a major departure from—Hollywood studios' products begs the question, What industrial conditions changed so drastically that once largely taboo cinema could make its way to the mainstream? The previous decade saw the collapse of the conventional studio systems, while the struggle to compete with the home entertainment offered by television continued. During the 1970s, studios continued to produce films but began acting mainly as distributors. From the late 1960s through the 1970s, American films varied widely in their style, budgets, and themes, evincing the industry's openness to new strategies for luring viewers, particularly the younger demographic, as the American audience was increasingly generationally and socially fractured. Along with the demise of the traditional studio system came the demise of the Production Code Administration's strictures; its subsequent replacement by the ratings system allowed for much-broader experimentation in depicting sex and violence. This change made possible, for instance, the advent of rated-R horror films that featured nudity as well as bloody and unflinching on-camera murders as opposed to the chaste and largely bloodless B-grade fright films from the studios, clear examples of how changes to film regulation also opened the door for traditional exploitation genres and spectacles.

The mainstreaming of exploitation, however, was a matter not only of content but also of personnel and distribution. With the studio system of talent-under-contract waning and seasoned directors retiring, studios offered opportunities to a young, new generation of directors and other artists, many of whom had just finished film school or had gained what little film experience they had from within exploitation houses like AIP. Hiring less experienced young talent was cheaper as well as an attempt to close a generation gap in viewing; it also made studios all the more willing to reduce risk by asking these directors to work in genre pictures.[17] This window, sometimes called "the New Hollywood," ended as the industry settled into the blockbuster strategy that would again seek to satisfy a wide range of viewers with a single film but ultimately resulted in far fewer and

Early seventies horror films like *Twitch of the Death Nerve* (1972) relied on the promise of a "savage" degree of gore as well as the classic exploitation marketing ploy of a moviegoer warning. (Display ad 31, *New Pittsburgh Courier*, October 7, 1972, 19, Proquest Historical Black Newspapers via the Library of Congress)

far more expensive pictures per year than previous approaches. Still, the blockbuster phenomenon itself relied on a marketing emphasis borrowed from exploitation cinema and the saturation booking practice that was the exploitation industry's standard. After *Jaws*' (1975) success with saturation booking (opening a film nationally on the same day) and a hefty prerelease advertising budget, mainstream Hollywood increasingly turned to this distribution pattern.[18]

Changes to the film audience also necessitated adjustments to Hollywood's way of doing business. As a result of the demographic patterns characterized as "white flight," by the dawn of the 1970s, black Americans represented about 30 percent of the urban market for first-run pictures, a hefty proportion given that at the time they constituted only 10 to 15 percent of the United States' total population. Moreover, black Americans were also a disproportionately large share of the sought-after youth market. This urban black "market" for movies, however, was also a community facing its own seismic changes. Black Power challenged the integrationist and uplift models of some civil rights movement leaders and rejected nonviolence. Cultural nationalism, including the Black Arts movement, emphasized the need to celebrate and cultivate distinctively black artistic perspectives, traditions, and aesthetics. Cities erupted into riotous protests. Black leaders were assassinated. As Mark Reid explains, "Images of black inner city life were formed or reinforced by the television images that portrayed blacks looting neighborhood stores while buildings burned."[19] That is, just as Hollywood turned toward a black America in turmoil as an important audience, it also participated in the mediation of black America as a signifier of violent urban turmoil. Paula Massood argues in *Black City Cinema* that highly televised social movements joined with the sociological discourses that framed urban public policy in terms of "the ghetto" such that "the trope of the black ghetto defined the American urbanscape as a whole."[20] While the postwar liberalism of the "Negro cycle" or "message movies" paralleled the era of the civil rights sit-in, as Black Power in its many forms gained traction and some black leaders began to challenge the commitment to nonviolence, blaxploitation's very different approach to imaging black life emerged.[21]

Black exploitation made a bid to win black moviegoers by adding three-dimensional black characters and an acknowledgment of racial politics to the usual lineup of exploitation appeals. But adding "more race" did not work like simply adding "more skin" or "more blood." Rather, adding race transformed the possibilities of exploitation aesthetics, while the exploitation mode of address also transformed the possibilities of reading race on the big screen. I am not arguing that blaxploitation achieved the "black aesthetic" as espoused by Larry Neal and others, nor that it represented "black independent film." The films of the black movie boom are by and large very far from the kind of political engagement or creative autonomy that those ideals demand. Exploitation did offer, however, a set of aesthetic conventions for telling stories of black life that broke with patterns in classical Hollywood cinema. Though doing so was part of a whites-driven business calculus, blaxploitation movies also addressed a black viewer as their ideal spectator.

Race operated significantly in this cycle of films, serving as more than a veneer updating cheap genre pictures or just another one of many exploitation appeals. Blackness added additional radicalism to sex and violence; rather than being just another in a string of sensational sights, race was both a spectacle on its own and force multiplier that changed the impact of other content. To see sexual activity was one thing; to see black love—so frequently the subject of taboos and stereotypes—was another. To see violence might be sensational, but to see interracial violence—and with the black characters prevailing!—was not only to further sensationalize but to politicize the scene. As Novotny Lawrence's analysis of blaxploitation supports, blackness tends to produce multiple transgressions of a genre's usual conventions. Lawrence's chapter on *Blacula* (1972), for example, makes a convincing case for how changing the race and backstory of the vampire transformed the "monster" of the movie into a sympathetic victim.[22] Ultimately, whatever other spectacles were offered, blaxploitation films always presented black viewers with a chance to see a spectacle that they could not have been accustomed to seeing in Hollywood media: the spectacle of self-determined black people, of black people winning.

The issues that had been glossed over with various forms of cinematic ellipses in Hollywood's message movies and stories of uplift were instead punctuated with exclamation points in exploitation. Efforts in blaxploitation to represent a black sensibility—however uncomfortably over-the top films like *Boss Nigger* (1975) may be—demand a confrontation with race as a spectacle of difference, opposing the way that the naturalized appearance of Sidney Poitier in *Guess Who's Coming to Dinner?* (1967) explicitly eschews the confrontation of otherness and enforced difference. Further, the obviousness of exploitation cinema's technique (or lack thereof) points to the constructed, performative nature of the types that appear on the screen. Gunning has described the aesthetic of attractions as a cinema "willing to rupture a self-enclosed fictional world for a chance to solicit the attention of the spectator."[23] I am suggesting that blaxploitation's often at once stereotypical, celebratory, and hyperbolic images of blackness (especially black masculinity) threaten to rupture the diegesis. The blackness of blaxploitation is larger than life and also, in a sense, larger than film; it solicits the spectator's attention to the limits of images and, perhaps, offers commentary on the ways that media representation itself has been part of the cultural apparatuses that work to manage "blackness" toward docility, otherness, or assimilation.

## THE DEBATE IN BLACK AMERICA

Reading the political possibilities of an affronting aesthetic is not, of course, the same as reading the audience's reactions to these images. The hard-to-crack mystery of why these films were so popular and what meanings black viewers took home with them plagued 1970s critics and observers. Proponents of the films tended to point out the simple pleasure of black main characters or that the films allowed viewers, particularly blacks exhausted with their treatment

These newspaper ads for *A Warm December* and *The Soul of Nigger Charley* appeared side by side, as if to illustrate the stark dichotomy of screen heroes offered to black audiences. (Display ads 120 and 121, *New York Amsterdam News,* May 26, 1973, D6, Proquest Historical Black Newspapers via the Library of Congress)

as second-class citizens, to escape to a world where whites got their comeuppance. Defenders also pointed to new black jobs and stardom and, with those, presumably, new black influence over Hollywood representations. In contrast, blaxploitation's opponents denounced the main characters as retreads of longstanding stereotypes given new force through the explicitness of the new black action films. A critic for the *Chicago Defender* lamented, "With black people shown as one dimensional honkeyhaters, oversexed and underbrained, blaxploitation 'entertainment' has its pursestrings [*sic*] securely in the hands of those same whites its story lines so mercilessly attack."[24] In addition to how much money from these productions still ended up in white pockets, blaxploitation's detractors attempted to calculate the cultural and political loss of the black community when black media images became dominantly exploitative rather than respectable.

Each of the aforementioned positions in their manifold articulations pointed to the images themselves and the producers and artists who made them. Moreover, each also relied on ideas about the black audience, how film representations affected them personally, and whether their moviegoing had political ramifications for the race. Implicit in blaxploitation advocates' and critics' perspectives were characterizations of black audiences as either active and discerning or passive and complicit. Black moviegoers were either demanding more radical representation and throwing off Hollywood conventions or being fed the worst of Hollywood's habits and being sold those images as "radical."

For the NAACP, CORE, and ultimately CAB, as scholar Eithne Quinn succinctly explains, "popular culture was seen to play a vital role in [the classic civil rights mobilization's] quest for black inclusion through the projection of progressive stories about black life and race relations."[25] Blaxploitation's images of pushers, pimps, criminals, and other violent racial avengers not only refused to participate in but deeply compromised that project of inspirational, respectable images of black integration into society. For another set of black leaders and artists, it was time to move past films dedicated to "social uplift." The ideal of a "black aesthetic," as promoted by Black Arts poet, critic, and activist Larry Neal, stressed the need for art that would address problems plaguing black Americans, would be valued according to a black-oriented (rather than white-defined) aesthetic criteria, and would be accountable solely to the black audience.[26] Films of the black aesthetic would be politically engaged and dedicated to the authentic treatment of black life. If not explicitly pedagogical or uplifting, such films would be obliged at the least to deal with social realities of black experiences rather than obscure them as had Hollywood's high-key, happy endings and well-meaning, "liberal" tomes such as *Pinky* (1949) and *Imitation of Life* (1959) had in previous decades.

Crucial to the achievement of a black film aesthetic was the necessary, but not sufficient, twin goal of black control of the means of production. The early 1970s cycle of commercially successful black films did employ black casts and crews in significant numbers. *Super Fly*, for instance, was the first Hollywood film financed mostly by black limited partnerships and the first to have a majority nonwhite crew.[27] When MGM hired a black marketing firm to provide advertising and public-relations campaigns for *Shaft*, it appeared that even nonfilm sectors of the black business world might benefit from the expansion of black film.[28] Yet the increased presence of African Americans behind and before the camera did not necessarily track with an increased "black" cinematic perspective as the Black Arts leaders defined it.

Black critics pointed out that despite a rise in film-related work for African Americans, many scripts were still written and produced by whites.[29] *Ebony*'s article on the blaxploitation controversy—"The New Films: Culture or Con Game?"—recounted complaints that, even in black-oriented films, the industry's persistent white perspective "[made] it difficult for black artists to work with any degree of integrity." Additionally, the article raised the suspicion that "white film-makers only use[d] black craftsmen to lend authenticity to exploitation films and as 'showcase' workers in the event that aware blacks complain[ed]."[30] While *Ebony* cautioned against a kind of symbolic tokenism meant to appease African American activists, the increased opportunities for black talent were also used as a "showcase" when three Russian directors visited the set of *Shaft* as guests of the State Department, the Directors Guild of America, and MGM. In addition to the largely black cast, they were encouraged to take note of the number of black technicians on the crew, including Academy Award nominee Hugh Robertson.[31] The *Shaft* set visit made clear that black film workers could be exploited as badges of Hollywood liberality rather than serve as bellwethers for substantive change in black access to film production.

While blaxploitation was not meeting black leaders' ideals for African American involvement in cinema, the cycle of film was exceedingly popular. Making sense of this popularity involved tacit and explicit acceptance of a market logic about the films being what black audiences demanded at the box office. Some of this was couched in the notion that black audiences were demanding "more realistic" portraits of black life, while others relied on the opposite assumption that the films were popular because they functioned as escapist fantasies. Ideals for black cinema aesthetics had put forth critiques of the systemic employment discrimination in Hollywood and sought to imagine how to best use rare opportunities for self-representation or, better, how to gain improved access altogether to the means of production. Put simply, these racial critiques tended to focus on problems of supply. As blaxploitation proved effective at attracting a robust black movie audience, critical approaches needed to also speak toward problems of demand. Leaders found themselves faced with explaining the black audience's demand for a cycle of films that fell far short of their hopes for black images, having to explain or otherwise weigh in on matters of black viewers' taste.

National media sources covered the black movie boom and speculated about why so many African Americans were patronizing the over-the-top, low-budget pictures. A common viewpoint was that taste for blaxploitation films would incrementally give way to demand for more sophisticated black cinema. "The black audience has gotten a cram course in junk films of all kinds and, paradoxical though it may seem, . . . this was a necessary first step in strengthening their image," explained one Catholic magazine.[32] "Perhaps the artists and decent entertainers will emerge when the audience gets over its first excitement at seeing blacks playing gangsters, cowboys and private detectives," speculated the *Atlantic Monthly*.[33] These (white) publications espoused the idea that the black audience enjoyed these films because they were unaccustomed to seeing themselves in positions of power and authority on film. This theory suggested that blaxploitation cinema represented an early stage of African American films that would eventually evolve into a more sophisticated era of black filmmaking. Even *Ebony*'s film writer Theophilus Green echoed these ideas about the appetite for blaxploitation as a function of both a film industry new to depicting black life and a black audience still nascent in its aesthetic discernment: "Before the audience can develop good taste in the new medium and exert its preference at the box office, the industry usually makes several dozen tasteless violent epics. . . . Black films and their heroes will undoubtedly have to follow the same cycle.[34] Of course, this common explanation completely ignored, whether intentionally or not, the early black cinema achievements of Oscar Micheaux and his contemporaries, positioning Hollywood productions as the full extent of black cinematic experiences.

In the black community, blaxploitation images played roles not only as cinematic products that blacks bought but also as concerns that animated protesters and proponents to enter the public sphere to make the case for their interpretation of the cultural politics of the black movie cycle. As previously noted, in 1972, in the wake of *Super Fly*, several civil rights organizations banded together to form CAB. Junius Griffin resigned his post as president of the Beverly Hills chapter of the NAACP in order to lead the group. Griffin's CAB also included local Los Angeles representatives of civil rights organizations such as the Southern Christian Leadership Conference (SCLC) and Congress of Racial Equity (CORE). The *New York Times* published Griffin's editorial on the spate of spectacle-oriented black action films, which warned that "the cancer of 'Blaxploitation' [was] gnawing away at the moral fiber" of the black community and that "if black movies [did] not contribute to building constructive, healthy images" of black life, then the community "shall have contributed to its own cultural genocide."[35] Conrad Smith, CAB member and leader of CORE's Los Angeles division, told *Newsweek*, "We're prepared to go all the way with this, even to the extent of running people out of the theaters."[36] In Chicago, FORUM staged "street drama" demonstrations in front of a theater showing *Super Fly*, during which a crowd of protestors stood outside and hung their heads in shame "to appeal to the conscience of black people."[37] In Washington, DC, Blacks Against Narcotics and Genocide (BANG) picketed *Super Fly*, while DC congressional delegate Walter E. Fauntroy and school board president Marion Barry publicly opposed the film as well.[38] Thus, those who rallied against blaxploitation appealed both to Hollywood and to black viewers to make changes and do better by the African American community.

Critics also imagined that the new brand of black screen archetypes contributed "toward crime and obnoxious behavior among black youth."[39] Dr. Alvin Poussaint, a prominent African American psychiatrist, then associate professor and associate dean of Harvard Medical School, wrote essays rejecting the notion that the films were "psychologically beneficial to the black viewer," as some supporters of the often-vengeance-oriented films argued. In contrast, Poussaint contended that blaxploitation encouraged violence, sexism, and antiwhite attitudes.[40] Dr. Roland S. Jefferson, a psychiatrist at the Watts Health Foundation, offered the opinion that "the flood of black movies [was] contributing to emotional disturbances among the young . . . [and was] responsible for much of the rise in black-on-black violence."[41] Reverend Jesse Jackson feared that black movies verged on advertisements for drugs to the black community.[42]

Many black artists countered suspicions of black audiences' taste and discernment and suggested that black audiences, like white ones, had every right to go to the movies to be entertained. In the furor over blaxploitation, it was easy to forget that exploitation had infiltrated not just black cinema but American cinema. The movie advertisements in the African American newspaper the *New York New Amsterdam News* illustrate vividly how black viewers (along with American audiences writ large) were being lured to theaters by a range of salacious appeals. Cinemation Industries—the distributor for *Sweet Sweetback's Baadasssss Song* (1971)—promoted one of its X-rated horror films with an advertisement that queried, "How long does it take a razor sharp knife to slice . . . From Ear To Ear."[43] Adjacent to the paper's review of *Shaft's Big Score* appeared the display ad for Sergio Leone's *Duck, You Sucker* (1971), which featured its smiling protagonists firing machine guns and wielding dynamite.[44] On the same page as a feature story focusing on acclaimed photographer and *Shaft* director Gordon Parks, Sr., ran ads for two different double features: one boasting (white) pornographic films and another for "back to back!" James Bond escapades.[45] The Bond advertisement's juxtaposition with an article about *Shaft* was particularly appropriate given that James Bond was the cinema icon to whom John Shaft was most frequently compared in both mainstream and black press coverage. As the reviewer for the *New Pittsburgh Courier* assured, "What if the movie is absurd, blacks will tell you. [*sic*] After all we have watched 'James Bond,' 'Nick Carter' and other white super-sleuths win out over all odds. So now it's time a black did the same thing."[46]

Blaxploitation traded in literally spectacular blackness, but racial politics were also used as part of character motivation in kung-fu and "angry white man" tales. Kung-fu pictures were originally conceived for an Asian American audience but found traction with other nonwhite moviegoers, especially blacks. They mixed the appeal of the defense of one's ethnic group with a less progressive dose of exoticism related to martial arts and Asian culture in general.[47] White warriors as vengeful cinematic counterparts relied less explicitly on racial identification but nonetheless rehearsed violent fantasies of white male domination, vindication, and competition that hinged largely on displays of masculinity in protection of the white home. Rural revenge films like *Walking Tall* (1973) and urban vigilante films such as *Dirty Harry* (1971) and *Death Wish* (1974) indulge in this tacitly racial, masculinist logic.[48] This is not to say that there were no representational styles, depictions, or objections peculiar to African Americans in the 1970s. Rather, it is a historical reminder that while black filmmakers, intellectuals, and audiences grappled with how to react to blaxploitation films, they did so while black neighborhood marquees were lit with a range of nonblack "exploitative" appeals and while theaters across the country drew in audiences of every race with cinema spectacles (even some that included racial politics of nonblack varieties).

Amid a sea of exploitation offerings and in light of the longer history of Hollywood's fantastic heroes and over-the-top adventures, some African Americans working in Hollywood regarded black viewers as but a subset of the larger American audience, and as such, it was reasonable for black audiences—even their right—to approach film with the expectation of finding typical, Hollywood-style pleasures. Gordon Parks, Sr., commented, "If [people from Harlem] see superheroes with fast cars and fancy clothes, well, that's the American dream—everyone's American dream," adding that it was an insult to think that seeing such images would only further disillusion black Americans about their own real-life experiences.[49] Director Gordon Parks, Jr., concurred with his father that black audiences that enjoyed films like his *Super Fly* were no different from other movie audiences who wanted to be entertained.[50] *Shaft* star Richard Roundtree also expected a measure of racial equivalence, not just difference, from the black audience: "Now I wouldn't suggest for one minute that 'Shaft' or 'Sweetback' are true depictions of Black life in this country by any means. But neither are the vast majority of films depicting the life style of white America," he said.[51] Samuel Arkoff, the white man at the helm of American International Pictures, expected that blacks would "resent the implication of this organization [the CAB] that black audiences are somehow not able to recognize something that is degrading to themselves."[52] This alternate understanding of the black viewer passed over ideas about deficient taste or deficient psychological wherewithal and instead imagined him or her as a having a trained, even cynical, eye for American mass culture as well as a desire to see more black characters at the center of those American stories.

Still, objections to these images as misogynist, violent glorifications of crime and drug use were not often wide of the mark. It takes little imagination to see why some critics felt the depictions were simply racist, not empowering appropriations but dangerous reinscriptions of racial stereotypes. Further, regardless of these popular films' indeed rather hefty import for black cultural politics, they were still confrontational, exploitation fare made outside the aesthetic tradition of more respectable Hollywood norms. Gunning reminds, "[The confrontational] aesthetic so contrasts with prevailing turn-of-the-century norms of artistic reception—the ideals of detached contemplation—that it nearly constitutes an anti-aesthetic."[53] Put specifically into the 1970s context, the very mode of address employed by blaxploitation was oppositional to conventional ideas about aesthetic appreciation. Blaxploitation's mode of address is that of bad taste.

The stakes of these representations and the black political ideologies through which they were understood were very much part of a 1970s shift in black leadership, the crises in American cities, and the rise of cultural nationalism. The black press, however, also had a historical role in critiquing Hollywood cinema and sometimes expressing anxiety about black moviegoing. When the 1970s critics and interviewers at the *Chicago Defender* or *Pittsburgh Courier* weighed in on black cinema, they did so from an institutional position within the black community and cultural life that had a tradition of critique. Anna Everett's *Returning the Gaze* makes a solid case that as long as there has been film, there has been black film criticism. She especially highlights the role of the black press as an institution that might rebuff censor boards, theater owners, and spectators—not just film producers—asking them to do better in terms of their commitment to black representation.[54] Jacqueline Stewart's work on black moviegoers in the Great Migration–era Chicago similarly recounts the role of newspapers in talking back to film representations and also to the avid black moviegoing public. Moviegoing was one of many sites in "the struggle for public respectability in the multiracial city," and papers took it upon themselves to help train recent migrants' comportment and desires in terms of black middle-class norms thought to be crucial to the progress of the black race.[55] The black newspapers and the civil rights leaders who appeared within them in the 1970s occupied a position that had precedent, attempting to use black owned and oriented mass media to critique Hollywood products as well as African American viewers whose relationship to Hollywood images did not square with the long-dominant model of representational "uplift."

Further, the discourses traded on taste and racial obligation while nonetheless trading on values and convictions associated with class. Class politics were just under the surface in conversations about black film in the 1970s. For instance, film scholar Jon Kraszewski has analyzed how blaxploitation advertisements played on 1970s anxieties about an increasingly class-divided black America; perhaps his most powerful example is a reading of how the ad campaign for *Dr. Black, Mr. Hyde* (1976) visually suggests that the doctor's new middle-class lifestyle is making him white.[56] Different beliefs about popular representation and what counted as "progressive" racial ideology were expressed alongside ideas about or through the language of class. Advocates who favored more positive or family-friendly representations of the black experience in the uplift model tended to talk about film representations as examples to (as well as images of) the black community and therefore favored images that emphasized middle-class respectability. In 1974, the Detroit NAACP, for example, reached a deal with downtown theater owners stipulating that at least 85 percent of the motion pictures shown would be family fare.[57] Class divisions were also prevalent in interviews with black artists as they tarred the antiblaxploitation camp with intellectual and moral pretenses that, they accused, superseded their loyalty either to the working class or to the arts. Though the films of James Earl Jones were not necessarily considered part of this new boom, the actor also expressed concern about these protestors, suggesting that they spoke only for a particular version or subset of the black community. He told the *Washington Post*, "The people criticizing these movies are mostly black middle-class intellectuals, and they don't produce anything. They don't support the arts. In a way they're asking for the nigger, pussy-footing act again when they demand positive images. They don't want art. They want inspirational images."[58]

Ultimately, the controversy over blaxploitation focused on black viewers' cultural tastes and their political import, as well as on film content and film producers. African Americans were actively struggling with one another, as well as with mass media, over competing constructions of blackness. As leaders vied to position themselves as spokespersons, they also imagined the constituency on behalf of whom they meant to speak. In other words, definitions of "black film" and approaches to blaxploitation tended to imagine a particular relationship between black film viewers and the good of the black community, one that figured movie viewers as sharing in the burden to represent the race. As Stewart has argued, "Black spectatorship was structured not only by limitations imposed by dominant practices, but also by expectations and pressures Blacks created for each other."[59]

Defenders of blaxploitation's fans and filmmakers made their cases by relying on an attribution of rights and possibilities to the black viewing position. Blaxploitation's detractors also identified viewing possibilities they wanted to seize, but those tended to trade more on ideas about the community obligations of the black audience and its continued susceptibility to white, commercial exploitation. The blaxploitation debate itself was a great moment of African Americans articulating the variety—not the monolith—of black viewing experiences and the ability to hold pleasure and politics in tension. It also raised and attempted to tease out questions about the enjoyment of what is clearly artifice (rather than "disidentifying" with nonnaturalistic representation) and how the pleasure provided by a black-dominated diegesis, even one compromised by less visual and narrative "continuity," is different or greater than the pleasures of classical Hollywood images that were "seamless" but unseemly representations of black life.

## CONCLUSION

That the term "blaxploitation" came to function not only as a term of protest but also as a pejorative tautological bundling of black and exploitation film aesthetics was overdetermined by three factors: Hollywood's focus on black Americans as a "market"; exploitation filmmaking practices already associated with "low" taste becoming widespread (especially in films to lure the young, urban, and black); and a long-standing tradition in the African American press of debating the political stakes of black moviegoers' community obligations, not just the racial stakes of film content. The studios' interest in making and distributing a bevy of black-oriented films was of a piece with its emphasis on courting specific markets—specifically reinvigorating the youth and urban markets—as part of its industry comeback strategy. The desire to cut costs and the need to try out new ways of doing business meant that exploitation filmmakers, production strategies, and aesthetics migrated to the mainstream.

The new prominence of exploitation storytelling and the new preoccupation with black moviegoers as a market segment were phenomena that overlapped not only in practice but also in theory as both marketing logics and exploitation distinctiveness traded on ideas about viewers' taste. As Hollywood searched out films to court black audiences, it also turned more broadly to the production of the low-budget and genre-driven fare previously supplied by B and exploitation outfits, fare that connoted low taste, not just low costs. As black audiences turned out in droves for blaxploitation films, box-office receipts appeared to confirm that blaxploitation was "what the audience wanted" rather than, for instance, interpreting those same choices as a preference for three-dimensional black characters when black viewers were given choices mostly between white exploitation fare and blaxploitation films. Exploitation cinema appeared to be the function of meeting black viewers' preferences in both popular discourse and popular memory not just because of the images in *Shaft* and *Super Fly* but also because of overlapping critical discourses in the 1970s that painted black viewers as a market with high demand for exploitation's sensationalism and with higher obligations to racial politics than to individual viewing pleasures.

## NOTES

1. Ed Guerrero's work addresses the controversy and the representational lineage of these films' protagonists. Recent work—for example, that of Stephanie Dunn and Jonathan Munby—has focused on blaxploitation's place in the history of representing black women or cultural archetypes like the trickster and gangster. Ed Guerrero, *Framing Blackness: The African American Image in Film* (Philadelphia: Temple University Press, 1993); Jonathan Munby, "The Underworld Films of Oscar Micheaux and Ralph Cooper: Toward a Genealogy of the Black Screen Gangster," in *Mob Culture: Hidden Histories of the American Gangster Film*, ed. Lee Grieveson, Esther Sonnet, and Peter Stanfield (New Brunswick, NJ: Rutgers University Press, 2005), 263–80; Munby, *Under a Bad Sign: Criminal Self-Representation in African American Popular Culture* (Chicago: University of Chicago Press, 2011); Stephane Dunn, *Baad Bitches and Sassy Supermamas: Black Power Action Films* (Urbana: University of Illinois Press, 2008). On the limits of black independent cinema, especially strong contributions have been made by Mark Reid, *Redefining Black Film* (Berkeley: University of California Press, 1993); and Jesse Algeron Rhines, *Black Film / White Money* (New Brunswick, NJ: Rutgers University Press, 1996).
2. Eithne Quinn, "'Tryin' to Get Over': *Super Fly*, Black Politics, and Post–Civil Rights Film Enterprise," *Cinema Journal* 49, no. 2 (2010); and Quinn, "Closing Doors: Hollywood, Affirmative Action, and the Revitalization of Conservative Racial Politics," *Journal of American History* 99, no. 2 (2012): 466–91.

3. Anna Everett, *Returning the Gaze: A Genealogy of Black Film Criticism, 1909–1949* (Durham, NC: Duke University Press, 2001).
4. Jacqueline Najuma Stewart, *Migrating to the Movies: Cinema and Black Urban Modernity* (Berkeley: University of California Press, 2005).
5. He explains, "The term 'blaxploitation' recognizes the addition of blackness but marginalizes the films by constructing them against whiteness and excluding them from generic categories." Novotny Lawrence, *Blaxploitation Films of the 1970s: Blackness and Genre* (New York: Routledge, 2008), 23.
6. David Bordwell, Janet Staiger, and Kristin Thompson, *The Classical Hollywood Cinema: Film Style and Mode of Production to 1960* (New York: Columbia University Press, 1985).
7. Thomas Doherty, *Teenagers and Teenpics: The Juvenilization of American Movies in the 1950s* (Boston: Unwin Hyman, 1988).
8. Eric Schaefer, *Bold! Daring! Shocking! True: A History of Exploitation Films, 1919–1959* (Durham, NC: Duke University Press, 1999), 4–6, 75–78.
9. Maitland McDonagh, "The Exploitation Generation: Or How Marginal Movies Came In from the Cold," in *The Last Great American Picture Show*, ed. Thomas Elsaesser, Alexander Horwath, and Noel King (Amsterdam: Amsterdam University Press, 2004), 107–30.
10. Guerrero, *Framing Blackness*, 69–70.
11. Eithne Quinn and Peter Kramer, "Blaxploitation," in *Contemporary American Cinema*, ed. Linda Ruth Williams and Michael Hammond (New York: McGraw-Hill, 2006), 189. David A. Cook historicizes the onslaught of blaxploitation, kung fu, and hard core and gives a useful history of the bloody evolution of horror in *Lost Illusions: American Cinema in the Shadow of Watergate and Vietnam, 1970–1979*, History of the American Cinema 9 (Berkeley: University of California Press, 2000), 20–38, 259–86.
12. Blair Davis, *The Battle for the Bs: 1950s Hollywood and the Rebirth of Low-Budget Cinema* (New Brunswick, NJ: Rutgers University Press, 2012). See esp. chap. 4, "Attack of the Independent: American International Pictures and the B-Movie. Also see Doherty, *Teenagers and Teenpics*, chap. 6, "The Horror Teenpics."
13. For a usefully concise summary of classical Hollywood narration, see David Bordwell, "Classical Hollywood Cinema: Narrational Principles and Procedures," in *Narrative, Apparatus, Ideology*, ed. Philip Rosen (New York: Columbia University Press, 1986), 17–34.
14. Tom Gunning, "An Aesthetic of Astonishment: Early Film and the (In)Credulous Spectator," in *Viewing Positions: Ways of Seeing Film*, ed. Linda Williams (New Brunswick, NJ: Rutgers University Press, 1997), 121.
15. Eric Schaefer, *"Bold! Daring! Shocking! True!": A History of Exploitation Films, 1919–1959* (Durham, NC: Duke University Press, 1999), 76.
16. Ibid., 80.
17. Mark Shiel, "American Cinema 1965–70," in Williams and Hammond, *Contemporary American Cinema*, 35; and McDonagh, "Exploitation Generation."
18. Cook, *Lost Illusions*, 15.

19. Reid, *Redefining Black Film*, 74.
20. Paula J. Massood, *Black City Cinema: African American Urban Experiences in Film* (Philadelphia: Temple University Press, 2003), 84.
21. Several authors address the way that race in films tracks with these ideological shifts within the black community. For a concise and helpful treatment of the topic, see Rhines, *Black Film / White Money*, chap. 4, "The Negro Cycle through Blaxploitation: 1945–1974."
22. Lawrence, *Blaxploitation Films of the 1970s*, 50–51.
23. Quoted in Schaefer, *"Bold! Daring! Shocking! True!,"* 78.
24. "Dig This Drama about the People on 47th and St. Lawrence," *Chicago Defender*, May 19 1975, 20.
25. Quinn, "Tryin' to Get Over," 100.
26. A short summary of Neal's take on film appeared in Hollie I. West, "Superblack at the Crossroads," *Washington Post and Times-Herald*, October 15, 1972, L6. A scholarly summary of his views on the "black aesthetic" is available in Reid, *Redefining Black Film*, 75.
27. *Superfly* was distributed by Warner Bros. Quinn, "Tryin' to Get Over," 90.
28. "MGM Retains Black Market Firm to Promote and Advertise 'Shaft,'" *New Pittsburgh Courier*, March 13, 1971, 13.
29. One review called the films "exploitation in the worst racial sense of the term, produced (and often written and directed) by whites interested only in giving a newly discovered 'market' a *Shaft* over and over." Richard Schickel, "A New Kind of Exploitation Flick," *Life*, June 9, 1972, 20. The *New Yorker* also brought attention to this ownership pattern. Pauline Kael, "Notes on Black Movies," *New Yorker*, December 2, 1972, 62.
30. B. J. Mason, "New Films: Culture or Con Game?," *Ebony*, December 1972, 60, 62.
31. Robertson was nominated for the Best Film Editing Oscar in 1970 for his work on *Midnight Cowboy*. "Soviet Directors Visit 'Shaft' Set," *New York Amsterdam News*, February 27, 1971, 19.
32. Moira Walsh, "One Vote for Black Films," *America*, September 1972, 211.
33. David Denby, "Getting Whitey," *Atlantic Monthly*, August 1972, 86.
34. Theophilus Green, "Black Man as Movie Hero," *Ebony*, August 1972, 146.
35. Junius Griffin, "Black Movie Boom—Good or Bad?" (letter to the editor), *New York Times*, December 17, 1972, D3.
36. "Blacks vs. Shaft," *Newsweek*, August 28 1972, 88.
37. FORUM is an acronym for Full Opportunity Redirected to Uplift Mankind. Michael L. Culbert, "New Group Joins 'Super Fly' Fray," *Chicago Daily Defender*, September 7, 1972, 5.
38. West, "Superblack at the Crossroads," L6. Guerrero's work reports that Marion Barry called the film "mind genocide." Guerrero, *Framing Blackness*, 102.
39. Leroy Thomas, "'Conrack' Still Lacks Good Movie Quality," *Chicago Defender*, March 30, 1974, A11. See also Mattie Robinson, "Super-Dummies," *Chicago Defender*, December 5, 1974, 21; and A Black Laboror, "Our Readers Write," *Chicago Defender*, November 12, 1975, 9.

40. His views were published in the February 1974 issue of *Psychology Today* and summarized in "Black Crime Films Degrading," *Chicago Defender*, February 6, 1974, 23.
41. Ralph Parker, "From Our Readers," *Chicago Defender*, May 22, 1975, 19.
42. Mason, "New Films," 66.
43. *New York Amsterdam News*, January 23, 1971, 19.
44. *New York Amsterdam News*, July 1, 1972, D6.
45. *New York Amsterdam News*, June 12, 1971, 19.
46. Hazel Garland, "Black Fans Enjoy 'Shaft's Big Score!' Playing at Stanley," *New Pittsburgh Courier*, July 22, 1972, 14.
47. Cook, *Lost Illusions*, 266–67.
48. Kyle Riismandel, "Under Siege: The Discursive Production of Embattled Suburbs and Empowered Suburbanites in America, 1976–1992" (PhD diss., George Washington University, 2010).
49. "Blacks vs. Shaft," 88.
50. West, "Superblack at the Crossroads," L1.
51. "Black Kids Identify with Shaft," *New Pittsburgh Courier*, April 22, 1972.
52. "Blacks vs. Shaft," *Newsweek*, August 28, 1972, 88.
53. Gunning, "Aesthetic of Astonishment," 123.
54. Everett, *Returning the Gaze*.
55. Stewart, *Migrating to the Movies*, 103.
56. Jon Kraszewski, "Recontextualizing the Historical Reception of Blaxploitation: Articulations of Class, Black Nationalism, and Anxiety in the Genre's Advertisements," *Velvet Light Trap* 50 (Fall 2002): 48–61.
57. "More Family Movies for Detroit," *Chicago Defender*, July 2, 1974, 2.
58. West, "Superblack at the Crossroads," L6.
59. Stewart, *Migrating to the Movies*, 101.

## WORKS CITED

A Black Laboror. "Our Readers Write." *Chicago Defender*, November 12, 1975.

"Black Crime Films Degrading." *Chicago Defender*, February 6, 1974.

"Black Kids Identify with Shaft." *New Pittsburgh Courier*, April 22, 1972.

"Blacks vs. Shaft." *Newsweek*, August 28, 1972.

Bordwell, David. "Classical Hollywood Cinema: Narrational Principles and Procedures." In *Narrative, Apparatus, Ideology*, edited by Philip Rosen, 17–34. New York: Columbia University Press, 1986.

Bordwell, David, Janet Staiger, and Kristin Thompson. *The Classical Hollywood Cinema: Film Style and Mode of Production to 1960*. New York: Columbia University Press, 1985.

Bourdieu, Pierre. *Distinction: A Social Critique of the Judgment of Taste*. 1979. Translated by Richard Nice. Cambridge, MA: Harvard University Press, 1984.

Cook, David A. *Lost Illusions: American Cinema in the Shadow of Watergate and Vietnam, 1970–1979*. History of the American Cinema 9. Berkeley: University of California Press, 2000.

Culbert, Michael L. "New Group Joins 'Super Fly' Fray." *Chicago Daily Defender*, September 7, 1972.

Davis, Blair. *The Battle for the Bs: 1950s Hollywood and the Rebirth of Low-Budget Cinema*: New Brunswick, NJ: Rutgers University Press, 2012.

Denby, David. "Getting Whitey." *Atlantic Monthly*, August 1972.

"Dig This Drama about the People on 47th and St. Lawrence." *Chicago Defender*, May 19 1975.

Doherty, Thomas. *Teenagers and Teenpics: The Juvenilization of American Movies in the 1950s.* Boston: Unwin Hyman, 1988.

Dunn, Stephane. *Baad Bitches and Sassy Supermamas: Black Power Action Films*. Urbana: University of Illinois Press, 2008.

Everett, Anna. *Returning the Gaze: A Genealogy of Black Film Criticism, 1909–1949*. Durham, NC: Duke University Press, 2001.

Garland, Hazel. "Black Fans Enjoy 'Shaft's Big Score!' Playing at Stanley." *New Pittsburgh Courier*, July 22, 1972.

Green, Theophilus. "Black Man as Movie Hero." *Ebony*, August 1972.

Griffin, Junius. "Black Movie Boom—Good Or Bad?" Letter to the editor. *New York Times*, December 17, 1972, D3.

Guerrero, Ed. *Framing Blackness: The African-American Image in Film*. Philadelphia: Temple University Press, 1993.

Gunning, Tom. "An Aesthetic of Astonishment: Early Film and the (In)Credulous Spectator." In *Viewing Positions: Ways of Seeing Film*, edited by Linda Williams, 114–33. New Brunswick, NJ: Rutgers University Press, 1997.

Kael, Pauline. "Notes on Black Movies." *New Yorker*, December 2, 1972.

Kraszewski, Jon. "Recontextualizing the Historical Reception of Blaxploitation: Articulations of Class, Black Nationalism, and Anxiety in the Genre's Advertisements." *Velvet Light Trap* 50 (Fall 2002): 48–61.

Lawrence, Novotny. *Blaxploitation Films of the 1970s: Blackness and Genre*. New York: Routledge, 2008.

Mason, B. J. "New Films: Culture or Con Game?" *Ebony*, December 1972.

Massood, Paula J. *Black City Cinema: African American Urban Experiences in Film*. Philadelphia: Temple University Press, 2003.

McDonagh, Maitland. "The Exploitation Generation: Or How Marginal Movies Came In from the Cold." In *The Last Great American Picture Show*, edited by Thomas Elsaesser, Alexander Horwath, and Noel King, 107–30. Amsterdam: Amsterdam University Press, 2004.

"MGM Retains Black Market Firm to Promote and Advertise 'Shaft.'" *New Pittsburgh Courier*, March 13, 1971.

"More Family Movies for Detroit." *Chicago Defender*, July 2, 1974.

Munby, Jonathan. *Under a Bad Sign: Criminal Self-Representation in African American Popular Culture*. Chicago: University of Chicago Press, 2011.

———. "The Underworld Films of Oscar Micheaux and Ralph Cooper: Toward a Genealogy of the Black Screen Gangster." In *Mob Culture: Hidden Histories of the American Gangster Film*, edited by Lee Grieveson, Esther Sonnet, and Peter Stanfield, 263–80. New Brunswick, NJ: Rutgers University Press, 2005.

Parker, Ralph. "From Our Readers." *Chicago Defender*, May 22, 1975.

Quinn, Eithne. "Closing Doors: Hollywood, Affirmative Action, and the Revitalization of Conservative Racial Politics." *Journal of American History* 99, no. 2 (2012): 466–91.

———. "'Tryin' to Get Over': *Super Fly*, Black Politics, and Post–Civil Rights Film Enterprise." *Cinema Journal* 49, no. 2 (2010): 86–105.

Quinn, Eithne, and Peter Kramer. "Blaxploitation." In *Contemporary American Cinema*, edited by Linda Ruth Williams and Michael Hammond, 184–98. New York: McGraw-Hill, 2006.

Reid, Mark. *Redefining Black Film*. Berkeley: University of California Press, 1993.

Rhines, Jesse Algeron. *Black Film / White Money*. New Brunswick, NJ: Rutgers University Press, 1996.

Riismandel, Kyle. "Under Siege: The Discursive Production of Embattled Suburbs and Empowered Suburbanites in America, 1976–1992." PhD diss., George Washington University, 2010.

Robinson, Mattie. "Super-Dummies." *Chicago Defender*, December 5, 1974.

Schaefer, Eric. *"Bold! Daring! Shocking! True!": A History of Exploitation Films, 1919–1959*. Durham, NC: Duke University Press, 1999.

Schickel, Richard. "A New Kind of Exploitation Flick." *Life*, June 9, 1972.

Shiel, Mark. "American Cinema 1965–70." In *Contemporary American Cinema*, edited by Linda Ruth Williams and Michael Hammond, 12–40. New York: McGraw-Hill, 2006.

"Soviet Directors Visit 'Shaft' Set." *New York Amsterdam News*, February 27, 1971.

Stewart, Jacqueline Najuma. *Migrating to the Movies: Cinema and Black Urban Modernity*. Berkeley: University of California Press, 2005.

Thomas, Leroy. "'Conrack' Still Lacks Good Movie Quality." *Chicago Defender*, March 30 1974.

Walsh, Moira. "One Vote for Black Films." *America*, September 1972.

West, Hollie I. "Superblack at the Crossroads." *Washington Post and Times-Herald*, October 15, 1972.

# 11

## FROM HARLEM TO HOLLYWOOD

### THE 1970S RENAISSANCE AND BLAXPLOITATION

#### WALTER METZ

ONE OF THE MANY REGRETTABLE THINGS ABOUT USING "BLAXPLOITA-tion" to group a set of African American–themed films produced in Hollywood in the early 1970s is that the label separates them from a wider critical context, delimiting them not just in time but also in quality and method. Exploitation films are a particular mode of independent cinema, frequently low budget but not always of low cultural significance. In this chapter, I propose a series of theoretical and critical interventions into the study of these films that seeks to correct this reductionism in thinking.

What if, instead of linking films such a *Blacula* (1972) to the tawdry cheapness of the postwar quickie exploitation market (Russ Meyer and the like), we link them to the Hollywood Renaissance, a formulation that celebrates the modernist genius of films such as *Easy Rider* (1969)? As Thomas Schatz argues, in the late 1960s, a series of American films made in the crumbling studio system—in which, absurdly, a shoe company (Kinney's) was using a major Hollywood production studio (Warner Bros.) as a tax write-off—projected the formal and thematic obsessions of the international art cinema onto American film screens.[1] As an example, in *The Graduate* (1967), Mike Nichols aggressively uses zoom and wide-angle lenses, focus pulls, jump cuts, and other formal trickery to express the isolation of a thoughtful young man in plastic, corporate Los Angeles.

If one looks at the list of films heretofore entered into the canon of the Hollywood Renaissance (from *Bonnie and Clyde* to *The Godfather*), we notice that, like the original Quattrocento, there are not that many black faces to be found. However, what is Melvin Van Peebles's *Watermelon Man* (1970) if not a Renaissance film? It uses a series of Brechtian modernist techniques to express the transformation in consciousness of a man who suddenly wakes up in the skin of another. Are not the truly great African American films of the early 1970s—*Ganja and Hess* (1973) and *Sweet Sweetback's Baadasssss Song* (1971)—interrogating the Othello complex of this latter-day Renaissance?

In the midst of that earlier encounter with black identity in western Europe—horrifyingly expressed by Ben Johnson's *The Masque of Blackness* (1605), for example—William Shakespeare offered his play about the difficulties of a Moor in Venice. Worse than the bubonic plague still closing theaters, these problems infect both people like Iago, who cannot overcome the blackness of his heart to accept a better man into the community, and Othello himself, who cannot escape internalizing the vile attitude of others toward him. Using Shakespeare as a model, we can come to see the 1970s films, both those inclined toward art cinema, such as *Ganja and Hess*, and also more commercial projects, such as *Scream Blacula, Scream* (1973), as full expressions of such transformational Renaissance themes.

Theoretically, it is not at all clear how to group the African American–themed films from the early 1970s. Genre fails as badly as usual: if *Shaft* (1971) is a genre film, then its connection should be backward to film noir, not sideways to *Blacula*. Indeed, *Shaft* is a remake of *The Maltese Falcon* (1941), but on either of genre theory's analytical axes, the relationships fail to illuminate much. Syntagmatically, *The Maltese Falcon* ends with abject pessimism, not with Sam Spade triumphant. Paradigmatically, the substitution of Richard Roundtree for Humphrey Bogart offers radical sea changes in each film's affective impact.[2] The sources of Roundtree's *aesthetique du cool*—as Thomas Cripps formulates the style of masculinity on display in films such as *Sweet Sweetback's Baadasssss Song*—are markedly different from Bogart's, even if both dangerously encourage regular men toward self-destruction.[3]

In an excellent essay on *Dead Man* (1995), Jim Jarmusch's "revisionist" Western, Susan Kollin suggests the formulation of "anti-Western," positing that there are some films which so assault their generic roots that they oppose the very foundational aesthetic, narrative, and ideological formulations of the original genre practice.[4] In this sense, *Ganja and Hess* would be a kind of anti-horror film, while *Sweetback* would be an anti-Western with as great a deconstructive impact as Jarmusch's film on the Western. However, by preserving the structuralist binaries of genre (if *Dead Man* opposes the Western, this implies the stability of the obverse Western typologies), the nonlinear complexities of cinema are once again restrained by genre's rigid logic.

In *Black Film as Genre*, Thomas Cripps led film studies astray, seeking out an organizational scheme that was doomed to reductionism.[5] Multiple dimensional genre definitions—such as Altman's semantic and syntactic approach—are problematic enough, reducing complex films to a few criteria while ignoring others equally important for understanding the texts. Seeing films through only one dimension, such as whether they represent black people or not, is disastrous, forcing criticism to discount the fascinating variety of such films. Instead, seeking to understand intertextual relationships, in their full multidimensional complexity, is the most productive way of thinking about how cinema works. Genre and history are mere subsets for understanding how a film exists in a web of formulations and hypotheses about the world. *Ganja and Hess* is a horror film, and an assault on horror conventions, but also an objet d'art, that is, an internally fascinating aesthetic experience, not to mention a meaningful engagement with the sociology and political configuration of New York City and its environs. *Sweetback* is similarly a negative engagement with the American film Western but also an articulation of the communal nature of subaltern Los Angeles and so much more. And yet what this study reveals is that *Scream Blacula, Scream*, certainly not an antiblaxploitation film but instead a commercial venture meant to extend the profitability of its predecessor, is every bit as compelling cinema as these other, more feted films of the early 1970s, in terms of both aesthetic practices and also political praxis.

In short, I want to celebrate the full aesthetic and political impact of black cinema in the early 1970s. Seeing these films within the frameworks of historical cycle or genre studies reduces them unnecessarily. Made by American International Pictures (AIP) in full exploitation mode, *Blacula* is perhaps more hindered by rigid adherence to genre conventions than is *Ganja and Hess*, but both films activate the metaphors of the vampire mythology in order to understand the racial experience of the United States in the early 1970s. Both of these films are properly located in the middle of a continuum of horror and anti-horror, genre and resistance to genre. We need to see such films in their full intertextual complexity to understand how they enter into a dialogue, not only with film history and the social history of the United States but also with the full array of human experience. I align my case studies according to three generic modes of experience—horror, Western, and comedy—suggesting that the slippages between these traditions outweigh any one film's rigid adherence to a particular genre tradition.

## HORROR

AIP's *Blacula* begins with a tour-de-force precredits teaser sequence. Prince Mamuwalde (William Marshall) and his princess, Luva, have arrived at Count Dracula's castle in order to demand a cessation of the slave trade. Rather than aligning with the forces of justice, as one might expect an outcast to do, Dracula defends the practice of selling souls as having "merit." Set in 1780, that is, shortly after the signing of the Declaration of Independence, *Blacula* lines up its metaphors with precision. Dracula is played by Charles Macaulay, born in Louisville, Kentucky, and played with an American accent that contrasts quite explicitly with the British Draculas who populate the twentieth century's monster movies, demonstrating their otherness through effete accents. Unlike the earlier films set in a dangerous and mysterious eastern Europe, *Blacula* establishes that the defense of the slave trade is a particularly American occupation. After Dracula turns lecherous, offering to pay Mamuwalde for the purchase of Luva, the prince becomes outraged, declaring, "I find your cognac as distasteful as your manners."

As played by William Marshall, Mamuwalde is civilization embodied. His resonant voice, familiar to *Star Trek* fans as Dr. Richard Daystrom, a genius scientist in the episode "The Ultimate Computer" (1967), commands the screen as no one else in the film. As Mamuwalde attempts to storm out of the castle in affront, Dracula grabs Luva. After a brief struggle, Dracula prevails and bites Mamuwalde in the neck, cursing him to forever suffer and naming him Blacula.

Alas, *Blacula* cannot sustain the political force of its opening sequence, falling back into genre clichés. After sealing Mamuwalde in a coffin, Dracula entombs Luva alive in his castle's dungeon, damning her to the full torment of consciousness as, in his words, "the black flesh rots from your bones." By invoking the stories of Edgar Allan Poe, *Blacula* easily falls back into the AIP horror tradition of the 1960s.

In the film's trite ending, the police chase Blacula to an underground chemical plant. A white cop shoots Tina, the reincarnation of Luva. Blacula avenges the second killing of his beloved, electrocuting one officer and throwing another over a railing at the facility. Distraught, Blacula climbs the stairs to expose himself to the sun. While he writhes in pain, Dr. Gordon Thomas, the film's Van Helsing, pulls away the vampire's cape. His face has melted in the sun, producing an ending that is far less shock than schlock. Nevertheless, *Blacula* proved a big hit at the box office. The film's $1 million gross doubled its production budget of $500,000, scoring a significant profit for AIP.[6]

*Blacula*'s success resulted not in a wave of movies seeking to expand on the film's opening political allegory but instead in a series of morally simplistic horror films, such as *Blackenstein* (1973), *Dr. Black and Mr. White* (1976), and *Abby* (1974), the latter a version of *The Exorcist* (1973). Film history tells us that one film resisted this moral simplicity, *Ganja and Hess*. The lore has it that the film's producers, Quentin Kelly and Jack Jordan, sought to take advantage of the success of *Blacula* and commissioned screenwriter Bill Gunn to craft a black vampire film. Gunn instead produced an allegorical art film about the nature of addiction. The producers viewed a cut of the film that they declared commercial poison and hired an editor to recraft the film into a sexploitation piece fit for drive-ins. Gunn and his creative team so loathed the film that they took their names off the new version, titled *Blood Couple* (more rereleases with worse titles followed).

There are a number of odd features of this oft-told story of the artistic corruption of *Ganja and Hess*. For one thing, Kelly and Jordan chose an extremely odd way of making exploitation films. They decided to bankroll five films, one an adaptation of a James Baldwin story and another a film to be directed by Maya Angelou. It seems unlikely that the producers were completely blind to the fact that they were assembling highly talented, radical African American artists and material.

Now let us stop to ponder for a minute the devastating effects that the blaxploitation label has had for the status of *Ganja and Hess*. Bill Gunn's masterpiece might be the most sophisticated horror film in all of American film history, never mind the Hollywood Renaissance period. My project, to reformulate *Ganja and Hess* as one of the masterworks of American cinema in the early 1970s, at least allows us to position its generic work alongside examples much closer to it in method. For instance, *Chinatown* (Roman Polanski, 1974) is one of the last great Renaissance films (before the return of the blockbuster, initiated by *Jaws* in 1975). As studied by John Cawelti in his seminal essay, *Chinatown* engages in generic transformation, the restructuring of material into a critique of the very foundations of those myths.[7]

*Chinatown* reworks film noir traditions in order to critique the very Los Angeles from which those cultural practices emerged. *Chinatown* reengineers film noir's obsession with the moral purification of rainwater into a full-blown critique of Los Angeles, whose water-use policies are riddled with corruption, greed, and murder. The building of a dream factory on a desert has vacuumed in the abusive fiscal policies that destroy any possibility of the American Dream. Furthermore, private investigator Jake Gittes (Jack Nicholson) is completely blind to the events unfolding around him. When Evelyn Mulwray's gardener (Jerry Fujikawa) mutters that the (salt) water is "bad for grass," Gittes's dismissive "yeah, bad for the glass" provides him the key to unraveling the mystery, but his racism prevents him from seeing the truth, beautifully allegorized by the fact that the clue hiding in the water at the Mulwray estate is Hollis's broken eyeglasses.

Director Roman Polanski himself slits Jake's nose, forcing him to walk around with an emasculating bandage on the middle of his face for the rest of the film, while he proceeds to fail at every step in helping the Mulwray women out of the clutches of the biblical beast, Noah Cross. That the incestuous rapist Cross is played by John Huston, the director of *The Maltese Falcon* (1941), one of the pillars of film noir, brings *Chinatown*'s critique of Hollywood into crystal clarity.

The appearance of the director Bill Gunn in *Ganja and Hess* serves a similar function to the filmmakers who populate *Chinatown*'s diegesis. Early in the film, George Meda (Gunn) comes to stay with Dr. Hess Green (Duane Jones), to assist him in his research into African tribal traditions. Driven insane by the pressures of black masculinity in racist America, Meda climbs a tree in despair. Gunn frames his own image next to a noose, invoking the central image of Jim Crow violence. Yet it is not the prying eyes of the white people in Westchester County (whose scorn Dr. Green rightfully fears) who bring the noose but Meda himself. This is the central conceit of *Ganja and Hess*, that horror comes not from without but from within. Here is the generic break with *Blacula* and the blaxploitation tradition. The white racist Dracula creates Mamuwalde's vampirism. In *Ganja and Hess*, the horrors of blood lust, while framed within a very clear critique of white racism, ultimately derive from an Afrocentric tradition, passed from the originating African tribe to Dr. Green's bourgeois lifestyle as a successful scientist and art collector in New York's most swank county.

Duane Jones's portrayal of Dr. Hess Green is haunted by his only other great role, as Ben in *The Night of the Living Dead* (1968). A necessary precursor to *Ganja and Hess*, the low-budget zombie film also presents race allegorically. Ben spends the entire film as the only African American hiding in a house with white folks, fighting together against zombies. Ben alone survives the night. When he awakens, he is immediately shot by a mob of white vigilantes, who mistake him for yet another zombie. When they begin burning the zombie bodies, including Ben's, Romero runs the end credits over grainy black-and-white photographs that look more like civil rights abuses in the American South in the 1960s than they do images from a zombie film.

Similarly, Gunn's film uses allegory to reframe the African American experience in cinema. *Ganja and Hess* assaults a number of the morally simplistic formulations of blaxploitation cinema. In *Blacula*, Dr. Gordon Thomas (Thalmus Rasulala) asks the coroner what could have happened to one of Mamuwalde's early victims, Bobby McCoy, a black gay man who bought the contents of Dracula's castle and shipped them back to America. The coroner suspects the wound around the neck to be a rat bite. However, Dr. Thomas does not accept the theory, since the young man's veins are completely empty. The coroner can go no further in his scientific exploration, since he did not get to examine the victim's white lover, also killed by Mamuwalde. "I don't get many whites in here," he observes.

It is the blaxploitation film's depiction of largely separate worlds between black and white folks that *Ganja and Hess* restructures. Dr. Green is introduced via his work at the Brooklyn Museum of Art. As the director, Jack Sargent, leads Hess around, they walk past the artworks. The camera comes to rest on a partially clothed white woman standing shivering in front of a tree. The image is a 1799 oil painting by Chevalier Fereol de Bonnemaison titled *Young Woman Overtaken by a Storm*. The allegorical piece expresses the drama of a world in the wake of the French Revolution.

Such turmoil frames the story of Hess Green, whose pursuit of knowledge of African culture will lead to his contracting the disease of vampirism, doomed to prey on the poor to supply his blood habit. The film is constantly attempting to situate Dr. Green, both in a world of blacks and whites cohabitating and also in one that is riven by class inequities, a world separate and woefully unequal. For Dr. Green has to drive out of his swank neighborhood to travel to the ghetto to prey on the black working class.

In the film's second part, "Survival," Hess pretends to deliver blood at a bank in the inner city. To distract the staff, he lights a wastepaper basket on fire, allowing him to steal all of the blood from the facility. He calmly walks down the street outside the blood bank carrying his satchel full of the plastic bags of that which will serve as his sustenance. Gunn's camera pans right across a bunch of kids playing in the street. A city bus passes by, with the word "Liberty" written clearly across the back. Gunn's film uses its mise-en-scène tactically to establish a series of ironies. Here, Dr. Green has attained the financial ability to collect the treasures of Western and African art and hire chauffeurs to drive him around in a Rolls Royce, but at the same time he is doomed to suffer the pains of his addiction. He is no freer than the black underclass that he exploits.

Gunn uses the intertextual language of cinema to tell his love story. In the film's third section, "Letting Go," Meda's ex-wife, Ganja (Marlene Clark), comes to stay with Dr. Green. Her search for her husband soon uncovers his dead body in Dr. Green's basement freezer. As Ganja has recently made love to Dr. Green, this presents her with a significant conflict of emotions. She and Hess

The "Liberty" bus passes by Dr. Hess Green. (*Ganja and Hess* DVD, Image Entertainment)

have dinner, sitting on opposite sides of a long dining table with many burning candles in between them. The setup invokes the breakfast sequence in *Citizen Kane* (1941), as Kane and his first wife's marriage crumbles, depicted without words, as the couple grows farther apart from each other at the breakfast table.

Gunn uses the tabular distance between his two lovers to express the conflict Ganja has over her having slept with the man who has frozen her husband's dead body. She declares simply, "I know that you killed my husband." Dr. Green quietly asks his butler to clear the dinner plates, as Ganja storms away from the table. Employing the deep focus for which *Citizen Kane* is famous, across two rooms deep into Hess's mansion, we see Ganja storming back and forth, tossing papers around the room, with Hess immobile in the foreground of the image.

This is one of the many complex cinematic moments in *Ganja and Hess*, seemingly rendering it head and shoulders above the Hollywood commercial cinema. Indeed, it is a sophisticated film about the relationship between African culture and Christianity. Early in the film, Meda says, "You are the despised of the Earth." The film comes close to invoking the postcolonial theorist Frantz Fanon. Indeed in *The Wretched of the Earth* (1961), Fanon formulates a three-pronged approach to colonization: (1) a phase in which the colonizers identify with the cultural and technological prowess of the "civilizers"; (2) another in which the colonized desire to return to the simpler state before the colonizers

Dr. Hess Green in the foreground, while Ganja storms away in deep focus. (*Ganja and Hess* DVD, Image Entertainment)

Deep focus is apparent as Charles Foster Kane (*left*) discusses his newspaper. (*Citizen Kane* DVD, Turner Home Entertainment)

arrived; and (3) the fighting phase in which the irrevocably changed culture of the colonized emerges into the future in a new idiom of progress and resistance.[8]

Fanon's ideas are a road map to *Ganja and Hess*. Hess is trapped between a nihilistic Meda, who destroys himself because he cannot reconcile himself to a world in which racism so determines his identity, and Dr. Green, who fares no better identifying so heavily with the world of white culture and commerce. Only Ganja survives to the end, struggling with the addiction she has been bequeathed by Hess yet finishing the film in close-up with a wry smile, awaiting the vampire lover she has created emerging out of Hess's swimming pool.

In short, *Ganja and Hess* is both aesthetically and politically a sophisticated film, a horror story in an allegorical register and told with cinematic complexity. However, we need to revisit the notion of its complete superiority over the blaxploitation films that surround it. One would think that if *Blacula* reverted so quickly to formulaic genre material after its first political antislavery, precredits sequence, its sequel would be far worse. However, it turns out that this sequel, *Scream Blacula Scream*, is a terrific film. First of all, it matches the aestheticism of *Ganja and Hess*. While not interested in the abstract art-cinema imagery of Gunn's film, it nevertheless stylishly tells its story of an outcast of a voodoo cult who brings Blacula back to life. The mise-en-scène and the editing work in concert to visually forward the film's story. As Lisa Fortier (Pam Grier), the talented voodoo priestess, talks with the ex-cop Justin Carter (Don Mitchell), they sit in front of a fire. The camera zooms into the logs, providing for the opportunity for a graphic match to the bones of Mamuwalde that Willis Daniels (Richard Lawson), the outcast, has laid out to perform his ritual. Sandy Dvore again provides an animated credits sequence, this time relying on the segmentation of bodies in black-and-white, inspired by the bones for the voodoo ceremony.

*Scream Blacula Scream* is an aesthetically inventive film. As Blacula returns to a party to strike at another victim, he sneaks in the back door and climbs the stairs. The point-of-view shot simulates his walking up the stairs in search of his victim. This was to become the standard horror film mode of the 1970s, most famously redone in *Halloween* (1978). It is of some significance that a much-earlier articulation of this technique occurred in a sequel to a blaxploitation film.

The film is also surprisingly—shocking if one accepts the reductionist definitions of blaxploitation—sophisticated in its treatment of Mamuwalde's plight. He pleads with Lisa to use her voodoo powers to "exorcise this demonic creature that inhabits [his] body." He rejects Dr. Green's solution of Christian immolation in *Ganja and Hess*: "My only alternative is to destroy myself." For a while, Lisa helps him with the exorcism. However, at the film's climax, Justin interrupts

Lisa's voodoo ritual precisely as it seems it is going to work. In a rage, Blacula attacks Justin, revealing to Lisa the monster that he truly is. As Blacula pleads, "You've got to help me. I need you," Lisa backs away in horror. Justin calls him Mamuwalde, to which he replies, "I am Blacula," for the first time embracing his destructive power without self-loathing.

The presentation of Blacula's triumph as a villain is presented with artistic flourish. As Lisa repeatedly stabs her voodoo doll of Blacula, the vampire writhes in pain. As he reaches his arms upward, attempting to turn into a bat, he fails to transform. The camera, mounted on a crane, spirals upward, ending in an extreme long shot from a bird's-eye view. The film ends on a freeze frame of Blacula, finally accepting of his identity as an avenging monster created by white racism but unable to return to the African civilization from which he came. Like *Ganja and Hess*, it is an ending resonant with Fanon's three phases of colonial liberation.

## COMEDY

What the preceding description of *Scream Blacula Scream* does not present is how funny the film is. As Willis awakens from having been bitten by Blacula and transformed into a vampire, he gets dressed in a flashy gray suit. He gets upset only when he cannot find his reflection in a mirror. He is upset that he can no longer primp. "I mean, a man has got to see his face," he shouts. He is upset not for being undead but for reasons of vanity. He questions Blacula not about their careers as vampires but to answer the question, "How do I look, man?"

The history of comedy is every bit as important as the dramatic in expanding our sense of the importance of blaxploitation cinema for understanding early 1970s American commercial cinema. In *White* (1997), Richard Dyer makes the simple yet game-changing observation that to study race by leaving white identity completely invisible dooms the project of breaking the shackles of oppression.[9] What results is that even within kindhearted liberal society, white identity is always assumed as the normative, from simple things like so-called flesh-colored Band-Aids to complexities like who is allowed to kiss Julia Roberts in a movie, something you may have already pondered by watching Denzel Washington inexplicably *not* get the girl at the end of the absurdly timid film *The Pelican Brief* (1993).

One of the most offensive expressions of racial discriminatory representational practice in the history of the United States is blackface. Refusing to allow people of color on the stage, American dramatic artists developed a way of having white people perform race by putting burnt cork on their skin. Deep into the twentieth century, this tradition continued in literal and symbolic forms. A blackface sitcom at its very core, *Amos 'n' Andy* (1951–53) remained into the 1960s CBS's most profitably syndicated show.

A civil-rights-inflected America began to gradually change. Most sitcoms of the 1960s and 1970s made use of what I suggest we call "liberal blackface," using blackface explicitly against its original goals of denying black people representation. An episode of *Bewitched* (1964–72) has Samantha step onto the set in blackface, invoking a spell to teach a bigot a lesson. In *Diff'rent Strokes* (1978–86), the white older sister to two adopted black orphans teaches her racist boyfriend not to judge others by their skin color by dressing for the prom in blackface. But these liberal one-off scenes did little to change the television landscape. They failed to decenter what critical theorists label the culture of white supremacy, in which the normative characters continue to be assumed to be white. With very few exceptions, such as Shonda Rhimes's *Grey's Anatomy* (2005–present), if you throw a dart at the TV screen, you are likely to hit a white character. *New Girl* (2011–present) may have a black friend, but she is surrounded by far more white ones.

In the 1960s, African American filmmaker Melvin Van Peebles fled to France to escape the remains of Jim Crow America. After making an exquisite film about a romance between an African American soldier and a white French woman, *Story of a Three-Day Pass* (1968), Columbia Pictures lured Van Peebles back to the United States. The studio had just made a fortune on 1969's *Easy Rider*, about the counterculture, and was looking for other safe and easy targets.

Van Peebles's bizarre but stunning *Watermelon Man* script tells the story of Jeff, a white insurance salesman, played by black comedic actor Godfrey Cambridge. Cambridge plays Jeff in whiteface in the first act of the film, until the character falls asleep one evening and wakes up black (that is, with Cambridge no longer in whiteface). Jeff soldiers on with his life, but it does not go well. Friends abandon him one by one. He is fired from his job after he is reassigned to the inner city and impudently helps black folks save money on their insurance policies.

Jeff's white, liberal wife leaves him when she can no longer stand living with what she cruelly terms the "race problem." And in a sparkling parody of a scene from Lorraine Hansberry's Tony-winning Broadway play *A Raisin in the Sun* (1959), Jeff's neighbors come to blockbust him out of his home, offering extra cash to remove him from their vicinity. Columbia butchered the edit of the final act of *Watermelon Man*, making its plot virtually incomprehensible, but what remains is clear enough. The film ends as Jeff joins a Black Panther–esque organization, comically wielding mop handles as spears, training in the basement of a karate studio.

Van Peebles's experience at Columbia was so brutal that he self-financed his next film, *Sweet Sweetback's Baadasssss Song* (1971), one of the masterpieces of American independent filmmaking. But it is worth remembering that, before that, in *Watermelon Man*, he made one of the great Hollywood comedy films of the Hollywood Renaissance, every bit as full of rage and disdain as *The Graduate*. When Van Peebles, full of exasperation, chants, "This ain't America, is it?" on the film's signature song, "Love, That's America," while Jeff is reduced to working at the dump, it is clear that the answer is unfortunately, "Yes, it is." That song has recently found a new life as a theme for Occupy Wall Street protesters, with Van Peebles's endorsement. But forty years earlier, Van Peebles used the absurdity of whiteface to criticize normative privilege, something that it took academic theory decades to discover in the otherwise-revolutionary work of Richard Dyer. The cinema can dream more easily that which we struggle to comprehend. While you would not know it from popular American film histories, the dreams of black liberation are just as cinematically present as those of Walter Mitty and Dorothy Gale.

## WESTERN

*Sweetback* delivers its critique of African Americans living under the yolk of white racism by using the traditions of the American Western. In the middle of the film, a biker gang traps Sweetback. In a bizarre sequence, he engages in a duel with the gang's leader, a white woman who goes by the name Big Sadie. They fight using the traditions of sex performance that the film has established as Sweetback's métier, but nonetheless, this is a kind of shoot-out that is most familiar from the American Western.

The film indeed ends with one of the central motifs of the American Western, the escape from civilized authority into the wilderness. There is nothing left for Sweetback, like Shane before him, in an America dominated by racist police who handcuff him. Sweetback beats those cops with their own handcuffs after witnessing the beating of a black protester, and he goes on the run for the rest of the film. In classic American Western fashion, he flees the city to the American Southwest. As the police dogs finally catch up to him, he rebaptizes in their blood, crossing the river of no return. The film ends with him crossing into Mexico, facing the mountains as far away as those that beckon Shane. Van Peebles ends with a textual warning, that Sweetback will return to collect some dues.

*Watermelon Man*'s Jeff Gerber loses his job in the insurance business and is reduced to working in a dump. (*Watermelon Man* DVD, Columbia Tristar Home Entertainment)

However, how do we reconcile the comedy of *Watermelon Man* with the horrors of *Sweetback*? We can find the middle ground between them by noticing that a commercial Hollywood film that would never have been seen as a blaxploitation piece in fact invokes these two generic traditions. *Blazing Saddles* (1974) is a blaxploitation film par excellence. It features a central African American character, Bart (Cleavon Little), and it is produced by Jewish filmmakers (Mel Brooks and Andrew Bergman) who had the good sense to hire the funniest man of the 1970s, Richard Pryor, as one of the screenwriters.

Like *Watermelon Man*, *Blazing Saddles* is rife with comic interventions into the racist nature of the American experience. When Bart and his friend Charlie (Charles McGregor), enslaved workers building the railroad, sink in quicksand while testing the track, Taggart (Slim Pickins) and his foreman, Lyle (Burton Gilliam), throw a rope. Taggart is relieved when they rescue the $400 handcart used by the men, but the African American men themselves are of no concern. When Bart barely keeps his feet on the rail to drag Charlie and himself to safety, Taggart jokes, "Don't just lay around getting a suntan." Like Sweetback, Bart has had enough: he responds to Taggart's order that he put his shovel to good use by whacking Taggart on the back of the head with it.

Throughout the film, Bart plays the trickster to the conventions of the American Western. When he learns that Taggart's boss, Hedley Lamarr

*Blazing Saddles* plays on the classic Western tradition to demonstrate the racist nature of the genre and American history. (*Blazing Saddles* DVD, Warner Bros. Home Entertainment)

(Harvey Korman), is building an army of villains to destroy his town of Rock Ridge, Bart and his buddy Jim (Gene Wilder) sneak into the line of applicants. Behind a rock, Jim distracts two Ku Klux Klan members by showing them his "prisoner," Bart. Bart quips, "Hey, where are the white women at?" When the Klansmen take the bait, Bart and Jim beat them up and steal their robes. When Bart and Jim arrive at the front of the line to apply to Lamarr, Lamarr's men notice that Bart's hands beneath the white robes are black. Bart jokes in direct address to the camera, "And now, for my next impression, Jesse Owens."

The postmodern comedy of *Blazing Saddles* offers a new turn of the screw for the genre play of Hollywood Renaissance cinema. Yet what we should notice is that the film's obsessions with the traditions of the American Western and its comic, irreverent, and trickster approach are aspects of blaxploitation cinema at its finest. Count Basie and his orchestra members at the beginning of *Blazing Saddles* are as out of place in the American West as Jeff the insurance salesman in *Watermelon Man* is holding a broom in the middle of the dump, set to the ironic tune "Love, That's America." Both offer acoustic tricksterism—replete with the complexities of the history of music and race in America—at their most scathing pitch. To expand our focus on a wide swath of early 1970s films to understand the changes in American film culture is to appreciate blaxploitation cinema more fully and to seek out the blaxploitation elements in Hollywood Renaissance films more generally.

# CONCLUSION

To explore the legacy of the blaxploitation cinema of the 1970s into the present, I want to collide the films of Spike Lee with those of Quentin Tarantino. When *Django Unchained* (2012) was released, Lee was very vocal about his opinions that a white filmmaker could take such liberties with the African American image on film. Indeed, Lee's critiques mirrored the critiques of 1970s African American film scholarship interested in forwarding positive images of black people. What I hope to have demonstrated in this chapter is that such a reductive approach to filmic meaning misses much of the complexity of film representation.

This is not to say that radical cinema does not have its place in defining for us the possibilities of what cinema can be beyond commercial genre restraints. And thus, I have celebrated both art cinema (*Ganja and Hess*, *Sweetback*) and commercial cinema (*Blazing Saddles*, *Watermelon Man*, even in its brutalized form; and most importantly, the blaxploitation sequel *Scream Blacula Scream*).

The legacy of these two lines of argumentation can be seen in Lee's remake of *Ganja and Hess*, *Da Sweet Blood of Jesus* (2014), and in Tarantino's homage to blaxploitation, *Django Unchained*. Lee takes a reverential approach to reconstructing Bill Gunn's radical project, at times reshooting the original à la Gus Van Sant's 1998 reconstruction of Alfred Hitchcock's *Psycho* (1960). In this way, Lee swallows whole the notion that blaxploitation was abusive to African Americans and that Bill Gunn's art cinema was its antidote. In short, *Da Sweet Blood of Jesus* attempts to be an antiblaxploitation film in Susan Kollin's sense that *Dead Man* is an anti-Western.

Tarantino, for his part, finds the blaxploitation moment, full of violence and rage at racist America, to be the proper idiom for *Django Unchained*. Like *Sweetback*, whose credits Tarantino's film emulates, the premise of *Django Unchained* ties it directly to the Hollywood Western, despite the film's music—featuring a song by Ennio Morricone—and periodic stylistic flourishes that evoke Italian spaghetti Westerns. Dr. King Schultz (Christoph Waltz), a bounty hunter masquerading as a dentist, frees the escaped slave Django (Jamie Foxx) so that Django can assist him in identifying his latest quarry. After successfully completing this first mission, Schultz teaches Django the business of bounty hunting, eventually coming to care about Django as a human being. Shultz discovers that Django and his wife, Broomhilda (Kerry Washington), have been separated by the slave trade. Shultz agrees to help Django rescue his wife from Calvin Candie (Leonardo DiCaprio), a notoriously cruel Mississippi plantation owner.

Tarantino effectively evokes the classical Hollywood Western's devotion to searching in order to unmoor it from its racist pilings. For example, as Django and Schultz wander around the snowy West, passing buffalo and elk herds, shots match those almost exactly in *The Searchers* (1956), a very different quest narrative. In John Ford's iconic mounting of the Western, the white Ethan Edwards (John Wayne) and the Native American Martin Pawley (Jeffrey Hunter) search for Ethan's niece Debbie (Natalie Wood), who has been kidnapped by an evil Comanche chief, Scar (Henry Brandon). *Django Unchained* reframes the captivity narrative that obsesses *The Searchers*, shifting its focus from hysterical white people afraid of being taken captive by savages to a far more historically grounded reality: the ripping apart of black families by the abhorrent everyday practices of the antebellum South.

Van Peebles's film makes us care about Sweetback, desperately rooting for him as he fights off attack dogs, and ends in a freeze frame of indeterminacy that implies that he made it to Mexico. Tarantino's film ends not with modernist indeterminacy but instead with classical Hollywood convention. Django blows up Candyland, Calvin's plantation manor, and exchanges in a passionate kiss with Broomhilda. In the third act of the film, Tarantino desperately throws in everything he can to save his project's great premise, but he has no viable endgame. After it appears that Django has been caught and is about to be castrated as punishment for the shoot-out inside Candie's manor, he escapes by tricking some improbably located Australian miners, one of whom is played quite terribly by Tarantino himself.

Not all of Tarantino's gambits are as disastrous as this. At the moment of the bloodbath at the plantation house, the editor cuts to a high-angle long shot of the proceedings, accompanied by a Negro spiritual on the soundtrack, "Motherless Child." The moment effectively invokes the ending of a very different film about white and black bonding in the South, *The Defiant Ones* (1958). In that liberal Hollywood film, Sidney Poitier sings a spiritual—"Bowling Green, sewing machine!"—holding Tony Curtis in his arms as the white police dogs hunt them down. Indeed, rescuing Poitier from radical criticism's unfair reduction of him to an "Uncle Tom" might be the next project of expanding our focus outward from blaxploitation, perhaps via Poitier's comic, political Western, *Buck and the Preacher* (1972).

The intertextual referencing is one of *Django Unchained*'s great strengths. Unlike previous Tarantino films, in which the references are showy and meaningless (the characters eat a Douglas Sirk burger for no apparent reason in 1994's *Pulp Fiction*), here a great many pieces line up quite effectively. For example, right before Schultz shoots Candie, he admires the books lining the mansion's walls. Recalling the slave D'Artagnan, whom Candie's men let be ripped apart by attack dogs, Schultz informs Candie that Alexandre Dumas, the author of *The Three Musketeers* (1844), was in fact the grandson of a black slave woman. When the bloodbath following Candie's death results in the destruction of these books, Tarantino effectively demonstrates that civilization built on barbarity will destroy itself. This theme is best expressed when Schultz becomes unglued, having witnessed the barbarism of slavery, accompanied musically by Candie's sister playing Beethoven's "Für Elise" on the harp. He finally has to rip her hands off the harp to keep her from sullying the radical Romantic Beethoven's memory.

In the tradition of *Blazing Saddles* and *Watermelon Man*, *Django Unchained* is joyous and funny in its first two acts. Indeed, I think it might be possible to understand the film as a black comedy. The film's funniest set piece involves the "bagheads," a group of Klansmen who pursue Schultz and Django for killing the three white criminals on their plantation. Led by Big Daddy (in a great comedic turn, Don Johnson), the white men don white cloth sacks. Tarantino begins the scene with the men riding triumphantly to surging orchestral music. However, the scene then abruptly retakes, as the men complain that they cannot see out of their masks. What begins as Griffith's iconic, racist *The Birth of a Nation* (1915) becomes a travesty. The moment brings to mind both the Coen brothers' *O Brother, Where Art Thou?* (2000), wherein John Goodman plays a Klan leader whose racist ceremony is interrupted by the comic hijinks of the Soggy Bottom Boys, but even more directly Mel Brooks's *Blazing Saddles* (1973).

In *Django Unchained*, Tarantino is on the hunt for a great modernist critique of American filmmaking traditions as they pertain to the tragedy of race relations. Indeed, the "Mandingo fighting" section of the film is not just a cheap reference to the horrid exploitation film *Mandingo* (1975) but is far more importantly the closest American cinema has ever gotten to adapting Ralph Ellison's 1952 masterpiece "Battle Royale," one of the stories within *Invisible Man*, the greatest piece of African American modernist literature.

However, without any constraint, Tarantino's film devolves into the sleazy exploitation violence of the films he seems to love too much. Most of his films—*Kill Bill* (2003–4) and *Inglorious Basterds* (2009), to name just two—suffer from not knowing when enough is enough. Spike Lee's *Bamboozled* (2000) also suffers as a film with a great premise ending in a whimper because all of its energies have been directed toward an orgy of violence, the gushing of blood diluting the thematic message to the point of illegibility.

In *Da Sweet Blood of Jesus*, Lee subsumes himself to the tight focus of Bill Gunn's masterpiece. If Tarantino is interested in wild postmodern referencing, Lee embodies a great deal of humility when confronted with Gunn's script.

Consider the way Lee refilms the *Citizen Kane* dining-room sequence from *Ganja and Hess*. The butler Seneschal (Rami Malek) cuts their roast beef and offers Ganja (Zaraah Abrahams) some red wine. It is not until a number of shots that we come to learn that Dr. Green (Stephen Tyrone Williams) is seated at the same table, many feet away.

Ganja abruptly asks Dr. Green why he killed her husband. Dr. Green replies, "I wouldn't do anything to hurt you." In an addition to the script, Lee adds Ganja telling a story about having been beaten up by her brothers when she was young. After these traumatic events, her father came to help her see the cruelty of the world. He told her, "This world is a harsh place, especially for a black woman. You'll have to deal with the double whammy, being a woman and black. . . . Life is as hard as hell. Ganja has got to learn to take care of Ganja." Ganja tells Hess, "I've been taking care of myself since I've been seven years old."

As opposed to Gunn's film, in which Ganja retreats into the deep focus of the frame, Lee has his Green break the logic of *Citizen Kane*. In response to Ganja's emotional story, he sits right next to Ganja at her end of the table. He explains that he drank the blood of Hightower (Lee's film's Meda, no longer played by the filmmaker but instead by Elvis Nolasco). Ganja declares Green to be a "freak." When he disputes this characterization, Ganja asks what he is. "I'm an addict," he explains. This closeness, the undoing of the marital separation of *Citizen Kane*, allows Ganja and Hess to unite. They drag Hightower's body out onto Green's dock, throwing his dead body into the ocean surrounding Green's home on Martha's Vineyard (changed from the white suburbs of New York City in Gunn's film).

This is the biggest change Lee makes to Gunn's version of *Ganja and Hess*. Gunn situated Hess within a high culture of white wealth. Lee's film imagines Dr. Green as almost purely Afrocentric. The only artwork he has in his home on Martha's Vineyard is African American. And even though he has retreated to the swank island off the coast of Massachusetts, the film still finds Green returning to Brooklyn frequently. Lee's film begins with a beautiful dance sequence of African American male dancers moving their bodies to a melancholy piano score on the streets of Red Hook. As in Gunn's original, Hess atones for his sin in a gospel church, accompanied in both films by the 1970s composer Sam Weymon's beautiful gospel song "Too Late."

The return of blaxploitation in both *Da Sweet Blood of Jesus* and *Django Unchained*, for all of their differences, indicates that African American–themed films from the early 1970s continue to hold our imaginations for their ability to imagine an America that is different from the one we have been bequeathed.

What I have attempted in this chapter is to argue that, to appreciate the full range of Lee's and Tarantino's approaches to that history, we need a less reductive understanding of that period of filmmaking. If we use the rubric of the Hollywood Renaissance more expansively, we can see that a fuller range of cinema, from the blaxploitation of *Scream Blacula Scream* to the antiblaxploitation of *Sweetback*, from the art cinema of *Ganja and Hess* to the commercialism of *Blazing Saddles*, serves as the fecund soil from which the work of Spike Lee and Quentin Tarantino spring.

## NOTES

1. Thomas Schatz, "The New Hollywood," in *Film Theory Goes to the Movies*, ed. Jim Collins, Hilary Radner, and Ava Preacher Collins (New York: Routledge, 1993), 8–36.
2. Rick Altman, "A Semantic/Syntactic Approach to Film Genre," *Cinema Journal* 23, no. 3 (1984): 6–18.
3. Thomas Cripps, "*Sweet Sweetback's Baadasssss Song* and the Changing Politics of Genre Film," in *Close Viewings: Anthology of New Film Criticism*, ed. Peter Lehman (Tallahassee: Florida State University Press, 1990), 238–61.
4. Susan Kollin, "*Dead Man*, Dead West," *Arizona Quarterly: A Journal of American Literature, Culture, and Theory* 56, no. 3 (2000): 125–59.
5. Thomas Cripps, *Black Film as Genre* (Bloomington: Indiana University Press, 1979), 3.
6. The budget figure comes from the Internet Movie Database: www.imdb.com/title/tt0068284/business. The box-office gross figure comes from Wikipedia: https://en.wikipedia.org/wiki/Blacula (accessed June 26, 2015).
7. John Cawelti, "*Chinatown* and Generic Transformation in Recent American Films," *Film Theory and Criticism: Introductory Readings*, 3rd ed., ed. Gerald Mast and Marshall Cohen (New York: Oxford University Press, 1985), 503–20.
8. Frantz Fanon, *The Wretched of the Earth* (1963), trans. Richard Philcox (New York: Grove, 2005), 3.
9. Richard Dyer, *White* (New York: Routledge, 1997), 2.

## WORKS CITED

Altman, Rick. "A Semantic/Syntactic Approach to Film Genre." *Cinema Journal* 23, no. 3 (1984): 6–18.

Cawelti, John. "*Chinatown* and Generic Transformation in Recent American Films." In *Film Theory and Criticism: Introductory Readings*, 3rd ed., ed. Gerald Mast and Marshall Cohen, 503–20. New York: Oxford University Press, 1985.

Cripps, Thomas. *Black Film as Genre*. Bloomington: Indiana University Press, 1979.

———. "*Sweet Sweetback's Baadasssss Song* and the Changing Politics of Genre Film." In *Close Viewings: Anthology of New Film Criticism*, edited by Peter Lehman, 238–61. Tallahassee: Florida State University Press, 1990.

Dyer, Richard. *White*. New York: Routledge, 1997.

Fanon, Frantz. *The Wretched of the Earth* (1963). Translated by Richard Philcox. New York: Grove, 2005.

Kollin, Susan. "*Dead Man*, Dead West." *Arizona Quarterly: A Journal of American Literature, Culture, and Theory* 56, no. 3 (2000): 125–59.

Schatz, Thomas. "The New Hollywood." In *Film Theory Goes to the Movies*, edited by Jim Collins, Hilary Radner, and Ava Preacher Collins, 8–36. New York: Routledge, 1993.

# CONTRIBUTORS

**Gerald R. Butters, Jr.** is a professor of history at Aurora University in Aurora, Illinois. He is the author of *From Sweetback to Super Fly: Race and Film Audiences in Chicago's Loop* (2015), *Banned in Kansas: Motion Picture Censorship, 1915–1966* (2007), and *Black Manhood on the Silent Screen* (2002). A Fulbright recipient, he has spoken to the European Union in Luxembourg on images of black leadership in American film and television. He has published articles in *Film History*, *Film-Literature Review*, *Choice*, *Scope*, *Flow*, and *Kansas History*.

**Allyson Nadia Field** is an associate professor of cinema and media studies at the University of Chicago. She is the author of *Uplift Cinema: The Emergence of African American Film and the Possibility of Black Modernity* (2015) and the coeditor with Jan-Christopher Horak and Jacqueline Stewart of *L.A. Rebellion: Creating a New Black Cinema* (2015). Field is co-curator of the L.A. Rebellion Project of the UCLA Film & Television Archive.

**Vivian Halloran** is an associate professor of English and American studies at Indiana University, Bloomington. She is the author of *Exhibiting Slavery: The Caribbean Postmodern Novel as Museum* (2009) and *The Immigrant Table: Food, Ethnicity, and Diaspora* (2016). Halloran specializes in genre fiction and film of the Caribbean and the African diaspora, food studies, and postmodernist fiction. She is working on a comparative study of the work Chester Himes and Frank Yerby produced while at the end of their lives in Spain.

**Laura Cook Kenna** is a writer, speaker, and independent scholar based in Washington, DC. She received her PhD in American studies from George Washington University, where she later served as a visiting assistant professor of American studies and professorial lecturer of film studies. Currently, Kenna is a faculty member in cultural criticism and writing at the Trinity Forum Academy in Royal Oak, Maryland, and is a regular guest instructor at the U.S. State Department's Foreign Service Institute. Kenna is completing work on her first book, tentatively titled *American Gangster*, which is a study of the gangster genre focused on efforts to either censor or celebrate these media from *The Untouchables* of 1960s television to the *Grand Theft Auto* videogame franchise. She has published an article on TV censorship approaches in the *Velvet Light Trap* and a chapter on Frank Sinatra's relationship to Las Vegas in the book *Frontiers in Chance*.

**Novotny Lawrence** earned his PhD in 2004 from the Department of Theatre and Film (now Film and Media Studies) at the University of Kansas. He is an associate professor in the Radio, Television, and Digital Media Department at Southern Illinois University, where he teaches courses such as "Understanding Electronic Media," "Media and Society," "Documenting the Black Experience," and "History of African American Images in Film." Lawrence is the author of *Blaxploitation Films of the 1970s: Blackness and Genre* (2007) and the editor of *Documenting the Black Experience: Essays on African American History, Culture, and Identity in Nonfiction Films* (2014). He has also published journal articles and book chapters on a variety of topics such as *The Jeffersons*, *The Twilight Zone*, the comedy of Dave Chappelle, and the indie film *C.S.A.: The Confederate States of America*.

**Alfred L. Martin, Jr.**, is an assistant professor in the Department of Communication at the University of Colorado-Denver. Martin's research focuses on queer media studies, black media studies, production studies, reception theory, and television genre theory. His forthcoming book argues that the black-cast sitcom is an explicit genre, and therefore its engagement with black gayness does not resemble any other contemporary genre. By examining audience reception, industrial production practices, and authorship, the book argues that representations of black gay characters are trapped into particular narrative tropes. Martin has published articles in both scholarly journals including *Popular Communication*, *Television and New Media*, the *Journal of Black Masculinity*, and *Spectator* and in the popular press, including PopMatters.com, FlowTV, In Media Res, and Antenna. He has also contributed work to the forthcoming anthologies *The Comedy Studies Reader* and *Dislike, Hate, and Anti-Fandom in the Digital Age*. Martin is an active member of several professional organizations including the Society for Cinema and Media Studies and the International Communication Association.

**Walter Metz** is a professor in the Department of Cinema and Photography at Southern Illinois University, where he teaches film, television, and theater history, theory, and criticism. He holds two bachelor's degrees, one in materials science and engineering and the other in the humanities, from the Massachusetts

Institute of Technology. He holds a master's degree in communication studies from the University of Iowa, and a PhD in radio-television-film from the University of Texas at Austin. He is the author of three books: *Engaging Film Criticism: Film History and Contemporary American Cinema* (2004), *Bewitched* (2007), and *Gilligan's Island* (2012). Currently, he is drafting a book manuscript titled "Molecular Cinema," a new theoretical exploration of materialism in cinema as a way of rethinking the relationship between science and film.

**Eric Pierson** is a professor in the Communication Studies Department at the University of San Diego. He has written on a variety of topics that include film distribution in the 1970s, hate group recruiting via the Internet, and film festival pedagogy. Among the journals in which his work has appeared are *Screening Noir*, the *Journal of Mass Media Ethics*, and *Scope*. His work on black images and audiences has appeared in the *Encyclopedia of African American Business History* and the *Encyclopedia of the Great Black Migration*. His most recent works, "The Promise of Roots" and "The Clinton 12 and Prom Night in Mississippi: Conversations in Integration," appear in *Watching While Black: Centering the Television of Black Audiences* and *Documenting the Experience: Essays on African American History, Culture, and Identity in Nonfiction Films*.

**Harrison M. J. Sherrod** is a Chicago-based writer, curator, and educator. He holds a BA from Sarah Lawrence College and an MA from the University of Chicago. He is the coordinator of the Karla Scherer Center for the Study of American Culture at the University of Chicago and programmer at South Side Projections, a grass-roots film organization committed to bringing screenings and educational opportunities to culturally disenfranchised pockets of the city. He also teaches classes around Chicagoland on film history, literature, and philosophy.

**Joseph S. Valle** is a PhD candidate in the Mass Communication and Media Arts Graduate Program at Southern Illinois University–Carbondale. He received an MA in film studies at Columbia University. Valle published a book review in *Senses of Cinema* and has a forthcoming book review in *Film International*. His research interests include Palestinian cinema, Hindi cinema, documentary studies, race in U.S. cinema, and queer studies. Valle is currently in the beginning stages of his doctoral dissertation, which will focus on blaxploitation cinema.

**Charles E. Wilson, Jr.,** is a professor of English and the dean of the College of Arts and Letters at Old Dominion University. He holds a PhD in English from the University of Georgia. Wilson has taught courses in southern literature, African American literature, and early American literature. He is the author of three books including *Gloria Naylor: A Critical Literature* (2005). In addition, he has written essays on black manhood and identity. Wilson is also the recipient of the Outstanding Faculty Award of the State Council of Higher Education for Virginia.

# FILM AND TELEVISION INDEX

*Abby* (1974), 229
*Airport* (1970), 64
*Amazing Grace* (1974) 15, 157, 166–79
*Amos n' Andy* (1951–53), 236
*The Arena* (1973), 159

*Baadasssss!* (2003), 10
*Baadasssss Cinema* (2000), 10–11
*Bad Day at Black Rock* (1954), 83
*Bamboozled* (2000), 108
*Beauty and the Beast* (1946), 117
*Betwitched* (1964–72), 236
*Beverly Hills Cop* (1984), 197
*Big Bird Cage* (1972), 142
*Big Doll House* (1971), 142
*Big Sleep* (1946), 9
*The Bingo Long Traveling All-Stars & Motor Kings* (1976), 180, 182
*The Birth of a Nation* (1915), 62, 202, 242
*Black Belt Jones* (1974), 5, 77
*Blackboard Jungle* (1955), 83
*Black Brothers* (1977), 78
*Black Caesar* (1973), 129, 166, 180
*Black Dynamite* (2009), 10
*Blackenstein* (1973), 12
*Black Gestapo* (1975), 5
*Black Girl* (1972), 165
*Black Godfather* (1974), 77

*Black Shampoo* (1976), 78
*Black Sister's Revenge* (1976), 165. See *Emma Mae*
*Black Vengeance* (1975), 78
*Blacula* (1972), 5, 12, 16, 103, 105, 119, 129, 159, 180–81, 183, 209, 225, 227–28, 230–31
*Blade Runner* (1982) 9–10
*Blazing Saddles* (1974), 238–40, 242, 244
*Blood Couple.* See *Ganja and Hess*
*Boarding House Blues* (1948), 166
*Body Heat* (1981), 9
*Bonnie and Clyde* (1967), 225
*Boss Nigger* (1974), 5, 159, 209
*The Boys in the Band* (1970), 181, 183, 189
*Bronze Buckaroo* (1939), 159
*Brother John* (1970), 62
*Buck and the Preacher* (1973), 159, 241
*Butch Cassidy and the Sundance Kid* (1969), 122

*Camelot* (1967), 83
*Car Wash* (1975), 15, 157, 171–74
*Centerfold Girls* (1974), 116
*Charley-One-Eye* (1973), 159
*Chinatown* (1974), 9, 229
*Citizen Kane* (1941), 232–33, 243

# FILM AND TELEVISION INDEX

*Cleopatra Jones* (1973), 5, 12, 123, 130–31, 166
*Cleopatra Jones and the Casino of Gold* (1975), 78
*Coffy* (1973), 5, 8, 123, 129–41, 142
*Come Back Charleston Blue* (1972), 166
*Cooley High* (1975), 1
*Cornbread, Earl and Me* (1975), 1
*Cotton Comes to Harlem* (1970), 5, 21–28, 81; and beginning of Blaxploitation, 2–3, 21, 24, 77, 114; and black audiences, 24, 32, 34–35; female characters, 34–36, 38; French origins, 2; impact on black detective genre, 2, 25, 32, 35

*Da Sweet Blood of Jesus* (2014), 240, 242–43
*Dead Man* (1995), 226, 240
*Death Wish* (1974), 215
*The Defiant Ones* (1958), 122, 241
*The Detective* (1968), 182
*Detroit 9000* (1973), 14, 77, 114–36; as black film, 115, 129–30, 133; and black sexuality, 126–27; change of title, 116; narrative- 117, 119, 124–25; promotional material, 128; soundtrack, 116, 132; trailers, 131–32; as white film, 129–30, 133; white protagonist as narrative focus, 123–26, 129–31
*Detour* (1945), 9
*Devil in a Blue Dress* (1995), 9–10
*Diff'rent Strokes* (1978–86), 236
*Dirty Harry* (1971), 215
*Django Unchained* (2012), 10, 240–43
*A Dog's Best Friend* (1959), 117
*Dolemite* (1975), 77
*Double Indemnity* (1944), 9
*Dr. Black and Mr. White* (1976), 229
*Dr. Black, Mr. Hyde* (1976), 217
*Drum* (1976), 159
*Duck, You Sucker* (1971), 214

*East Side/West Side* (1963–64), 183
*Easy Rider* (1969), 16, 122, 225, 236
*Emma Mae* (1976), 165
*Escape From the Planet of the Apes* (1971)
*The Exorcist* (1974), 7, 229

*The Farmer's Daughter* (1947), 83
*Four Brothers* (2005), 10
*Foxy Brown* (1974), 5, 12, 15, 129, 138–53; as melodrama, 138, 142–43, 151; music, 146–47; narrative, 142–43, 145–46; and revenge, 143; and suffering, 144–45, 149–51; pre-production, 141–42; rape scene, 146–49
*French Connection* (1971), 86
*Friday Foster* (1975), 181, 183, 187
*Friday the 13th* (1980), 8

*Ganja and Hess* (1973), 14, 16, 103–13, 227, 234, 240, 244; critical reaction, 104; as masterpiece, 104, 226, 229; readings of, 104, 230–31; truncated version, 104, 229; visual language, 108–9, 230–33, 243
*Girls in Prison* (1956), 115
*The Godfather* (1972), 7, 225
*The Graduate* (1967), 16, 182–83, 225, 237
*Grey's Anatomy* (2005–present), 236
*Guess Who's Coming to Dinner?* (1967), 209

*Halloween* (1978), 234

*I'm Gonna Get You Sucker* (1988), 10
*Imitation of Life* (1959), 211
*In Living Color* (1990–94), 197
*In the Heat of the Night* (1967), 82, 122–23
*Inglorious Basterds* (2009), 242

*Jackie Brown* (1997), 10, 110
*Jaws* (1975), 8, 207

*Kill Bill* (2003), 242
*Killer Diller* (1948), 166
*The Killers* (1946), 9

*LA Confidential* (1955), 9
*La Permission.* See *The Story of a Three Day Pass*
*Lady Sings the Blues* (1973), 7, 180, 182
*The Landlord* (1970), 103
*Laura* (1944), 9
*The Learning Tree* (1969), 82, 86
*Legend of Nigger Charley* (1972), 159
*Lethal Weapon* (1987), 123
*Linda Lovelace for President* (1975), 116
*Love Story* (1970), 63

*The Mack* (1973), 5
*Mahogany* (1975), 112
*The Maltese Falcon* (1941), 9, 226, 230
*Man and Boy* (1971), 159
*Mandingo* (1975), 159, 242
*Melinda* (1972), 5
*Midnight Cowboy* (1969), 122, 183
*Monkey Hustle* (1977), 77
*Murder, My Sweet* (1944), 9
*The Mothers* (1976), 151

*Naked City* (1958–63), 81
*Naked Paradise* (1957), 115
*Night of the Living Dead* (1968), 104, 230
*Nightmare on Elm Street* (1984), 8
*Norman, Is That You?* (1975), 15, 180–88, 195–197; closing credits, 191; decentered gayness, 182, 184, 186–88, 191; jewish to black translation, 180–81; opening credits, 185; promotional material, 186, 189, 193; ratings, 181; structure, 190

*O Brother, Where Art Thou?* (2000), 242
*One Potato, Two Potato* (194) , 117
*Original Gangstas* (1996), 10

*Operation Bottleneck* (1961), 117
*Out of the Past* (1947), 9

*Parachute to Paradise* (1969), 85
*Passing Through* (1977), 173
*Passion Plantation* (1976), 159
*The Pawnbroker* (1965), 82
*The Pelican Brief* (1993), 235
*Perils of Pauline* (1914), 143
*Personal Problems* (1980), 111
*Pinky* (1949), 121, 211
*Preacher Man* (1983), 166
*The Princess Diaries* (2001), 78

*Reflections in a Golden Eye* (1968), 182
*Revenge of the Nerds* (1984), 197
*Rio Conchos* (1964), 78
*Route 66* (1960–64), 81

*Sanford and Son* (1972–77), 181, 184
*Sanford Arms* (1977), 184, 189
*Saturday Night Fever* (1977), 8
*Saturday Night Live* (1975–present), 197
*Scream, Blacula, Scream* (1973), 16, 226–27, 234–35, 240, 244
*The Searchers* (1956), 241
*Shaft* (1971), 5, 9, 10, 14, 21, 77–101, 114, 126, 132, 182, 194, 211–12, 214–15, 226; benefit screenings, 94; budget, 83, 86–87; and Blaxploitation, 6–7, 77–79, 97; casting, 84–85; critical reaction, 92; distribution, 94; location shooting, 86–87, 89–90; marketing strategy, 91–92; novel origins, 79–81; opening scene, 88–89; promotional materials, 92; script revision, 84; soundtrack, 90–91; test screenings, 92–94
*Shaft* (2000), 10, 78
*Shaft's Big Score* (1972) , 214
*Sin City* (2005) 9
*Skin Game* (1971), 159

*Slaughter* (1972), 5, 129
*The Soul of Nigger Charley* (1973), 210
*Soul Soldier* (1970), 159
*Sounder* (1972), 1, 7, 180, 183
*Space is the Place* (1974), 111
*The Spook Who Sat By the Door* (1973), 12, 111
*Star Wars* (1977), 8
*The Story of a Three Day Pass* (1968), 3, 60, 236
*Sugar Cookies* (1977), 116
*Sugar Hill* (1974), 151
*Sunset Boulevard* (1950), 9
*Super Fly* (1972), 5, 6, 8, 10, 107, 114, 126, 132, 160, 194, 201, 211, 213–215, 219
*Sweet Sweetback's Baadasssss Song* (1971), 1–2, 13–14, 21, 59–73, 110, 114, 119, 123, 132, 160, 181–82, 214, 226, 237–38, 240, 244; advertising and promotion, 62, 170; aesthetics, 4, 61–62; and black press, 65, 69–70; box office, 3, 61–62, 70; criticism of, 61, 65–70; impact on Blaxploitation, 3, 5, 59, 68, 70, 88; and sexuality, 4, 60–61, 67–69, 182–183, 187; victorious film, 4, 61; X-rating, 4, 62

*The Swimmer* (1968), 82

*Take a Hard Ride* (1975), 159
*The Third Man* (1949), 9
*Thomasine and Bushrod* (1974), 5, 159
*Three Outlaws* (1956), 117
*Three the Hard Way* (1974), 77
*Top of the Heap* (1972), 111
*Touch of Evil* (1958), 9
*Trouble Man* (1972), 5
*Twitch of the Death Nerve* (1971), 207

*Undercover Brother* (2002)

*Village of the Damned* (1960), 82
*Vixen* (1969), 62

*Walking Tall* (1973), 215
*A Warm December* (1973), 210
*Watermelon Man* (1970), 3, 12–13, 15, 42–58, 60, 157, 161–64, 226, 236, 238–41, 242; advertising, 11–12; narrative, 44–56, 60
*What Do You Say to a Naked Lady?* (1970), 85
*Woman in the Window* (1944), 9

*Youngblood* (1978), 107

# SUBJECT INDEX

Academy Awards, 82, 86, 89, 91, 122, 183, 212
action films, 142, 167
advertising, motion picture, 162–64, 166, 172, 214–15, 217
*aesthetique du cool*, 226
Affordable Care Act, 43
African American actors, 9, 84, 85, 158, 160
African American actresses, 9, 11–12, 142, 144–45
African American audiences, 1, 3, 5, 7–8, 24, 63–64, 70, 91–92, 94, 97, 121, 125, 130, 133, 165–66, 182, 202, 204–5, 207, 211–12, 214–16, 210; critical views of, 32–33, 204–5, 209, 211–12, 216, 219
African American directors, 2–3, 6, 9, 26, 60, 82, 84
African American film criticism, 33, 65–67, 70, 240
African American history, 105, 107
African American masculinity, 68, 79, 194–95; and gay characters, 183, 188–89, 195; in 1970s, 194
African American political leadership, 170
African American press, 65, 69–70, 166, 192, 202, 214, 316–17

African American sexuality, 4, 35, 38, 60–61, 63, 67–69, 79, 84, 115, 126, 183–85, 189, 194, 208
African American women, 33–34, 38, 67, 121, 141–42, 144, 243
African American youth, 6–7, 65, 67, 70, 170–71
Afrocentrism, 31, 35, 189
American International Pictures (AIP), 5, 115–16, 128–29, 131, 141–42, 148, 205–6, 216, 227–28
Altman, Rick, 8
Angelou, Maya, 229
Apollo Theater, 22–23, 28, 30, 32, 35–36, 38
Arkoff, Samuel, 216
Ashby, Hal, 103
Atlanta, 59, 61
Aubrey, Jim, 83, 87
audiences, white, 708, 78, 92, 121

Back to Africa movement, 2, 22, 30–31, 34
Bailey, Pearl, 181, 186, 188, 193
Baldwin, James, 229
Baraka, Amiri, 7
Bar-Kays, 91
Barry, Marion, 214
Barrymore, Ethel, 121

Battle Royale, 242
Beavers, Louise, 144–45
Bell, Al, 92
Bell, Jeannie, 11–12
Bennett, Jr., Lerone, 66–67, 69, 114
Bergman, Andrew, 238
Bergman, Ingmar, 104
Black, John D. F., 84
black aesthetic, 21–22, 28, 32, 37–38, 61–62, 69, 208, 211
Blacks Against Narcotics and Genocide (BANG), 214
Black Arts movement, 21–22, 26, 31, 33, 37, 66, 208, 211–212
black church, 19, 172–173
black crime novels, 35
blackface, 192–193, 235–236
black family, 189
black film criticism, 64–65, 69
*Black Film as Genre,* 174, 227
black film history, 68, 157–58, 160, 165, 168, 174, 203
black heroism, 2–4, 7, 41, 61, 65, 67, 91, 95, 97, 123, 139–41, 145
black homophobia, 195
black identity, 26–27, 56, 108, 193
"black is beautiful," 30–32
black nationalism, 30, 67
blackness and homosexuality, 192–193
black objectification, 50, 55, 60, 108
Black Panthers, 61, 110, 149
Black Power, 3, 12, 26, 56, 59, 107, 137, 140–41, 160, 172, 208
black representation, 15, 67, 78, 140, 202, 204, 216–17
black romance films, 208
black spectatorship, 59, 63, 67, 165, 202, 218
black-themed motion pictures, 69, 129–30, 180, 182, 202–4; and blaxploitation, 1, 7, 98, 157–58, 165–66, 180, 201, 218
black westerns, 159
blaxploitation, 103, 181; aesthetics, 13, 16, 21–22, 28, 208, 211, 216, 217; and academic attention, 10–12, 77; and Black Arts movement, 13, 21–22; and black audiences, 1, 5, 8, 132–33, 209, 211–12; and black cast films, 7, 98, 157–58, 165–66, 180, 209; black control over, 211–12; and black employment, 7, 9–10, 26, 86, 97, 210–12; and black masculinity, 194, 202, 209; and blackness, 21, 61; characteristics of, 2–3, 41, 97, 115, 123, 139; and class, 27–28, 217; controversy over, 5–7, 114, 159, 167, 204; debates over, 5, 110, 167, 213–14, 217–18; as discourse, 175, 213; economic impact on studio system, 8, 10, 98, 121, 182, 204; and exploitation, 7, 203–4, 208, 219; as form of production, 78, 97, 205; and gay characters, 183, 194, 197; and gender, 137–38, 144–45, 151; as genre, 8, 12–13, 42, 138, 203; history, 8, 98, 114, 175, 180, 202; heroines, 123, 139, 141–42, 146–48; iconography, 11, 127; legacy, 243–44; and melodrama, 137–38, 150–51; as movement, 5, 9, 41, 138, 151, 205; origins of, 6, 15, 77, 114, 140, 201, 204; perioidization, 8, 158; political ramifications, 110, 119, 123, 140, 194, 202, 209, 211, 216–18; problems with term, 12, 14–16, 114–15, 133, 158–59, 201–3, 205, 218, 225; and quality of films, 11; and real lived experiences, 119, 211–12, 218; revenge, 5, 148, 150, 209; role of villain, 41, 145, 148, 150; struggles against, 61–70, 159, 213–14, 217–18; and urban space, 4–5; white control over, 97, 208, 212
Blockbuster films, 7
blood, 107

# SUBJECT INDEX

Bogle, Donald, 11, 159–60, 174, 192–93
Bond, James, 214–215
box office, 2–3, 5, 8, 62–63, 94–95, 121–23, 132, 182, 228
Brandon, Harry, 241
Brestoff, Richard, 172
Brooks, Gwendolyn , 60, 68
Brooks, Mel, 238
Brooks, Peter, 138–39, 150
Brown, Claude, 24
Brown, Jim, 6, 78, 85, 167–69
Brown, Juanita, 146
Brown, Peter, 146
"browning" of America, 13, 42–43, 51
buddy film, 122
burlesque, 35
*Buzz the Fuzz,* 125, 127

Calloway, Earl, 167
Cambridge, Godfrey, 22, 30, 44–45, 158, 162, 236
cameo appearances, 161, 171–72, 195
Cannes Film Festival, 104
Cannibalism, 107
Carlin, George, 171–72
Carroll, Noel, 106
Carter, Terry, 84, 142
Casey, Bernie, 84–85
Cash, Rosalind, 169
Chan, Charlie, 160
Chandler, Raymond, 25
Chicago, 14, 59–60, 66, 69–71, 94, 214
*Chicago Defender,* 66, 68, 70, 117, 216
Chicago Theater, 129, 132
cinema of attractions, 205, 209
Cinemation Industries, 4, 214
civil disobedience tactics, 141
Civil Rights Act, 123
civil rights movement, 47, 54, 69, 140–41
Clark, Larry, 173
Clark, Marlene, 231
Clark Theater (Chicago), 62

Coalition Against Blaxploitation (CAB), 159–60, 201, 211, 213, 216
code switching, 161–62
Columbia Pictures, 60, 162
comedy film, 163, 165
coming-out episodes, 182, 184, 188
Congress of Racial Equality (CORE), 7, 159, 211, 213
coon stereotype, 159–60, 165, 169
Corey, Irwin, 117
Cosby, Bill, 4
Cotton, 23, 27–28, 33–34, 37
Cotton Club, 33, 35
crack cocaine, 103
Crain, Jeanne, 121
Crain, William, 103
crime, 124, 127; black-on-black, 29, 125
Cripps, Thomas, 174, 226–27
Crosse, Robert, 84
crossover film, 91–92, 94, 182
Curtis, Tony, 241,

Davis, Ossie, 2, 21–26, 32–33, 37, 158, 165
De Jesus, Luchi, 132
Dee, Ruby, 23
detective film, 22, 24–25
detective novel, 79–80
Detroit, 14, 59, 61, 116–19, 121, 124–25, 129–30, 133; race riots, 117–19, 121
Diawara, Manthia, 104
DiCaprio, Leonardo, 240
Dimension Pictures, 115
Directors Guild of America, 212
Dixon, Ivan, 174
Dobson, Tamara, 11–12
Doherty, Thomas, 132, 203
Donaldson, Melvin, 123
Dozier, Lamont, 116
*Dracula,* 103, 106, 228
drugs and drug addiction, 107, 142, 146–47, 149, 214

257

## SUBJECT INDEX

Duchisne, Ernest, 102
Duke, Bill, 174
Dumas, Alexandre, 241–42
Dyer, Richard, 235, 237

Earth, Wind, and Fire, 5
*Ebony*, 69, 189, 192, 194–95
Edwards, James, 121
Elder III, Lonnie, 7
Ellison, Ralph, 242
*The Emancipation Orgasm*, 69
Everett, Anna, 12, 202, 216
exploitation films, 92, 132–33, 225; mainstreaming, 203, 206, 215; in the 1970s, 203, 205–6, 214–15; qualities of, 132, 205–8

Fanon, Franz, 67, 107, 232
Fargas, Antonio, 142
feminism, 144
Fetchit, Stepin, 15, 158–10, 166–70
film genre, 8
film noir, 9–10
*Film Quarterly*, 160
FORUM, 214
Foxx, Jamie, 240
Foxx, Redd, 27, 181, 185–89, 193
*Framing Blackness*, 7, 122
Freeman, Joel, 14, 79, 82–92, 97
Frank, Nino, 9
French Revolution, 138–39, 231; and melodrama, 137
*From Sambo to Superspade*, 120
Fuller, Hoyt, 31–33, 66

Gates, Raquel, 12, 60
gay black men as antiblack, 189
gay black men in popular culture, 181, 189, 192–93, 196
gay face, 192–93, 195–96
gay film, 180–81, 183
gay rights protest, 89–90
gay slurs, 150, 188
Gaye, Marvin, 115

Gaze, 203
General Film Corporation, 115–16, 122, 129, 132–33
germ theory, 14, 105, 109–10
ghetto, 22, 25, 32, 208
Goines, Donald, 35
Gold, Ronald, 3, 24
Golden, David, 91
Goldman, Martin
Goldstein, William, 191
Goldwyn Jr., Samuel , 2, 22–24
Goodman, John, 242
Gordy Jr., Barry, 115–16
Green, Theopolis, 213
Grier, David Alan, 197
Grier, Pam, 11–12, 15, 137, 141–42, 145, 234
Griffin, Junius, 5–6, 114, 133, 158–59, 213
Griffith, David Wark, 242
Guerrero, Ed, 7, 10–11, 122–24, 158, 190, 204
Gunn, Bill, 103–104, 108, 110, 229–231, 242
Gunning, Tom, 205, 209

Haggerty, H. B., 146
Hampton, Orville, 116–17
Hansberry, Lorraine, 236
Harlem , 1, 21–22, 24, 26, 34, 79
Hayes, Isaac, 89–91, 132
hegemony, 191
heroin, 107
heteronormativity, 184, 188–91, 197
heterosexual gaze, 184, 188
Hill, Jack, 138, 142, 148–49
Himes, Chester, 2, 21–22, 32–33, 35, 37
hip hop, 78
Hitchcock, Alfred, 240
Hoffman, Dustin, 183
Holland, Eddie, 116
Holland, Brian, 116
homonormativity, 190
homophobia, 52, 80–81, 195–96

# SUBJECT INDEX

homosexuality, 15–16, 182, 184, 189–90, 196–97; detection of, 185, 187–88; in film, 181, 183, 195; and professions, 193–94; and sports, 193–94
hooks, bell, 10
horror film, 8, 12, 106, 128, 205, 227, 234
Houston, Thelma, 191
Hunter, Jeffrey, 241
hustler, 67

Huston, John, 230

Iceberg Slim (Robert Beck), 35
individualism, 56
Innis, Roy, 7, 159
integration, 121, 141
interracial buddy film, 122, 124
interracial relationships, 3, 54–55, 60, 93, 117, 121–23, 235

Jackson, Jesse, 110, 214
Jarmusch, Jim, 226
Jarrett, Vernon, 68
Jefferson, Roland,, 214
Jeffrey Theater (Chicago), 70
*Jet,* 192, 195–196
Jewison, Norman, 122
Johnson, Don, 242
Johnson, Lyndon, 118
Jones, Duane, 194, 230
Jones, James Earl, 217
Jordan, Jack, 229
Julian , Isaac, 10–11

Kelly, Quentin, 229
Kennedy, Robert, 147
Kerner Commission, 118
Kerner, Otto, 118
King Jr., Martin Luther 47, 133, 172
Klotman, Phyllis, 104
Korman, Harvey, 239
Ku Klux Klan, 52, 239, 242

kung-fu movies, 205; and black audiences, 215
KUUMBA Workshop, 66–69, 110

Lathan, Stan, 157, 168, 175
Lawrence, Novotny, 12, 140, 203, 209
Lawson, Richard, 234
Leab, Daniel, 11, 120, 174
Lee, Spike, 107–8, 240, 242–44
Little, Cleavon, 238
Lockhart, Calvin, 22
Loder, Kathryn, 142
*The Lonely Crusade,* 2

Mabley, Moms, 166–69, 171
Malcolm X, 26
Mapp, Edward, 174
Marks, Arthur, 115–16, 123, 129, 131, 133
Marlowe, Phillip, 14
Marshall, William, 228
Mask, Mia, 145
masculinity, white, 122–23, 215
*The Masque of Blackness, 226*
Massood, Paula, 32–33, 37
Mayfield, Julian, 31
McBride, Joseph, 160
McDaniel, Hattie, 144–45
McGee, Vonnetta, 117, 131
McGregor, Charles, 238
McQueen, Butterfly, 166, 169
melodrama, 15; definition, 138–40; and performative style, 138; racial, 140, 149, 151; and revenge, 148, 150–51; and suffering, 137–38, 140, 148, 151
Metro Goldwyn Mayer (MGM), 5, 10, 78, 81, 83–84, 86–87, 90–92, 94, 211–12
Micheaux, Oscar, 213
Mims, Greg, 167–68
Minstrelsy, 108, 193
Mitchell, Don, 234

Mitchell, Elvis, 10
Monaco, James, 104
Moreland, Mantan, 15, 158, 162, 164–65, 169–70
Morgan, Boyd Red, 146
Morricone, Ennio, 240
Morris, Garrett, 122
Motion Picture Producers of America (MPPA), 4, 62, 181
Motown Productions, 115–16, 132–33, 182
*Muhammad Speaks*, 65
Murphy, Eddie, 197
Muse, Clarence, 15, 158, 160, 172–173
Museum of Modern Art, 104

National Advisory Committee on Civil Disorder, 118
National Association for the Advancement of Colored People (NAACP), 5–6, 159, 161, 211, 213, 217
Nation of Islam, 65–66
Neal, Larry, 208, 211
Negro faggotry, 195
neo-noir, 9–10
Netflix, 77
Netter, Doug, 91
New American Cinema, 182, 225
New Hollywood, 206, 225, 237
New Woman, 143–44
*New York Times*, 213
Newton, Huey, 61, 110, 160
Nichols, Jerry, 125–26
Nichols, Mike, 225
Nicholson, Jack, 229
nudity in film, 128, 142, 148, 182, 203

Obama, Barack, 13, 42
one-drop theory, 103
Ongiri, Amy Abigo, 24, 26–27, 33, 35
Oriental Theater (Chicago), 62–65, 69; changing racial reception, 64–65

Parks Jr. , Gordon, 159, 215

Parks Sr., Gordon, 6, 21, 78, 82–90, 92–95, 97, 215
Penicillin, 102
Perry, Lincoln. *See* Stepin Fetchit
Pickens, Slim, 238
Pines, Jim, 174
Plessy, Homer, 102
*Plessy v. Ferguson*, 102
Pointer Sisters, 71, 73
Poitier, Sidney, 62–63, 65, 78, 122–23, 159, 209, 241
Polanski, Roman, 229–30
police, 30, 79, 122–23, 125, 127–28; brutality, 60, 118, 124
pornography, 3–4, 149, 205
Poussaint, Alvin, 214
prison industrial complex, 52
Production Code Administration (PCA), 183, 203, 205
prostitution, 146–48
Pryor, Richard, 171–72, 238

queerness, 197
queer representation, 2, 183

race riot, 208
racial otherness, 56
racial pride
racism, 3, 10, 41, 45, 50, 54–55, 108, 123–25, 140, 151, 161; institutional, 42–44, 52, 118
*A Raisin in the Sun* (play, 1959), 236
rape, 55, 146–49, 194
Raucher, Herman, 163
Regester, Charlene, 144–145
*La Reine de Pommes*, 2
Revenge films, 1, 4, 150
Rhodes, Hari, 117, 131
Riggs, Marlon, 195
Riley, Clayton, 95–96, 114
Roberts, Julia, 235
Robertson, Hugh, 232
Robinson, Mabel, 22
Robinson, Matt, 168

Robinson, Smokey, 115, 185, 191
Romney, Mitt, 43
Rocco, Alex, 117
Roosevelt Theater (Chicago), 90, 94
Ross, Diana, 182
Roundtree, Richard, 14, 85–86, 88, 189–90, 215, 226
Sampson, Henry T., 174
Schaeffer, Eric, 203, 205
Schlatter, George, 181
Schultz, Michael, 157, 172, 174–75
Scott, Larry B., 197
*Screening Noir*, 12
Senghor, Leopold, 62
serial queen melodrama, 137, 143, 145, 151
sexuality, 35–37, 51, 60, 67–69, 167, 182, 188, 197, 237
sexual revolution, 182, 186
Shaft, John (novel character), 78–81
Sieving, Christopher, 12
Silliphant, Stanley, 81–82, 86, 92
Sims, Yvonne, 11–12
Singleton, William, 91
Sirk Douglas, 241
sitcoms, 190, 197
slasher films, 8
slavery, 53, 105–6, 119, 147–48, 228, 240–41
Smith, Conrad, 213
social problem film, 120, 122, 208
Solow, Herbert, 84
Southern Christian Leadership Conference (SCLC), 213
St. Jacques, Raymond, 22
Stax Records, 90 92
Steiger, Rod, 122
Steinberg, Martha Jean, 125–26
stereotypes, racial, 6, 10, 52, 67, 78, 108, 140, 160, 193, 202, 208, 210, 216
Stewart, Jacqueline, 165, 202, 216–17, 218
Stoker, Bram, 103

Stowe, Harriet Beecher, 140
Supremes, 115

Tarantino, Quentin, 11, 78, 110, 240–42, 244
theaters, motion picture, 4–5, 94, 217
Tideyman, Ernest, 78–79, 81, 83–84, 86

*Uncle Tom's Cabin*, 140
United Artists, 2, 121, 166, 168
U.S. Catholic Conference, 181

Valenti, Jack, 62
vampire film, 103, 105–6, 110, 227–35
vampirism as slavery, 105–7, 228
Van Peebles, Melvin, 1–5, 12–14, 21, 41, 46, 57, 60–61, 65, 68–69, 110, 157–58, 160–61, 163–65, 175, 236–37
Van Sant, Gus, 240
*Variety*, 5, 69, 97
Vietnam War, 107
vigilante justice, 150
villains in film, 148–49
violence, 5, 47–48, 68–69, 79–80, 115, 128, 145, 149–51, 167, 203, 209
Voight, Jon, 183
Voting Rights Act of 1965, 123

Waltz, Christoph, 240
Ward, Frances, 66
Ward, Val Grey, 66, 68
Warner Brothers, 5, 10, 83
Warren, Michael, 182, 184, 187, 191, 193–96
Washington, Denzel, 10
Washington, Kerry, 240
Wayans, Damon, 197
Wayne, John, 7
West, Cornel, 109
Westerns, 227, 237, 240–41
WGBH, 166–67
White, Armond, 10
white flight, 207

whiteness, 43–44, 47, 49–50
Wilder, Gene, 239
William Morris Agency, 84
Williams, Billy Dee, 84, 182
Williams, Linda, 140
women-in-prison films, 143
Wood, Natalie, 241
World War II, 120–121
Worthington, Sam, 65

*The Wretched of the Earth*, 232
Wright, Richard, 35

X-rated films, 214. *See also* pornography
X-rating (for Sweetback), 4, 62

Zarzosa, Agustin, 138

www.ingramcontent.com/pod-product-compliance
Lightning Source LLC
Chambersburg PA
CBHW082104250426
43661CB00079B/2629